EARTH'S DAUGHTERS

Stories of Women in Classical Mythology

Betty Bonham Lies

fulcrum resources
Golden, Colorado

For
Elaine, Brian, Laurel, and Maddy
with love

Library of Congress Cataloging-in-Publication Data
Lies, Betty Bonham.
     Earth's daughters : stories of women in classical mythology / Betty Bonham Lies.
        p.   cm.
     Includes bibliographical references and index.
     ISBN 1-55591-414-4 (pbk.)
     1. Women—Mythology. 2. Goddesses, Greek. 3. Goddesses, Roman. 4. Mythology, Classical. I. Title.
     BL795.W65L54 1999
     1292.1'3—dc21   98-47862
                                        CIP

Cover design by Alyssa Pumphrey
Interior art © 1999 www.arttoday.com

Printed in the United States of America
0 9 8 7 6 5 4 3 2 1

Fulcrum Publishing
350 Indiana Street, Suite 350
Golden, Colorado 80401-5093
(800) 992-2908 • (303) 277-1623
www.fulcrum-resources.com

CONTENTS

INTRODUCTION
WHAT ARE MYTHS?

HERE WE ARE, WE HUMAN BEINGS, SMALL CREATURES ON A BIG PLANET, WITH A VAST, MYSTERIOUS universe beyond. *How did I get here?* we have to ask ourselves. *How did this all begin? Who am I and why am I alive? What is my proper relationship with Earth and its creatures? What powers exist that are greater than I am? What is the meaning of death?*

People try to answer these urgent human questions in many ways; one way is to create stories. The stories we call myths probably began when ancient people sought to make sense of the world and their own existence by telling each other these tales.

Myths explain many things that puzzle people about life. They pass on the ethics and values of a society and give guidelines for behavior. Sometimes they contain hope for human beings, other times they contain terror. But, even though figures called gods and goddesses appear in them, myths should not be mistaken for the religion of a culture. They are stories—stories that surmise how the world came to be, stories that entertain, stories that inspire and uplift.

Some classical myths seem to suggest facts that modern scientists have discovered about the Earth. For example, the original monsters of Greek myths resemble the earthquakes and volcanoes that occurred when the world was formed. It's interesting that the mythologies of many civilizations contain very similar stories, such as the creation of humans from clay, or the destruction of the world through a flood, with just one good family saved.

And always, myths start with the Earth: always female, always Mother Earth, life-giving and fertile.

The myths of many early civilizations are frightening and dark, full of black magic and inexplicable happenings. Deities may be strange and inhuman, given to wrath at human beings and demanding terrible things of them, even human sacrifice. Gods and goddesses might have the heads of cats or birds, the body of a lion, or simply exist as elements of nature, likely to turn angry at any moment for no apparent reason.

The gods of Greek myth are very different. For the first time in human history, gods were portrayed as men and women and not as terrifying inhuman beings. They were more comfortable to live with than the irrational deities. They were still mighty, and people had to be very respectful of them because of their great powers, but they had reasons for the things they did. If they were angry at a mortal, it was most likely deserved. If they rewarded one, that too was probably because of something the person had done.

The gods and goddesses of Greek mythology look like men and women and have human characteristics, both noble—pride, courage, wisdom, and love—and base—jealousy, petty anger, hate, a desire to get even. They move easily between Heaven and Earth and mingle freely with mortals, falling in love and marrying, having children, helping or hindering mortals. Heaven is like Earth, only better. The gods eat and drink, amuse themselves in various ways, and sometimes quarrel just as people do—but they are immortal; they cannot die.

The world of Greek mythology is a world of beauty, where trees and rivers are inhabited by deities that watch over them, where one might run into a god just around the next corner. There is little nasty magic, no ugly witches, no demons, no fearsome ghosts (the shades of the dead are never frightening). It's true that there are some rather awful monsters, but they can usually be defeated, or at least avoided, by cunning mortals, or those with divine help.

The Roman myths are, by and large, the same as the Greek myths, with new names given to the gods. Slight changes in the stories and the ways they are told reflect differences between the two civilizations. The Roman writers, coming from a more scientific society—one of great engineering and military feats rather than of great art—seem to view the myths simply as stories. Any element of belief is missing, as is some of the beauty and mystery.

STORIES OF
TRANSFORMATION

MANY OF THE CLASSICAL MYTHS TELL STORIES ABOUT A *METAMORPHOSIS*, IN WHICH A PERSON IS changed into another form. Usually the transformation is performed by a goddess or god, sometimes as a kind of punishment for bad behavior, sometimes as a reward, a wish fulfilled, a means of escape from an unbearable situation. Or it may just occur at random, falling on somebody who was in the wrong place at the wrong time.

The transformation of things is a thread of stories from many cultures. Shape-shifters appear in fairy tales, folktales, and ghost stories. Some of our most familiar legends—Cinderella, for example—depend on our willingness to believe that change is possible: a pumpkin may become a golden carriage, mice may turn into horses, a dirty urchin into a glowing princess.

Why is metamorphosis so common in old stories? Maybe it's because the nature of the universe is change. From the moment the world was created, its physical features have undergone tremendous transformations. Mountains rise and are leveled, oceans flood and then dry up, species of creatures rise and fall. Some changes are so gradual that we don't even realize they are happening, while others are swift. A tornado flattens an entire town in minutes, a flood sweeps away bridges and homes, sources of food are suddenly wiped out by weather, insects, or disease.

Human life is ruled by change too. Babies are born and grow up. When we haven't seen someone for a while we often say, "Oh, you've changed!" The human body goes through constant transformations throughout life, and we change inside as well. Sometimes when we look back at the past, it's difficult to connect ourselves with who we were at an earlier age.

Perhaps people in the past, who lived closer to nature than we do in modern civilizations, were more closely attuned to the constant changes of the world. Day and night, weather, the turns of season—all must have had a bigger impact on human life without machines, artificial light, or home heating. Before such inventions, it may have been more natural to understand life as flowing in and out of transformations.

Some stories of metamorphosis explain how things of the world came to be the way they are: a weaver becomes the spider, constantly spinning her web. Others define the relationships between gods and mortals: the god turns a girl into a heifer to hide her from his wife, and would rather let her suffer from the gadfly than confess that he loves her. Still others mark a natural sympathy in relationships: a father protects his daughter from the unwanted advances of a god by turning her into a laurel tree.

In a strange way, the transformations that appear in classical mythology confer a level of permanency on those who undergo them. The girl who has become a constellation or a tree or a statue will never have to worry about what the future has in store for her, although she has no potential to change her life. Perhaps humans long for both the possibility of change and the possibility of an unchanging eternity.

WHO'S WHO IN CLASSICAL MYTHOLOGY:
Names of the Goddesses and Gods

THE NAMES OF THE GODDESSES AND GODS IN CLASSICAL MYTHOLOGY MAY BE A LITTLE CONFUSING AT first. Why is one goddess sometimes called Athena, then Pallas, and other times Minerva? That's because the deities have different names in Greek and Roman mythology, and sometimes they are given a kind of nickname, called an *epithet*. But once you understand the difference, it's not really a problem to know who's who.

Roman civilization flourished later than Greek civilization, and the Romans admired the earlier people very much. Ancient Greece gave them much to base their culture on, and in particular they took ideas from Greek art and architecture, literature, and mythology.

This book uses Greek names if a story appears in both Greek and Roman myths, since such stories originated in Greece. Some tales appear only in the works of Roman writers, either because they were not Greek originally or because the older story has been lost. In that case, the Roman name is used.

Here is a list of the major goddesses and gods of classical mythology and their names in Greek and Roman myths.

The Twelve Great Olympian Deities

Greek Names	Roman Names
Zeus, *the supreme ruler*	Jupiter *or* Jove
Hera, *the wife of Zeus*	Juno
Poseidon, *god of the sea, Zeus's brother*	Neptune
Hades, *Zeus's other brother, god of the underworld*	Pluto
Athena *or* Pallas Athena, *Zeus's daughter, goddess of war and wisdom*	Minerva
Apollo *or* Phoebus Apollo, *Zeus's son, god of music, healing, and the sun*	Apollo
Artemis, *Apollo's twin sister, goddess of the hunt and the moon*	Diana
Aphrodite, *goddess of love and beauty*	Venus
Hermes, *messenger of the gods*	Mercury
Ares, *god of war*	Mars
Hephaestus, *god of fire*	Vulcan
Hestia, *goddess of the hearth*	Vesta

Other Important Deities

Greek Names	Roman Names
Eros, *god of love*	Cupid *or* Amor
Demeter, *goddess of grain*	Ceres
Persephone, *queen of the underworld*	Proserpina
Dionysus, *god of wine*	Bacchus
Ilithyia, *goddess of childbirth*	Lucina
Hebe, *goddess of youth*	Hebe
Iris, *goddess of the rainbow*	Iris
Hecate, *goddess of witchcraft*	Hecate
Themis, *goddess of justice*	Themis
Pan, *god of nature*	Faunus

Women in Classical Mythology

On first reading the Greek and Roman myths, it might seem that men play the most important roles. Perhaps that's because so many books about classical mythology have titles like "Heroes and Gods." Perhaps it reflects the power of two of the world's great epic poems, Homer's *Iliad* and the *Odyssey,* which tell stories about wars and the adventures of men. Or perhaps it's simply that Western societies have traditionally valued "masculine" qualities more highly than "feminine" ones.

A closer look, though, reveals something interesting: there are as many females, both mortal and immortal, in the stories as males. They may not venture as far from home, nor do they usually fight battles or seek to become heroes as men do. Still, their influence is enormous. They have a powerful effect on every aspect of human life; sometimes they even control it.

The men of myth undertake all kinds of exploits. They go on journeys, looking for adventure, and find it everywhere. They fight wars, perform deeds of daring, and outwit monsters; mortal men challenge the gods and suffer for it. The primary and most powerful god is male: Zeus, considered the father of all the gods and humans.

But women find adventures, too, although they usually happen closer to home. Women fight their own battles, often taking a strong stand for what they see as right. They show tremendous courage when they forgo traditional feminine roles to stand up against the injustices of society. They can be as heroic as men.

"Women are sometimes warriors, too," says Orestes in *Electra*. He means it metaphorically; usually a woman's physical strength and ability to fight wars are not of primary importance. Yet story after story depicts the courage and moral strength of women. Some women choose an independent life, wishing not to marry but to live on their own terms.

Many Western cultures that came after ancient Greece and Rome assigned women only one of two roles in their stories: either the all-good, pure mother figure, or the all-bad woman, temptress, and evildoer. As the stories in this book make clear, women in Greek and Roman mythology play a wider range of roles and are much more morally complex.

Goddesses figure prominently among the important deities of Olympus. And the goddess Earth, called Ge or Gaia in Greek myths, was the first of all deities.

Of course, nobody is perfect in classical mythology. Men and women of myth, gods and goddesses, all have flaws. They all make mistakes and, at times, behave badly. They can be petty, arrogant, jealous, mean; they can do things they later regret. Usually they have to pay for such behavior, whether they are male or female.

There is one interesting difference between the mythical males and the mythical females, though. Normally, the men must be seen as individuals, forever testing their strength and daring against other men. Comradeship can be important, but in the long run it is the individual male standing alone who defines his role.

Mythical women stand out as individuals too. But females frequently appear as a group, sometimes human, but more often as goddesses or demigoddesses. These clusters of women are crucial to the lives of everyone on Earth, for better or worse. Let us begin where the myths begin, with the nine Muses, whose presence has inspired the arts and all of human knowledge.

The Muses

The Muses are the daughters of Zeus and Mnemosyne, whose name means "memory." It is the Muses who give artists the gift of memory and help them create works of all kinds. Poets, particularly, call upon the Muses for inspiration.

There are nine of these divine inspirers. Hesiod, the earliest of ancient storytellers, opens his book of myths by describing how they appeared before him as he tended his lambs at the foot of the mountain Helicon, one of their sacred dwelling places. According to Hesiod, the Muses bathe in the streams of Helicon, then "dance on their soft feet round the violet-dark spring" and the altar of Zeus. "From there they go forth, veiled in thick mist, and walk by night, uttering beautiful voice." The Muses' songs tell of what is, of what shall be, and of what has been. They breathe poetry into the shepherd and give him the voice with which he can pass on all he has learned from them, to tell the wonderful tales that will follow.

And what names they have! Clio *(fame-spreading)*, Euterpe *(gladness)*, Thalia *(good cheer)*, Melpomene *(singing)*, Terpsichore *(dance-delight)*, Erato *(lovely)*, Polyhymnia *(many songs)*, Urania *(celestial)*, and Calliope *(beautiful voice)*. Calliope is the chief among them.

Each Muse is associated with a particular intellectual area: Clio with history, Euterpe with lyric poetry and flute players, Thalia with comedy, Melpomene with tragedy, Terpsichore with dance, Erato with love poetry, Polyhymnia with music and mime, Urania with astronomy, and Calliope with epic poetry.

Born on Mount Pierus, the Muses have homes on other mountains, including Helicon, Parnassus, and Olympus. They are closely associated with Apollo, the god of music and prophecy. Indeed, the musician Orpheus is the son of Apollo and the Muse Calliope.

The Nymphs

Wherever there are woodlands, water, or hills, there are nymphs. These lovely and graceful spirits inhabit all places of natural beauty. Tree nymphs are called dryads and hamadryads; the nymphs of brooks, rivers, and springs are naiads; sea nymphs are Nereids or oceanids; and the nymphs of the hills and mountains are oreads.

Although they are of divine origin, nymphs are closely bound to the Earth and to the particular places where they dwell. As lesser deities, nymphs are immortal, or at least so long-lived that they are almost immortal. They look like radiant young maidens and are prone to falling in love. They interact with both gods and mortals. To humans they bring fortune and fertility. Although nymphs are usually kind and loving, occasionally they can be cruel, just like people.

The Graces

The three Graces are the daughters of the gods Zeus and Eurynome. Their names are Aglaia *(splendor* or *brilliance)*, Euphrosyne *(joy* or *mirth)*, and Thalia *(bloom* or *good cheer)*. The personification of beauty, grace, gentleness, and friendship, the Graces are inseparable, presiding over banquets, dances, and other social events. When they dance or join their voices in song, gods and men rejoice. It was said that they "gave life its bloom."

The Hours, or Seasons

Daughters of Zeus and Themis, the Hours, or Horae, are the goddesses of the changing seasons. Their name does not mean "hours of the day" but rather "times of the year." In most stories there are three Hours: Spring, Summer, and Winter.

The Hours attend on the god of the sun, Phoebus Apollo, harnessing his horses each day so that he is able to make his passage across the sky. As guardians of the sky, they open the gates of Olympus by rolling aside the clouds whenever the gods want to ride forth in their chariots.

The Fates

Night has many offspring, and among them are the three Fates, the goddesses who determine the course of human life. Clotho spins the thread of life; Lachesis assigns every mortal his or her destiny, holding the thread and measuring its length; and Atropos, the smallest but most fearsome of the three, cuts it off, ending a mortal's life.

But how much power do the Fates have? Are they the subjects of Zeus? Can he change their decisions? Or is even the most powerful god subject to the Fates? The stories vary. Usually the Fates are assumed to cause both the good and the bad things in life. Many classical writers believed they were superior to the gods. Homer and Virgil describe Zeus holding up a scale with human lives in it, to determine what the Fates had in store for them. Zeus could not even intervene to save his son Sarpedon, who was fated to die in the Trojan War. Still, the gods could sometimes trick the Fates into changing their minds, as Apollo did in the story of Alcestis and Admetus.

Hesiod first calls the Fates the daughters of Night, but later says they are the children of Zeus and Themis, the goddess who personifies everything that is right and proper in nature and society. This implies that although the Fates' power over human life is frightening, it is the way things are supposed to be.

The Furies, or Erinyes

These terrible female spirits are the goddesses of retribution, demanding justice and exacting punishment from those who have committed serious crimes. They are usually said to have been born from drops of Cronos's blood falling on Gaia, the Earth, although sometimes they are called the daughters of Night.

There are three Furies: Alecto *(unceasing)*, Megaera *(grudging)*, and Tisiphone *(avenging murder)*. It is their duty to persecute any man or woman who transgresses a natural law, especially the killing of a clan or family member.

The Furies are horrid-looking crones. Their heads are dogs' heads, their hair made up of snakes with the wings of bats. They stare from gaping, bloodshot eyes, and carry torches and brass-studded whips, with which they scourge culprits. Their intent is to drive their victims to madness, to a fury, finally to die in torment. They are considered so terrifying that their real name cannot be spoken; to avoid insulting them, people often call them Eumenides *(kind-hearted)*.

When they are not visiting Earth to punish living sinners, the Furies dwell in Tartarus, or Hell, where they spend their time inflicting eternal torture on mortals whose sins have damned them to everlasting punishment.

The Harpies

The Harpies are horrible winged monsters, half bird and half woman. They have sharp claws and powerful hooked beaks with which they attack helpless victims. Their names suggest that they are as violent as storm winds: Aello *(squall)*, Okypete *(swift-flying)*, and Celaeno *(dark as a storm-cloud)*. Everything they touch they foul, and wherever they go they bring with them an unbearable stench that sickens any creature who smells it.

The Harpies are called "the hounds of Zeus" because the god sometimes uses them as instruments of punishment. Their usual method is to swoop down on their victim just as he or she is beginning to eat, befoul the table, and snatch away the food. Because their feathers are steel and tougher than swords, it is almost impossible to keep them away.

The Sirens

The Sirens are temptresses, also said to resemble birds, although, because nobody who has seen them has ever survived, it is hard to prove what they look like. Their number and their names differ in various stories, but it is significant that the meanings of the names are always similar: *maiden-voice, gentle-voice, enchanting speech, persuasive, lovely speech, song.*

These creatures dwell on a flowery island close to the strait where the monsters Scylla and Charybdis lurk. Whenever a ship passes, the Sirens raise their voices in song, so sweet and enchanting that any man who hears it is compelled to leap into the sea and swim to their island, where he must listen forever. Bleached bones of sailors whiten the shoreline around these entrancing singers.

Only twice have the Sirens failed to lure their intended victims. On the first occasion, the Argonauts were passing by the island and would have succumbed, but Orpheus sang louder and more sweetly than the Sirens and drowned out their music. The second time, Odysseus became the only mortal man to hear the Siren song and live. Following the advice of Circe, he plugged his sailors' ears with beeswax so they could not hear it. Then he had himself tied to the mast so firmly that he could not leave the ship, however strong the temptation.

Once, the Sirens entered a singing contest against the Muses, but of course they lost, and the victors plucked out their feathers to make crowns. Another story says that the Sirens were the friends of Persephone who were picking flowers with her on the day she was carried off by Hades. Because they had let the abduction happen, the Sirens were punished by being turned into grotesque forms.

The Gorgons

The Gorgons are three terrible sisters, daughters of the sea rulers Phorcys and Ceto. They live in the far west by the ocean stream and are monstrous creatures with serpents for hair, staring eyes, horrible tongues, beards, claws, and tusks like a boar's. A single glimpse at these horrible beings would instantly turn any living creature to stone.

The Gorgons are named Stheno *(strength)*, Euryale *(wide-leaping)*, and Medusa *(ruler* or *queen)*. Although her sisters are immortal, Medusa was not, and eventually she was killed by the legendary warrior Perseus.

The Graiae, or Gray Ones

The Gray Ones, who are the sisters of the Gorgons, live in a cave in the mountain of Atlas. Enyo *(warlike)*, Pemphredo *(waspish)*, and Deino *(dreadful)* were old hags from the moment they were born, with gray hair and deeply wrinkled faces. They are blind and toothless, but together they own a single eye and a single tooth. When one of them needs to see or to bite, the others pass her the eye or the tooth; they share these parts equally.

The Writers of Classical Mythology

Unlike legends, folk stories, or fairy tales, the classical myths as we know them were written by artists, people who deliberately shaped their stories into poetry or plays. Most of these writers no doubt had heard the old myths told and retold, and then wrote them down to become lasting works of art. Here are some of the important writers of the Greek and Roman myths.

Homer was perhaps the oldest and best known of all storytellers, a blind Greek poet who created two great epics around 1000 B.C. The *Iliad* tells the story of the great war between Greece and Troy, and the *Odyssey* describes the adventures of the hero Odysseus as he returns home after the Trojan War.

Hesiod was apparently a shepherd and farmer who lived sometime in the ninth or eighth century B.C. He was the first to record his wonder about how everything began. In *Theogony,* he describes the creation of the universe and the world, the origin of the gods, and how life on Earth began. Another book, *Works and Days,* tells how to live a good life in a hard world.

Homeric Hymns are poems, apparently written in the late eighth or early seventh century B.C. in honor of specific gods.

Pindar was a great lyric poet at the end of the sixth century B.C., who wrote odes to celebrate the victors at the great Greek games. All of the odes tell myths and are the source of many of the stories as we know them.

Many of the stories come from Greek playwrights. **Aeschylus, Sophocles,** and **Euripides,** who lived between the sixth and the end of the fifth century B.C., wrote the great tragedies that have made so many mythological characters come alive for Western civilizations. The comic playwright **Aristophanes,** who also filled his plays with myths, wrote in the late fifth and early fourth centuries B.C.

Herodotus, a Greek historian, and **Plato,** a philosopher, who lived at the end of the fifth century B.C., included many myths in their writings.

Ovid, one of the most important sources of classical mythology, was a Roman poet who lived at the end of the first century B.C. and the beginning of the first century A.D. Ovid's *Metamorphoses* retell more than two hundred mythical stories of gods and mortals, most of which involve a transformation of one of the characters. His *Heroides,* or "Letters of Heroic Women," invent letters written by famous women in mythology to their husbands or lovers.

Virgil lived at about the same time as Ovid and was perhaps the greatest poet of ancient Rome. In his epic, the *Aenead,* he tells the story of the hero Aeneas, who alone of the Trojans survived the fall of Troy, later to found the city of Rome.

Pausanias was a Greek who traveled widely in the second century A.D. In the guidebook he wrote after his journeys, he retold all the stories he heard from people at the various sites he visited.

Apuleus, a Roman, recorded some of the myths in the second century A.D. while **Lucian,** a Greek, wrote satires of the myths. **Apollodorus,** another Greek of that time, also wrote down many of the stories.

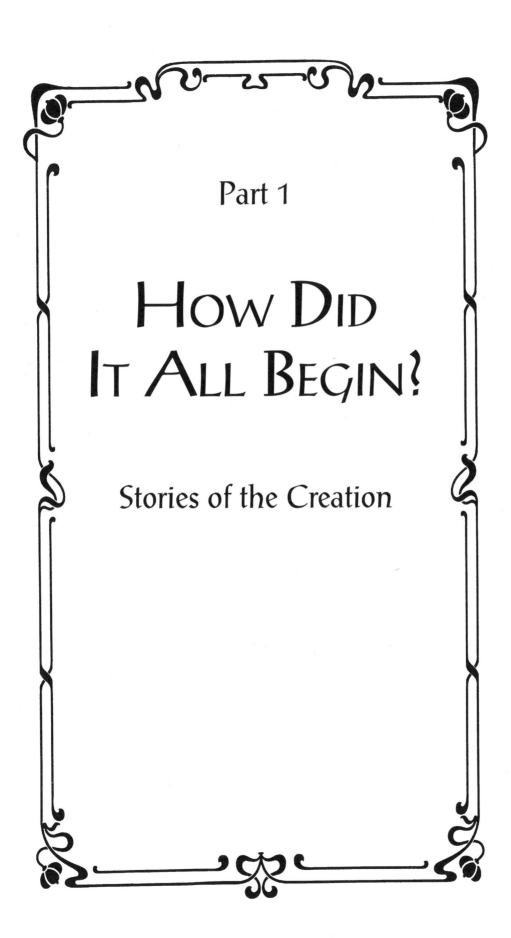

Part 1

How Did It All Begin?

Stories of the Creation

Gaia:
The Mother of Everything

FIRST THERE WAS CHAOS, A DEEP CHASM IN WHICH NOTHING EXISTED. OUT OF IT ROSE GAIA, THE broad-breasted Earth, mother of the immortals who occupy Mount Olympus. Then came Tartarus, hidden in a remote corner of the wide Earth, and after it, Eros—Love— the most beautiful of the immortal gods, who overcomes reason in gods and mortals alike. From Erebos, the realm of darkness, and Night, came Day and Bright Air.

Now, Earth gave birth to one who was equal to herself—starry Heaven—to surround her and make a home for the blessed gods. Next, she bore the long mountains, the beautiful haunts of the goddesses, the nymphs who live in the valleys and hillsides. And she bore the sea, the turbulent and undraining water, but also Oceanus, the great river that encircles the world, who came of her union with Heaven.

Also born of the marriage of Earth and Heaven were the Cyclopes and the three mighty giants with a hundred arms. The youngest child was Cronos, whose name means "time."

Heaven loathed his own children. As soon as each of them was born, he hid them away in a cavern, and would not allow them to see light. He reveled in this wicked work, while Earth groaned and was sore at heart because of the father's lack of love for her children.

She created adamant, a metal of great hardness, and made a huge sickle, a tool for reaping. Then she spoke to her children, saying, "We could make amends for your father and his cruel behavior. Who will help me?"

But they were afraid, and all the children remained silent—all except Cronos, who replied, "Mother, I will undertake this task. After all, our unspeakable father began it by his cruelty."

That night, when Heaven came and covered Earth with night, Cronos leaped out from ambush, and struck at his father with the sickle. The blood of Heaven fell in great drops, and was received by Earth. From it grew the Furies and giants, and the tree nymphs. Aphrodite, the goddess of love, rose from the foam where her father's wounds had touched the sea.

Heaven railed at his children and gave them the name of Titans. Later, there would be a great fight between the Titans and the gods, and the gods would be victorious.

But Gaia, Earth, was the mother of everything, gods and mortals alike.

This is the story Hesiod tells to explain the beginning of the world. There are other stories, as you will see.

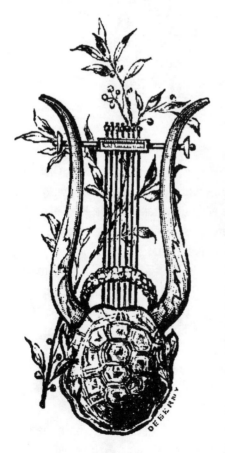

In the Beginning

BEFORE ANYTHING EXISTED, THERE WAS CHAOS, a shapeless nothingness. Out of Chaos rose Eurynome, the Goddess of All Things. When she had risen, naked and alone, she found there was no place for her to rest her feet. She divided the seas from the sky, but still she had no resting place. Eurynome began to dance upon the waves, moving toward the south, and her dancing created a wind that danced too, following behind her. This was something new, so Eurynome took the wind in her hands and rubbed it until it became the great serpent Ophion. The serpent curled itself around her and she became pregnant.

Now the goddess took on the form of a great dove and brooded over the waves. In time, she produced an enormous egg, the Universal Egg, which contained everything that was to come. At her request, the serpent Ophion coiled around it seven times to keep it warm until it hatched and split in two. From the egg tumbled out all the children of Eurynome: the sun, the moon, the planets, and stars. The last child was Earth with its wonderful features: mountains and valleys, rivers and streams, trees, plants, and all living creatures.

Eurynome and the serpent took up residence on Mount Olympus, until they quarreled. When he claimed that he, not she, had created everything, she banished him to a dark cave deep underground. Next the goddess created seven planetary powers, and set a Titan and Titaness to rule over each. Then she made the mortals. The first human was Pelasgus, who sprang from the soil of Arcadia. He became the ancestor of all mankind.

Well, that is a second version of creation, anyway. There is still another.

How the World Began

Before anything existed, there was Chaos, a shapeless nothingness. Its children were the black-winged goddess, Night, and Erebos, the place of death. Night, the all-powerful, was courted by the wind and laid a silver egg in the depths of darkness. When the egg hatched, Love emerged, golden-winged and shining, and began to create order and beauty. Love created light and day, then earth and sky.

The marriage of Mother Earth and Father Heaven—whose names were Gaia and Uranus—brought forth the first inhabitants, huge creatures with all the force of volcanoes, earthquakes, and hurricanes. The first three were giants with a hundred hands and fifty heads. The next three were the gigantic Cyclopes, each with one eye, huge as a wheel, set in the middle of his forehead. The last were the Titans, as large and powerful as their brothers, but not all violent or destructive. Some of them, in fact, were to be the benefactors of a new race: mankind, yet to be invented.

Uranus hated his children. As soon as the monstrous giants were born, he imprisoned them in caverns deep underground. Earth was furious, and she appealed to the other children, the Cyclopes and the Titans, to do something about this outrage. Cronos, the youngest Titan, was the only one of her children who had enough courage to help his mother. He fought Uranus, wounding him horribly. From the blood that spilled onto the ground sprang the giants and the Furies.

Cronos was now the sovereign of Heaven and Earth, ruling with his queen, his sister Rhea. They became the parents of the gods, but Cronos too was a jealous father. The dying Uranus had predicted that Cronos would suffer the same fate as he: that one of his sons would dethrone him. But Cronos thought he had figured out a way to prevent this. As each of his children was born, he swallowed them—first the three daughters, Hestia, Demeter, and Hera; then his sons, Hades and Poseidon.

Now it was Rhea's turn to be enraged at the father of her children. When the youngest, named Zeus, was born, she did not let Cronos see him, but quickly gave him to Mother Earth to care for. Then she wrapped the infant's swaddling clothes around a stone, and Cronos swallowed it, thinking that it was the baby.

When Zeus was grown to manhood, he determined to take vengeance on his father and rescue his siblings. Secretly he returned home to confer with his mother Rhea, who agreed to help him. She gave Cronos a drink that made him sick, and he began to throw up. First the stone came up, then each of Zeus's older brothers and sisters, unhurt and grateful to their younger brother for their deliverance. Understandably displeased about their treatment by Cronos, they begged Zeus to lead them in a war against the Titans.

In the long struggle for possession of Heaven and Earth that followed, the Titans and gods fought fiercely. The Titans, led by Atlas, were huge and more powerful than the young gods. They seemed most likely to win. But Zeus enlisted the aid of his father's siblings, the Cyclopes and the hundred–handed monsters, who held a mighty grudge against their brother Cronos.

The Cyclopes were blacksmiths who could work wonders with metal. They had created some amazing weapons, which they were glad to contribute to their brothers for this epic struggle. To Zeus they gave a thunderbolt, to Hades a helmet that would make the wearer invisible, and to Poseidon a sharp, three-pointed weapon called a trident. With such tools, the balance of power tipped toward the gods. Wearing the magic helmet, Hades entered his father's chamber unseen, and threw the door open for his brothers. While Poseidon held Cronos at bay with the trident, Zeus hurled his thunderbolt. The head of the Titans was dead.

At last, the gods were victorious. As their first act of power, they banished the Titans and chained them deep in the Underworld, from which they could never escape.

Because he had led the Titans in battle, Atlas was condemned to stand forever in the place where day and night meet, holding the heavens up on his shoulders. There he stands, carrying his burden, to this day.

The three brother gods now had control of the universe. It only remained to decide how they would rule it. There were four realms: Heaven, Earth, the seas, and the Underworld. Earth seemed too insignificant for them to bother with, so they dismissed it. Then they threw dice for the others. Zeus won the first pick, and he chose Heaven as his realm. Poseidon was next, happy to choose the seas, which he had really wanted in the first place. Hades was left with the only undesirable place, the Underworld, the realm of night, sleep, and death.

Now the attention of the gods turned to the Earth. How should they arrange it? First they created all the natural features they could imagine to make it beautiful. They raised mountains and carved out valleys, set water flowing in rivers or gathering in pools, and brightened it all with trees, green plants, and flowers. Then they were ready to populate this lovely place with living creatures.

To Prometheus—a Titan who had fought on the side of Zeus—and his brother Epimetheus, the gods gave the task of creating the animals and mankind. Prometheus's name means "foresight," and he was wiser even than the gods. But Epimetheus means "aftersight;" he had none of his brother's wisdom. Without thinking ahead, this scatter-brained brother went to Earth and began endowing the animals with their qualities. He gave them speed and courage, cunning and strength; he gave fins, feathers, claws, and beaks, fur to keep them warm. Suddenly he realized he had nothing left to give to humans! Epimetheus called on his wiser brother for help.

Prometheus had already begun to mold a clay figure. Now he picked it up and changed its shape. He made it into the very image of the gods, standing upright and looking toward Heaven. Then the goddess Athena breathed life into this creation. Mankind was born!

But one thing still was missing: if mortals only had fire, they would be the most powerful creatures on Earth. Out of love for his creation, Prometheus went up to Heaven holding a hollow fennel stalk, and took fire from the sun, then carried it back to Earth. With this gift, mankind became more than a match for the other animals.

Zeus was outraged. He had never wanted humans to have fire; that was an attribute of the gods. He blamed Prometheus for taking the mortals' side and stealing fire for them, even for teaching them civilization and the arts. As a punishment, Zeus condemned Prometheus to be chained on a high cliff, far away from mankind. There, every day, an eagle tore at his liver, which renewed itself again every night, to be ready for the next day's agony. After a very long time, Zeus agreed that his captive could be freed. Hercules came to his rescue, killed the eagle, and released Prometheus from his chains.

Zeus's Revenge: Pandora

ZEUS WAS STILL ANGRY, BOTH AT PROMETHEUS AND AT THE MORTALS WHOM THE FIRE-GIVER SEEMED to love so much. Not content with bringing them his marvelous gift, Prometheus had arranged matters so that humans would keep the best parts of every animal they sacrificed, while the gods would get only the scraps.

This is how he pulled such a trick. He killed a fat ox, then cut the animal up and wrapped the meat in its hide, covering the whole thing with entrails. The bones he put in a second pile and covered them with juicy fat. Prometheus offered Zeus his choice between the two piles. The god chose the one that looked far better, the one with the fat on top. When he lifted the fat and saw only bones, he was furious, but there was nothing he could do. He had made his choice. Now, when men sacrificed an animal before the altar, they got to keep the meat for themselves, burning only the bones and fat for the gods.

But Zeus was not a god who could be tricked lightly. Revenge he must have, and of course he had no problem coming up with a plan. Up to this time, you see, only men had inhabited the Earth. Zeus would give them something that would cause them trouble! He called Hephaestus, the god of fire and a master blacksmith, and ordered him to shape a mortal being out of clay, modeled after the beautiful Aphrodite. When the figure was finished and brought to him, Zeus breathed life into it and called it "woman."

Now Zeus assembled all the gods and asked them to give gifts to this woman–creature, gifts that would make her desirable to man, but not helpful to him. Zeus himself gave her extraordinary beauty, but also vanity and foolishness. Athena taught her to spin and weave, but did not impart any of her wisdom. From Demeter she learned the art of gardening, from Aphrodite how to attract the attentions of men. Hera gave her curiosity and suspicion.

When the woman was finished, all the gods clothed her in shining garments embroidered with wreaths of flowers, and set a golden crown on her head. They named her Pandora, which means "the gift of all." Then Hermes handed her a box, elaborately carved and gleaming with gold. With the instruction never, ever to open the box, the gods sent their creation down to Epimetheus, the foolish brother of Prometheus. Although his brother had warned him to beware of any gift from Zeus, Epimetheus was so stunned by Pandora's beauty that he forgot this caution and gladly accepted her.

The box, of course, teased Pandora's mind unbearably. What could be in it that was so secret? Why couldn't she just peek in to see? Surely, that could do no harm! At last, curiosity overcame her; she simply had to open the box. But as soon as she lifted the lid, misfortunes began to fly out; sorrows and plagues such as the Earth had never before experienced—all whizzed by her head. Pandora tried to close the lid, but by the time she did, all the woes of the world had escaped. There was only one thing left at the bottom of the box. That thing was hope, and it is all that remains to mankind to fight against the evils that Pandora had set loose upon the world.

Zeus had his revenge.

The Five Ages of Man

HERE IS ANOTHER STORY ABOUT THE CREATION OF HUMANS. AFTER THE WORLD WAS FORMED, THIS story says, it was vast and empty, a flat disk divided into land and sea. Around the disk flowed Ocean, the great river with no storms. It was time for the gods to make man.

Creation did not go bad at once. No, in the beginning, mortals behaved quite well—better, you could say, than the gods themselves had at the beginning of the world. Mankind was innocent and happy, and life was wonderful. The Earth gave abundantly of its riches; mortals did no work, but ate wild fruits, acorns, and honey that dripped from the trees; they drank the milk of sheep and goats. They lived without care, dancing and singing, laughing and joyful all day long. There was no old age and no fighting among people, who treated each other with truth and justice. This was the Golden Age of the world.

But then things started to decline. Next came the Silver Age, when life was harder. Winter appeared, and people had to toil for their food. They raised grains and made bread to eat. Humans became ignorant and quarrelsome, but they did not fight against each other.

In the Bronze Age, mortals ate meat as well as bread. These humans had fallen to Earth already armed with bronze weapons. Violence filled their hearts; soon wars broke out. People were pitiless toward their fellows, treating each other with the utmost cruelty.

Then came an upturn in the fortunes of mankind. The people of the second Bronze Age had gods for fathers, although their mothers were mortal. This race was nobler than the one before it, and more generous. Still, they loved wars, and during this period were fought all of the famous ancient battles, such as the siege of Thebes and the Trojan War. The great heroes of mythology, the warriors and adventurers, lived during this age.

But that period, too, had to end. By the Iron Age, all virtues had fled from the Earth. Selfishness and brutality had become the whole nature of humans. Mortals were cruel and treacherous, unjust, untruthful, malicious. This, says the myth, is the age in which we live today, forever looking back and yearning for the innocence and happiness of the Golden Age.

The Flood:
Pyrrha and Deucalion

ONCE AGAIN, ZEUS WAS IN A RAGE AGAINST MANKIND. IT WAS TIME TO DESTROY THAT VICIOUS race of beings, the mortals, and create a new one. First he thought of using fire to wipe out everything on Earth, but fearing that a fire might spread and burn the heavens as well, he withheld his thunderbolt. Instead, he unleashed all the waters at his command. The sky darkened, clouds gathered and teemed with rain, and the rivers overflowed their banks. Then Zeus called on his brother Poseidon, the god of the seas, to add to the flood.

Soon it was impossible to tell where land had ever been. Crops were swept away, houses and temples disappeared, birds found no place to light, fish swam among the branches of trees. The only dot of land that was visible was the very peak of Mount Parnassus.

To this spot floated a wooden vessel. Some say it was a chest, some say an ark. What matters is that from this vessel emerged the last living humans: Pyrrha, daughter of Epimetheus and Pandora, and her husband Deucalion, the son of Prometheus. Foreseeing the flood, Prometheus had warned his son to build an ark and store it with provisions. For nine days and nine nights the couple had floated over the water before they touched on Mount Parnassus. When Zeus saw them set foot on land, he recognized that Deucalion was a just and honorable man, and that Pyrrha was a good woman, a faithful follower of the gods. Deciding to let them live, Zeus made the waters recede and dry land emerge.

At once, the pair made their way to the nearest temple, where they threw themselves facedown before the goddess Themis, seeking her wisdom. The oracle told them what to do: "You must veil your faces, loosen your clothing, and cast behind you the bones of your mother." Deucalion and Pyrrha stared at each other, shocked. Both of their mothers were long buried. It would be a terrible sacrilege to follow this advice!

Then they had a new thought. Who was the mother of everyone? Why, Earth, of course. And her bones are not like human bones. The good couple walked forth, throwing over their shoulders stones, the bones of the earth. As the stones touched the ground, they began to soften and take human shapes, men if Deucalion had thrown them, and women if they came from the hand of Pyrrha. Thus a new race of humans was created, a race that had new virtues, the virtues of stone: hardness, the ability to labor, and endurance to bear whatever one's lot on Earth.

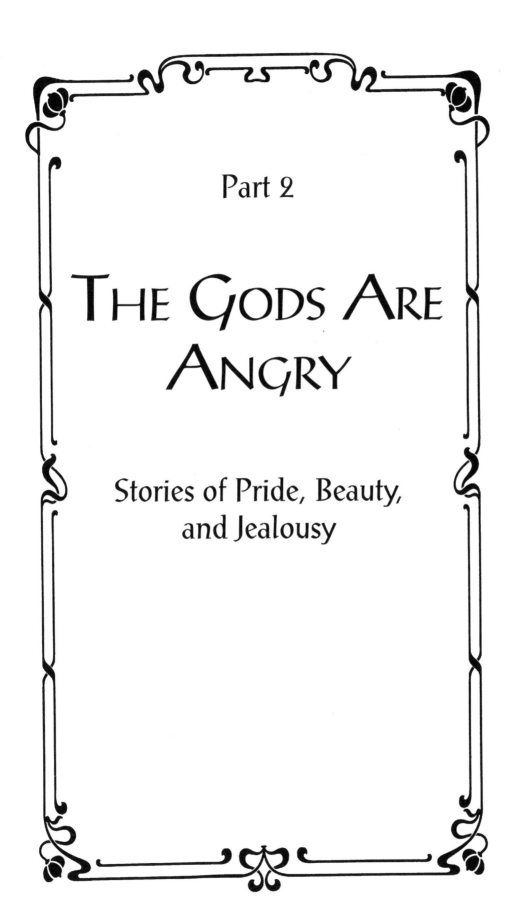

Part 2

THE GODS ARE ANGRY

Stories of Pride, Beauty, and Jealousy

PROUD WOMEN, ANGRY GODS

The Unforgivable Sin: Pride

IN THE GREEK AND ROMAN MYTHS, IT IS NOT UNUSUAL FOR GODS AND MORTALS TO MINGLE QUITE freely with each other. The gods answer petitions for help—if it pleases them to do so. They take sides in human affairs, helping their favorites among the mortals to achieve their goals. Sometimes they fall in love with, or even marry, humans.

Nevertheless, there is a clear boundary between the three worlds: Olympus, the home of the gods; Earth, the home of living mortals; and the Underworld, the realm of the dead. The distance between the three is measurable. If you drop an anvil from Heaven, it will fall nine days before it reaches the Earth, landing on the tenth day. The distance between Earth and the Underworld is the same.

The gods ruled over all three worlds, and no matter how casually they might sometimes show themselves on Earth, their power was supreme. It was essential for mortals to remember that they were lesser beings. To challenge the power and authority of the gods was to commit the worst of sins: the sin of pride, called hubris.

Still, now and again people would forget. Knowing their own strength and pleased with their accomplishments, they would believe they had succeeded on their own merits. Men who resolved to launch an adventure without leaning on the strength of a god, and women who thought they were as good as—even better than—a particular goddess doomed themselves through such pride. The gods would not tolerate arrogance, and took care to visit a terrible fate on anyone who boasted of superiority.

The following stories tell of women who forgot this.

The Eternal Weaver: Arachne

IN LYDIA THERE LIVED A YOUNG GIRL NAMED Arachne. She was the daughter of a humble man, whose work it was to color wool with the beautiful purple dyes of Phocaea. Arachne had lost her mother when she was small, but even so, she had become amazingly adept at the art of weaving. Indeed, she was so skilled in working with wool that her fame had spread throughout all the towns of Lydia.

Everyone came to watch Arachne at her weaving. Even the nymphs would come down from the vine-covered hills or the streams where they lived, just to look on. Her way of working was as lovely and graceful as the things she created. First she would take the raw wool as it came from the sheep and make a cloudlike ball. Then she would pull out strands of wool and spin them into long, soft threads, nimbly twirling the spindle with her slender thumb. With the thread she had spun, she would weave and embroider beautiful patterns of cloth.

After a time, people began to gossip. "How could the girl have acquired such miraculous skill?" they asked. Surely she had been trained by a superb teacher. It must have been the goddess Minerva! But Arachne, despite her humble birth, had grown proud. She refused to give any credit to the goddess, denying that she had had a teacher so distinguished. In fact, in her conceit the girl went even further. Fame had turned her head, and one day she dared to challenge the great Minerva herself. Arachne proposed a contest: she and the goddess should compare their skills in weaving. She swore she would pay any penalty if she lost, so sure was she that her art would surpass Minerva's.

When she heard this arrogant boast, Minerva was furious. Who was this mere mortal girl who dared to think she was better than Jove's daughter? The goddess decided to check it out. Disguising herself as an old, old woman with ragged clothing and gray hair that straggled in wisps around her forehead, Minerva descended to Earth. She pretended to walk with tottering steps, leaning weakly on a cane. In a quavering voice, she spoke to Arachne.

"I am old, and I have seen many things in my long lifetime. You may think that everything about old age is bad, but it's not. Let me tell you something: my years have given me both experience and wisdom. So you ought to listen when I speak to you.

"True, it's good to seek fame down here on Earth among the mortals, but you must never challenge the skill of a goddess. That can only bring disaster on your head! It's not too late, though. If you will humble yourself before Minerva and beg forgiveness for your arrogance, I know she will find mercy in her heart and pardon you."

Arachne's eyes flashed with pride and anger. She almost hit the goddess-in-disguise as she snapped, "Why should I listen to anyone as old and shabby as you? I think your brain has softened with age! If you really need to feel powerful, you can tell your daughters and daughters-in-law what to do, but leave me alone. I don't need anyone's advice! And since you're so smart, tell me this: why is Minerva afraid to come down here to talk with me herself? I'll tell you why. She doesn't dare to match her skill with mine!"

When she heard these arrogant words, the goddess could no longer contain her rage. She flung off her disguise and cried out in a voice that struck terror in her listeners: "She *has* come!"

When they recognized the great Minerva, all the Lydian women and the nymphs fell to their knees in awe and reverence. But Arachne stood her ground, though for a moment her cheeks grew red, then pale. She was determined to have this match, sure that she would win.

Common sense should have told the girl to beware of conceit: a mortal must not issue such a dare. To challenge a goddess is simply foolhardy! But Arachne had gone beyond common sense, and Minerva no longer tried to warn her. The goddess was eager to begin the contest, and agreed to start at once.

Both contenders set up their looms. With sure hands, they wound the threads that would form the warp, and tied them to the cross-beam. Rapidly, they began to pass back and forth the shuttles that wove the threads of the wool. As each thread went through, a fine comb pulled it back and firmed it into place. The goddess and the girl pulled their dresses up close around them to free their arms, which now moved firm and sure. They worked fast, and excitement made the work seem light.

As they watched the two contestants deftly weave their patterns, the spectators gasped in wonder. The colors of the threads were delicate and subtle, like the colors of the rainbow when the sun shines against a showery sky, melting from shade to shade imperceptibly, and yet each arc different. The weavers added strands of Tyrian purple, and of gold wire, and silver. And the tapestries began to take their shape.

For her design, Minerva chose to show her own victorious conflict with Neptune over the naming of Athens: which one of them would become its patron deity? She depicted twelve gods, with Jove in the middle, all sitting regally on thrones. Neptune, the ruler of the sea, stood with his long trident in his hand, and struck down through solid rock, bringing up a great gush of salt water. The goddess herself appeared fully armed in helmet and shield. With her sharp-tipped spear she struck the earth and brought forth an olive tree heavy with fruit. The gods judged her the winner, for a tree bearing olives would be more useful to the city than a spring of brackish water.

This should have been the first warning to Arachne: not even a god could win a contest with Minerva!

To make her point still stronger, the goddess wove into each corner of her tapestry a scene that showed what had happened to other mortals proud enough to dare to compete with gods. There was a couple, Rhodope and Haemon, who had lovingly called each other by the names of the highest gods, and had been changed to snow-covered mountains. Another corner showed the Pygmy queen Oenone, whom Juno turned into a crane, which attacked the people she had once ruled. The third depicted Antigone, who compared herself to Juno, and as punishment was turned into a stork, clacking and clashing her bill. Finally, there was the weeping Cinyras, whose daughters had been transformed to marble temple steps. And around the border, Minerva wove a running olive branch, the branch of peace.

Foolish Arachne, swollen with pride, paid no heed to the warning so clearly pictured in the goddess's work. She chose for her subject the failings and wickedness of the gods. Arachne filled her tapestry with scenes of Jove, who had come down to Earth and taken on various disguises, to deceive women. The first victim she pictured was Europa, with Jove as a bull, woven so skillfully he looked alive, and the sea in which he swam looked wet. Europa gazed back at the shore in terror, calling to her friends for help. Other scenes showed Asterie struggling with Jove in the guise of an eagle, and Leda with the swan, then Jove disguised as a satyr with Antiope, as a shower of gold with Danae, a flame with Aegina, a shepherd with Mnemosyne, and a spotted serpent with Proserpina.

Other gods, too, appeared in other disguises, to deceive other women: Neptune as a bull, a ram, a horse, a bird, a dolphin. All of the scenes were filled with fine and accurate detail, both of faces and scenery. There was Apollo dressed as a herdsman, a shepherd, wearing a lion's skin and a hawk's plumage; then Bacchus and Saturn, also in disguises meant to fool women. Instead of the olive branch, Arachne's border was a pattern of flowers and ivy intertwined.

When she had finished, Arachne's tapestry was perfect. Minerva could find no flaw anywhere. Despite her envy, she had to admire the splendid work. But she could not forgive the young upstart her success, nor her calculated insult to the gods. In a rage, the golden-haired goddess lashed out at the tapestry and ripped it to pieces. With her boxwood shuttle, she struck the girl on the forehead three times, then a fourth.

Arachne was both mortified and outraged. Hardly knowing what she was doing, she ran off; then, in her fury, she threw a noose around her neck and hanged herself. When Minerva saw what had happened to the girl, she was surprised by a momentary pang of pity. She raised Arachne up and declared, "All right, you wicked girl! You have touched my heart. You may live! But you must never forget that a mortal cannot challenge a goddess. And to make sure that you remember, this will be your fate: you will dangle forever by a single thread, you and all your descendants after you."

As she spoke these words, Minerva sprinkled the unhappy girl with the juices of aconite, the drug sacred to Hecate, queen of the witches. At the first touch of the drug,

Arachne's hair fell off, and then her nose and ears. Her head began to shrink, and her body too, until she was tiny. Those wonderfully nimble and slender fingers stretched out into long, thin legs. And all the rest of her was body, out of which, to this very day, she spins her thread and weaves her web.

Arachne still practices her art, and her weaving is unsurpassed. But you can often find her hanging from her thread, dangling just as she was at the moment Minerva touched her and turned her into a spider.

Sorrow in Stone: Niobe

ALL THE DESCENDANTS OF TANTALUS WERE doomed to misfortune because of his wickedness. But of them all, none suffered a more terrible fate than his daughter Niobe.

At first it seemed as if Niobe had been singled out for good fortune, not ill. She was most happily married; her husband, Amphion, was the son of Zeus, and a superb musician. Amphion had a twin brother named Zethus, who was known for his great strength. Zethus often teased his twin because he spent his time on art instead of sports, a more manly pastime, Zethus thought. Yet when the two brothers decided to strengthen the defenses of Thebes by building a high wall all around it, only Amphion could move the heavy stones. He played on his lyre, and the stones were so enthralled by the music that they got up and followed him to Thebes. This act won him fame and riches.

Niobe and Amphion had a splendid family, seven strong and handsome sons and seven beautiful daughters, children any parent would be proud of. But Niobe's pride in her children was excessive, almost to the point of madness. It was doomed to a tragic end.

In her girlhood, Niobe had been a good friend of Arachne. She should have learned something from the terrible story of what had happened to her friend. That story had passed quickly from person to person throughout Lydia; everyone had talked about what had become of the girl because of her incredible pride.

But Niobe paid no heed to that lesson. She had so much to be proud of: her own high birth and her husband's skill, their power and position, and most of all, of course, her children. She would have been the happiest of all mothers on Earth, if only she had not thought she was. But alas, her arrogance led her to believe that she was happier even than the gods.

One day, the seeress Manto, burning with the fire of prophecy, went through the streets of the city calling out: "Women of Thebes! Listen to what I have to tell you. Adorn your hair with laurel wreaths and go at once to the temple of Leto, taking incense to worship the goddess and her children. This order comes from Leto herself, so pay attention!" At once, the women caught up their hair with garlands and made a procession to the holy shrine, to burn the incense and offer prayers.

They had just begun their rites when Niobe appeared, surrounded by a throng of courtiers. She looked splendid in robes of purple embroidered with threads of the brightest gold. Even though she was angry, she was beautiful. Niobe tossed her graceful head, letting her radiant hair fall over both of her shoulders. She stopped, holding herself very tall, and ran her proud eyes over the scene.

"Are you mad," she asked, "to prefer gods you have only heard of to the gods you can see? Why should you worship Leto at her altar, and offer no incense to me? You know I too am divine. My father is Tantalus, the only mortal the gods ever invited to their banquet table. My mother is sister of the Pleiades. The giant Atlas, who bears the heavens on his shoulder, is one of my grandfathers; great Zeus himself is the other, and he is my husband's father as well, I'm proud to say. I am the mistress of the beautiful palace built by Cadmus, and through my husband, I am queen of Thebes, whose very walls he erected with his music. Wherever I cast my eyes, I see evidence of our enormous wealth. And my beauty is equal to that of any goddess. But above all that, glory is due to me because of my seven sons and seven daughters. Before long I will add their wives and husbands to my fine family. Do you have to ask why I am so proud?

"How dare you prefer Leto to me!" she went on angrily. "She is lowborn, the daughter of Coeus, whoever he is! There was a time when Leto could find no place to bear her children, not the tiniest spot. Neither Earth nor sea nor sky would take her in, and she was forced to roam throughout the world, homeless, until the island of Delos took pity on her and offered her room. Delos himself was a vagrant, a wanderer on the sea as she was on land. Her only refuge was a little floating island!

"And how many children did she finally bear?" Niobe sneered. "Only two! I have seven times as many children as she! Who can deny my happiness? Who dares to doubt that I'll remain happy in the future? My riches keep me safe from the blows of Fortune; I am too great for her to injure me. And just suppose I should lose a few of my children— whatever the loss, I'll never be reduced to a paltry two, like Leto. She might as well be childless!

"So, women, go away and leave your foolish worship! Away at once! Take those laurel wreaths out of your hair! Stop making sacrifices to Leto, and be quick about it!"

Niobe was so commanding that the women at once took off their garlands and left the temple, the rites unfinished. But as they went, they continued to murmur words of praise to the goddess softly, under their breath.

Of course, Leto was outraged when she heard Niobe's speech. She called her children to her—and her children were none other than the god and goddess of the sun and moon, Apollo and Artemis.

"Look at me!" Leto spluttered. "I am your mother, and I am proud to have borne two such glorious children! The only goddess I would ever defer to is Hera, the queen of Heaven herself—yet this mere mortal woman has cast doubts on my greatness! My children, unless you avenge me, I will never again be worshiped at any altar.

"To add insult to injury, Niobe has the gall to say that her children are better than mine. She called me 'childless!' Well, she shall see my power at work! Childless, indeed! Let that fate happen to her instead!"

She would have added more, but the furious Apollo interrupted. "You've said enough! The longer you talk, the longer her punishment is delayed!" Artemis agreed with him. The two wrapped themselves in a cloud and swiftly glided down to the citadel of Thebes.

From their vantage point, the god and goddess could look far out over the broad plain that lay outside the Theban walls, where a hard track had been worn by the pounding of many hoofs and the wheels of chariots. There, Niobe's older sons were riding their high-mettled steeds, on bright crimson saddlecloths, their harnesses blazing with gold. The oldest son, Ismenus, was just leaning in to make a turn, pulling hard on the bit, when he suddenly cried out in pain. An arrow had pierced his heart. He dropped the reins, and slowly he sank sideways to the ground.

His brother Sipylus heard the rattling of an invisible quiver, and urged his horse to fly ahead. But the divine arrow was faster than Sipylus. It struck him in the back of the neck, the blow so fierce that the barb came out through his throat. Hit just as he was leaning forward to gain more speed, he went flying over the horse's head and down between the galloping feet. The ground was stained scarlet with his blood.

The next unfortunate sons, Phaedimus and Tantalus, were finishing their usual morning exercise with a bout of wrestling. Their bodies glistening with oil, the two boys were struggling breast to breast when a single arrow pierced them both, fastening them together. As one, they groaned, writhed in pain, and fell, rolling their eyes until only the whites showed. Alphenor saw this happening, and ran to them, beating his breast. He tried to lift the bodies, but was struck himself in this act of devotion. Apollo's arrow pierced him through the chest, and when he tried to pull the shaft out of the wound, part of his lung came with it. Blood spouted through the air.

Young Damasichthon was hit more than once, first behind the knee; then, as he bent to pull that arrow out, a second, swifter and more accurate, struck him through the throat, driven in up to the feathers. A great spurt of blood sent the arrow flying out.

Now there was only one left of the seven sons. Ilioneus begged for his life. "Oh gods in Heaven! Have mercy on me! Spare me!" Of course, he needn't have prayed to all the gods, but the boy didn't know that. And although Apollo was moved by his plea, it was too late. The arrow had already left his bow. Still, the god slowed its flight, so that the wound that killed Ilioneus was the least cruel of all: it only reached his heart.

Rumors of a terrible tragedy began to spread through the city. The streets filled with sorrowing people, and the lamentations of her own household brought Niobe the news of her sons' deaths. So shocked and bewildered was she that Niobe could not take it in, could not believe that the gods would be so daring, so violent. But when her husband Amphion, maddened by grief, drove his sword into his own heart, she understood it all, and knew what power the gods held.

It was a different Niobe who went out of her house, different from the one who had driven the women away from Leto's altar. Then she had been haughty and proud, envied by all who met her. Now she was pathetic, a woman even her enemies must pity. She threw herself on the cold bodies of her sons and covered them with kisses. Then she raised her arms to Heaven and cried, "Cruel Leto, feast on my sorrow! Let your heart be glutted with it! My seven sons are dead, and I will go to my grave from grief. Yes, exult! Triumph in your victory!"

But Niobe's pride was not yet quenched. She could not keep herself from adding "But is it victory? I still have more children, in spite of my sorrow, than you! Even with these deaths, I am the winner!"

Scarcely had she finished speaking when a bowstring twanged. The seven sisters, clad in robes of black, their hair let down in sorrow, were standing by their brothers' funeral biers. As one of them bent over to pull an arrow from her brother's body, she fell dead, her cheek against his. A second, trying to comfort her mother, suddenly grew silent, stricken by an invisible wound. A third tried to escape, and fell as she was running; a fourth tripped over her and died beside her sister. One attempted to hide, and one tried to be brave out in the open; both of them trembled violently, then died. Now six sisters were dead, and only the seventh was left alive, youngest of all the children. Her mother bent over her, trying to shield the girl with her robe and her own body. She cried to Heaven, "Oh, leave me this one child, my littlest one! Of all of them I ask you only for her!" But even as she prayed, the little girl was dead.

Niobe was childless. She sat among the bodies of her seven handsome sons and seven beautiful daughters and her husband, frozen into complete stillness. Not a muscle of her body moved. The breeze did not even lift her hair while her cheeks slowly grew pale, as white as marble. Her eyes were fixed and staring. Here was the very picture of grief, a picture lifeless and still. Her wayward tongue turned stiff, her jaws were hard; no pulse beat in her veins. Her neck could not bend, her arms could not move, her feet could not go forward. All was changed to stone.

And yet she wept and wept. Then, as her tears kept falling, a mighty whirlwind caught her up and carried her to her native land. There on a mountaintop Niobe sits, still weeping for her children. To this day, the marble drips with tears.

The Pierides Challenge the Muses

ONE DAY, THE GODDESS MINERVA CHOSE TO PAY A visit to the Muses high atop their sacred mountain, Helicon. As she spoke with one of the nine sisters, the air filled with the whirring of wings, and then from the boughs of the trees overhead came words of greeting. Jove's daughter looked up into the leaves, certain that she was hearing words, human words spoken in human voices.

But all Minerva could see was a bird perched on the branch. In fact, nine birds sat there, chattering at her in raucous voices. They were magpies, those master imitators of any sound they hear, and they were complaining in human tones about misfortune and the sad fate that had befallen them.

Surprised, the goddess turned to the Muse, who began to speak in low, confidential tones, one goddess to another.

"Don't pay any attention to them." she said "They have not been birds for very long. They used to be women, but then they dared to challenge us, the Muses. Of course they lost.

"Here's how it all came about. Their father was Pierus, a rich landowner, and their mother was called Euippe. Nine times she gave birth; nine times she called on Lucina, the goddess of childbirth, to come to her aid. Nine times she brought forth a girl-child.

"What a pack of fools those girls were! Just because there were so many of them, they thought they were superior to everyone else, the rarest of the rare. They traveled through all the towns of Thessaly and Achaea, swollen with pride and boasting of their artistic skill. Finally they arrived here at Helicon and challenged us, the Muses—taunted us, if you can believe it!

"They said, 'Quit trying to fool these ignorant people, the silly mob, with your feeble attempts at poetry and song! We dare you to come and sing against us! If you trust your own art, you won't be afraid to compete with us. Look, there are just as many of us as of you, and our skill and voices are at least equal to yours. We'll outsing, outdance, outplay anyone!

" 'Here's our offer. If you lose, you give us two of the clear springs you own. If we lose, we'll give you all the beautiful plains of Macedonia right up to the snowline, halfway up the mountain. Come on, don't be shy! Let's go! Call on the nymphs to judge our contest!'

"It was a disgrace to have to compete with those braggarts, but it would have been even more shameful to ignore their challenge. And so we chose nymphs to act as judges, agreeable to both sides. Each nymph took an oath, by her own stream, that she would be unbiased and fair. Then they sat down on benches made of living stone, ready to listen and to judge.

"The girl who challenged us didn't even wait for lots to be drawn to determine the order of contestants, but started singing, grabbing the first position for herself. Her song told of the great war in Heaven, the battles between the gods and giants. She praised the giants and belittled the achievements of the gods. She sang that the monster Typhoeus came out of Hell and terrified the gods, making them run until they were exhausted and sought refuge in Egypt by the seven-mouthed Nile.

But, she sang, Typhoeus still chased the gods, until they had to take on disguises to hide themselves. Jove turned into a ram; Apollo hid himself in crowskin, while his sister Phoebe became a cat, Bacchus a goat, Juno a great snow-white cow, Venus a fish, and Mercury an ibis.

"She sang and sang, accompanying herself endlessly on the lute until our time finally came to answer her …

"But"—here the Muse broke off— "you must be bored by this story, my dear goddess! Perhaps we should postpone our talk; maybe you're busy and have something else to do?"

At once Minerva answered, "No, no, please go on. I can't wait! Give me the whole story the way it should be told, from beginning to end." So the Muse continued.

"We chose only one of us to represent all nine: our great sister, Calliope. Proud and tall she stood, an ivy wreath holding back her flowing hair. When she ran her thumb across the strings of her lute, sweet sounds rose to heaven. The song she sang was in praise of Ceres, goddess of the life-giving Earth.

"As soon as my sister had finished singing," the Muse chuckled, "the nymphs rose with one accord, and gave the victory to us, the goddesses of Helicon.

"They were terrible losers, those defeated sisters, those Pierides. They cursed and hurled abuse at us. I had to tell them, 'It wasn't enough for you to challenge us in song, it seems. Now that you've lost this disgraceful contest, you add insult to injury. We've put up with a lot from you, but even our patience has a limit! We've listened to you too long. Now it's time for anger, time for punishment!'

"They kept on mocking, laughing at my threats. But as they jeered, as they tried to shout us down and thumb their noses, they saw feathers sprout between their fingers and spread across their hands and up their arms. They watched each other's faces change in profile, grow pointed and hard, with stiff yellow beaks.

"Another new bird had been added to the forest! When they tried to beat their breasts, they found black wings lifting them into the air. And there they hovered, magpies now, the chatterboxes and scolds of the woodlands.

"Still, they love the sound of their own voices, and go on day after day, making that dreadful din as they talk, talk, talk."

The Sisters Who Scorned Bacchus

A new god had appeared, and everyone rushed to welcome him. Everyone, that is, except Alcithoe, a daughter of the rich king Minyas. Bacchus, she said, might be the son of Jove or he might not, but for her part, she chose to think he was not. She refused to worship him or to take any part in the ceremonies that had been announced to celebrate his arrival. Her sisters joined in her rebellion; none of them would recognize Bacchus, this upstart god.

The priest who had ordered the day of celebration called on everyone to join in its festivities. Servants must be given the day off, he said, and maid and mistress alike should dress in animal skins, letting their hair flow free from its usual ribbons, twining it instead with garlands of grape and myrtle. The celebrants were to come to the temple carrying vine-wreathed staffs in their hands. Bacchus would be enraged, the priest added, if anyone balked at this order.

Old and young, the women all obeyed. They put away their unfinished work—spinning, weaving, sewing, and their daily housework—to flock to the altar. There they burned incense and called the god by all his names and titles. They hailed him as *Deep-Sounder, King of the Noises, Deliverer from Sorrow, Son of the East, God of the Vine, the God of Night*. "Be with us forever, gentle god!" they cried.

Only the daughters of Minyas, Alcithoe and her sisters, kept aloof from the sacred rites. They stayed indoors, spoiling the festival by going about their usual activities. All day they kept busy, and kept their maids busy too, spinning, weaving, and doing their regular chores.

Outside, the streets had grown very quiet, and it did seem a little odd to be the only ones in town who were not rejoicing at the temple. Alcithoe had an idea to make the time pass pleasantly. As her agile fingers spun the thread, she said, "Those other women have all run off to worship what's-his-name, abandoning their duties and wasting their time with silly, false rites. But we worship a better goddess, Pallas. So let's forget about them. Why don't we while away the time by telling stories as we work?" All the sisters agreed, and they spent the day happily, weaving wool and wonderful tales at the same time.

Many stories later, the day was almost gone. Still the sisters worked on, still scorning Bacchus and the festival that had honored him. Suddenly, as they sat at their looms, a great noise burst over them, the sound of unseen drums and flutes, cymbals and trumpets, and the air was filled with the sweet scents of myrrh and saffron. Then—oh, miracle!—their weaving turned to green, and all across the finished cloth grew luscious vines of ivy and grape. The threads became clinging tendrils, leaves grew over the warp, and lush bunches of grapes covered all the pattern that had been woven in purple.

Now the magic hour came on, the hour that lies just between daylight and darkness, when the sun's red glow is low on the horizon. The whole house began to tremble and shake, the lamps flared bright as if crimson fire were leaping from room to room. Phantom forms seemed to fill all the spaces—great howling, savage beasts of prey. The sisters cowered in the corners.

Then, as the rooms filled with smoke, they tried to flee, to escape the flames and glare. Groping for their way, they tripped and began to fall. Oddly, though, they did not reach the floor. Delicate membranes began to spread over their legs and feet; thin wings wrapped around their arms.

The house had grown dark, and none of the sisters could see, at first, how they had changed. They found themselves lifted up on wings, featherless and light, thin as parchment, wings so frail anyone could see right through them. When they tried to speak, their voices made only a shrill squeak, as tiny as they themselves had become.

To this day, the bats, who were once the daughters of Minyas, prefer houses to the forest, hiding in the rafters and swinging from the highest beams. They hate the light and fly only in darkness. Even their name, Vespertiliones, means "the evening flutterers."

The Proud Queen: Cassiopeia and Her Daughter Andromeda

THE QUEEN OF ETHIOPIA WAS PROUD, AS PROUD AS she was beautiful. Cassiopeia was the granddaughter of Hermes, but it was not her heritage she prized so highly, nor the rank of her husband, King Cepheus. It was beauty. Not just her own beauty: Cassiopeia had a daughter named Andromeda, whose loveliness, her mother thought, was unsurpassed by anyone, mortal or immortal.

One day Cassiopeia boasted that her daughter was more beautiful even than the Nereids, the nymphs of the sea. That was foolish enough, but even worse, she did her bragging right on the seashore, where the nymphs could hear her! Of course, they were outraged. They went straight to their father, the sea god Poseidon. He must avenge this terrible insult to his daughters, they urged. Poseidon agreed. He would send a cruel sea serpent to ravage the land of Ethiopia and terrify the people away from their homes, until the whole country lay in ruins.

King Cepheus was stunned. What could he do to save his country and his people? Unable to think of a solution, he sought advice from an oracle. The answer was terrible. In order to rid his land of the monster, the oracle pronounced, he must sacrifice his beloved daughter, Andromeda, to the serpent. Only that would satisfy the beast and send it back to the ocean depths.

Cepheus and Cassiopeia cried out in horror. Condemn their daughter to such a fate? Never! For a very long time, they resisted the oracle's demand, but the people begged them to do their duty. The land must be saved! At last, in agony, they agreed.

So Andromeda was chained to a rock at the base of a cliff that towered over the ocean, there to wait for sunrise, when the serpent would come to devour her. The king and queen hovered nearby, distraught. They wept, but could think of no way to save their daughter. The innocent girl must pay the price of her mother's pride and boastfulness.

But chance took a hand in events. The young hero Perseus, returning from his defeat of the terrible Gorgon, Medusa, noticed the scene below as he flew overhead on his winged sandals. He saw a black rock, washed by the waves of the sea, and the figure of a lovely maiden, her arms firmly fastened to the stone. At first he thought she was a marble statue, but then the breeze stirred her hair and he saw hot tears flow down her lovely face.

Dazed by this vision, Perseus almost forgot to beat his wings, but quickly recovered himself. He glided down to confront the girl. "What has happened to put you in these iron chains?" he demanded. "You are meant to be held only by the chains of love! Tell me: who are you, what country is this, and why have you been bound to this dark rock?"

Andromeda was too shy to look at him, and would have covered her face with her hands, but she could not move them, chained as they were to the stone. She could only gaze down, with tear-filled eyes, until Perseus gently urged her to speak. At last she told him the whole story.

Even before she had finished, a terrible noise rose out of the depths of the ocean. Looking seaward, everyone was horrified to see a monstrous beast riding the waves, heading straight toward them. Andromeda screamed in terror. Her parents, panicked but helpless, wrung their hands and hugged their daughter.

Now Perseus spoke. "Later there will be plenty of time to cry, but right now there's very little time for rescue!" He turned to King Cepheus. "If this were a normal situation, I would come to you as a suitor for Andromeda's hand, and I think you'd look kindly on me. I am a son of Zeus, the one who rides the air on wings, the slayer of the snake-haired Gorgon. But now I will do one more deed: with the help of the gods, I will defeat this dragon. If I am successful, will you give me Andromeda in marriage?"

What could they say but *yes?* To save their daughter, Cassiopeia and Cepheus promised they would give Perseus not only her hand, but their rich kingdom as well.

The monster swam on, as fast as a swift ship that cuts the waves with its prow, sending out a great wake of white water. Now it was no farther from the rock than the little distance a slingshot can send its stone flying.

Suddenly Perseus sprang into the air, soaring up to the clouds. The beast saw his shadow fall across the sea. Then, as an eagle swoops down on a snake sunning in an open field, Perseus fell on the dragon, thrusting his sword up to the hilt into its shoulder. The wound was deep, and it burned terribly. The monster reared up into the air, then plunged down through the waters, twisting and turning in agony, then rose again to the attack. The winged Perseus dodged its snapping fangs, and as the beast turned over and over, he deftly jabbed with his sword wherever he saw an opening. He struck now on the belly, now on the neck, now on the ribs, now between the barnacles that covered its back, now at its fishy tail.

The dragon spewed purple blood. The famous winged sandals grew heavy with a mixture of blood and sea spray, and Perseus began to fall. Then he saw a rock that stood out of the water whenever the waves drew back, and leaped to safety. Bracing himself against the cliff, he plunged his sword deep into the monster's vitals, again and again. Perseus had won; the shore rang with cheers that echoed up to Heaven.

Cassiopeia and Cepheus were rapturous. They hailed Perseus as their new son, the savior of their house. Andromeda's chains were loosened, and shyly the girl stepped forward, both his reason for this fight and his reward. Before he took her hand, Perseus washed his own clean of the monster's blood.

Then, mindful of what he owed to the gods, he built three altars on the shore, one for Hermes, one for Zeus, and one for the warrior goddess, Athena. Before these altars he made his sacrifices to the three gods: a calf, a bull, and a cow.

Joyfully Perseus took Andromeda as his bride; he needed no further reward. The gods of love and marriage themselves carried the torches to lead the wedding procession. Merry sounds of lyre, flute, and song rose to heaven; the heady perfume of incense filled the air; and in all the streets, houses were hung with garlands to celebrate the happiness of the land. The great doors of the palace swung open to reveal a gleaming golden hall, where a lavish banquet was spread for all the nobles of Cepheus's country.

The newly married couple lived in Ethiopia for a time with Andromeda's parents. When their first son was born, Perseus renounced his claim to the kingdom, giving his son the right to inherit the throne when Cepheus died. Then he returned in triumph to his native city, Argos, where for many years he ruled as king.

Perseus and Andromeda remained together until death. Then Athena placed them all into the heavens as constellations—Andromeda, her husband, her parents, and even the sea serpent. But because Cassiopeia's pride had caused so much trouble and anguish, she hangs forever upside down, her feet in the air.

You don't always have to boast to be found arrogant by the gods. In this story, Galanthis was only trying to help her mistress, but she did outsmart a goddess. Not a good idea, as she learned.

<hr>

Galanthis the Gallant

ALCMENA WAS ABOUT TO BECOME A MOTHER, AND HER SON would be the hero Hercules. But when the day came for her to give birth, things were difficult. Juno was angry at Alcmena, and she had persuaded the goddess Lucina, who attends women at this time, to refuse her help. More than once, Alcmena called on the goddess of childbirth and her two midwives, begging them to come to her, but she received no answer. For seven days and seven painful nights, she waited in vain for assistance.

At last Lucina came, but she had promised Juno that instead of assisting the birth, she would prevent it. Without a word, the goddess took up her position by the altar outside Alcmena's door. She crossed her arms, locked her fingers together, and crossed her legs, the right over the left. Then she began to chant spells to hold back the birth. Alcmena's tears would have moved a stone to pity, but Lucina was harder than a stone. She just sat, chanting, with her arms crossed, her fingers locked together, and her legs crossed, the right over the left.

Then Alcmena's best-loved servant, a little golden-haired peasant girl named Galanthis, had an idea. Going in and out of the room, she had noticed the figure who was always sitting there, crossed and locked, as still as a statue except for her low mutterings. The servant guessed that spiteful Juno was working mischief against her mistress, and would never let her have this baby.

Galanthis left the room where Alcmena lay, and cheerfully greeted the goddess. "I don't know who you are," she said, "but you must congratulate my lady! Her prayers have been answered by the gods, and she has given birth to a healthy baby boy."

When she heard these words, Lucina sprang up, shocked to learn that her curse had failed. In her dismay, her arms uncrossed, her fingers unlocked, her legs uncrossed. And at that very moment, Hercules was born.

The ruse had worked. But naughty Galanthis began to mock the goddess she had deceived. At the sight of Lucina's bewilderment and wrath, she began to laugh. The more she laughed, the angrier the goddess grew; but the angrier the goddess grew, the more Galanthis laughed. As she doubled up in merriment, Lucina grabbed the girl and yanked her hair, pulling her to the ground. There she held her until her arms and legs began to grow short, and her body long and sinewy. When Galanthis tried to get up, she could not; she could no longer stand on two feet.

Although her shape is different now, Galanthis has kept her pretty golden hair, and she is still as busy and cheerful around the house as she was when she was a gallant little serving girl instead of a golden ferret.

SECTION 2

BEAUTIFUL WOMEN, JEALOUS GODDESSES

The Jealous Goddess: Hera

HERA WAS THE QUEEN OF HEAVEN; THERE WAS NO DOUBT ABOUT THAT. AS THE WIFE OF THE GREAT god Zeus, her position as chief among the goddesses was secure. At least, it appeared to be. But Hera never felt secure, because her husband was always attracted by beauty, and there were many beautiful women to capture his attention.

It was her own beauty that had first drawn Zeus to her—her handsome appearance and her stately bearing. He courted her for a long time, and still she would not agree to marry him. Perhaps even then she did not quite trust him.

One day, before she had said yes, Zeus watched Hera walking in the woods of Argos, and he thought he could wait no longer for her to become his wife. He raised a tremendous storm: wind raged and rain pounded; all creatures sought shelter from the blast. Zeus turned himself into a cuckoo. Wet and bedraggled, he flew to Hera, looking at her with piteous eyes. Touched by such helplessness, she drew the little bird under her cloak for shelter. There the god changed himself back into his real form and kissed her. At last Hera promised to marry him.

Their wedding filled Olympus with celebration. Of course, all the gods brought lavish presents, but the most beautiful of the gifts was the one from Gaia, Mother Earth herself. She gave the bride a tree that bore gleaming golden apples. Hera planted it in the center of the garden of the gods.

But alas, in spite of all the gods' blessings, the marriage of Zeus and Hera was not destined to be a happy one. Zeus could not keep away from beautiful women, and his love affairs were many. It's true that Hera was bad-tempered to begin with. Certainly she was always noted for her pride—after all, she had taken the peacock for her special bird! Still, both her temper and her pride worsened during her marriage, and increasingly she fell prey to tremendous fits of jealousy.

Although anyone who crossed her was bound to suffer, most of Hera's anger was directed at the objects of Zeus's love. Never mind that almost all of those women were entirely innocent, and had never wanted to be involved with the god. More often than not, he had disguised himself when he approached them, so they didn't even know that it was Zeus. Still, Hera spent her days seeking them out and inflicting the most terrible punishments on them. Often the punishment would fall on their children as well. This was a goddess who never forgot or forgave anything!

Once, Hera's anger turned against her husband. Zeus had taken too much power on himself; his arrogance had grown intolerable, especially to his wife, his brother Poseidon, and his son Apollo. With the support of all the other Olympians except Hestia (who never engaged in quarrels), the three decided it was time to curb the supreme god's temper and pride. They waited until the time was just right, a night when, having eaten his fill, Zeus fell asleep on his couch. The other gods slipped up quietly and fell on him. They bound his arms and legs with rawhide thongs, which they tied in a hundred knots. Zeus awoke, roaring with anger, and threatened them all with instant death. But they had put his dread thunderbolts out of reach, and they only laughed at his rage.

During all this uproar, someone was cowering in a corner. Thetis, a Nereid whom Hera had raised, was terrified. "What if there were to be another war among the gods?" she worried. That was unthinkable! Silently, she stole away to Tartarus and brought back the hundred-handed monster Briareus. Quickly, his hundred hands untied the hundred knots, and Zeus was free.

Now it was Hera's turn to be punished. Zeus decreed that she should be hung from the sky, with golden manacles binding her wrists and heavy anvils attached to her feet. None of the gods dared to listen to her pitiful cries; none of them tried to rescue her. But Zeus himself took pity on her at last, and agreed to release her if she swore never again to rebel against him.

In spite of her bad temperament, Hera was noted for her faithfulness as a wife. She was the goddess who protected marriages and married women. Many people prayed to her. Of course, that might have been because she could be so persistent in her torture of those who made her angry. In Greece today, if something is irritating—an insect that keeps biting, or ants attacking a picnic, for instance—people will say, "Careful! It looks like Hera is out to get you."

Hera was gifted with the power of prophecy, not always a happy gift, and she could bestow this power on anyone she chose. Usually, the people so favored could foretell nothing but disaster. But who wants to listen to such gloomy talk? Death and destruction, love doomed to disaster, failures of all kinds—to foretell such things was not a gift that anyone looked forward to receiving.

Hera kept very busy involving herself with mortals and their affairs. Some people she favored, some she hated. Her intervention had great consequences in the stories of mythology. For instance, when she was on Jason's side, he succeeded in his search for the Golden Fleece. When she abandoned him, everything in his life turned out badly.

Hera's wrath at the Trojan prince Paris was unquenchable: he had awarded the title of most beautiful goddess to Aphrodite, not to Hera. If she had not been so furious, the Trojan War might have ended in a truce between Greece and Troy. But Hera would not rest until Troy and all the Trojans were utterly destroyed—and they were.

Hera and Zeus had several children: Ares, the god of war, and his twin Eris, the goddess of discord; Hebe, the goddess of youth; and Hephaestus, the blacksmith—though some say that Hephaestus had no father, but was the child of Hera alone.

In Roman myths, Hera is named Juno, and in those stories she is somewhat more dignified, less vindictive, more regal. Rather than spending time punishing girls who catch her husband's eye, Juno is the true protector of the married, a proper Roman matron. With quiet pride and dignity, she walks just a few steps behind her husband to show her respect for her station in life. She is nicer than Hera, but less spirited. She understands her place. Perhaps something has been lost.

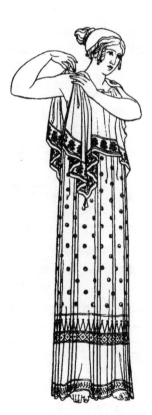

The Terrible Punishment: Io

IN THESSALY THERE IS A VALLEY ENCLOSED BY STEEP CLIFFS AND GROWN over with forest. It is called Tempe, and from this place flows the River Peneus. One day, all the rivers of the land came to visit Peneus—that is, all except one: Inachus, a river with a terrible sorrow. He had withdrawn into his cave, where he wept unceasingly, making the water of his river deeper and deeper. He mourned for his daughter Io, who had disappeared. Was she alive or dead? Inachus feared the worst.

This is what had happened. One day, as Io was coming away from her father's river, the great god Zeus saw her, and was smitten by her beauty. "Oh!" he exclaimed. "Lovely creature, how beautiful you are—worthy of the love of Zeus himself! But this sun is too hot for you. Why don't you go and rest in the shade of the woods? Don't be afraid that some beast will hurt you. I'll go with you, and you know, if you are with a god you will be safe. I'm not just any ordinary god, either, but the one who holds the scepter of Heaven in his hand and hurls the mighty thunderbolt.

"No, don't run … !" For Io had started running away. Through the meadows she ran, through the leafy woodlands. But the god had many powers, and he hid the entire countryside in a thick black cloud, so that it was too dark for Io to keep running. Zeus caught up with her.

Meanwhile, from where she sat in the heavens, Hera was gazing down at the country she loved so well, and she noticed a dark cloud hanging over just one spot—and in the middle of the brightest day, too. This could not be mist from the river, or fog rising from damp earth! Her suspicions were aroused along with her curiosity, and she looked around for her husband. Zeus had a way of falling for other women; she'd caught him at that more than once. "Either I'm wrong or I am being wronged," Hera said to herself, and she glided down to Earth, scattering the cloud.

But Zeus had sensed that his wife was coming, and when the cloud blew away, there stood, instead of Io's form, a sleek white heifer. The god had transformed her. Even as a cow, Io was beautiful. Hera gazed on her with admiration and envy, and began to question her husband: "What herd does she come from? What pasture? Who is her owner?" To satisfy his wife and to keep her from asking more questions, Zeus lied. He said that the heifer had just sprung out of the earth, full-grown, at that very instant. He had never set eyes on her before, not he!

Hera didn't believe this story for one minute. She thought briefly, then asked her husband, "Will you give the heifer to me?" Now what could Zeus do? It would be cruel to put the transformed maiden into the hands of his wife, but if he refused so slight a present, it would look very suspicious. Hera would know this was no ordinary animal.

So Zeus gave her the cow, but she still distrusted her husband. To keep him away from the heifer, Hera handed her over to Argus to guard. Of course Argus made a splendid watchman, because he had one hundred eyes, spaced all around his head. No more than two eyes ever slept at a time, and which way his head was turned, he could watch out of the other ninety-eight eyes. Io could never escape his gaze.

During the daytime, Argus let the heifer graze, but as soon as the sun went down, he locked her in the stable with a halter around her tender neck. Io fed on green leaves from the trees, and the bitter herbs that grow along the riverbanks. To sleep, she lay on the cold ground, often not even softened by a covering of grass, but rocky and bare. She drank from streams that were roiling with mud. Again and again she longed to stretch out her arms toward Argus to plead for mercy, but she had no arms to stretch. When she wanted to complain, the only sound she could make was the lowing of a cow. Her own voice frightened her.

One day, seeking new pastures, Io chanced upon her father's land, where she had so often played as a girl. Lowering her head to the river to drink, she saw her muzzle and horns reflected in the water. Terrified by the sight of herself, she ran. When her family saw her, none of her sisters guessed who she was; not even her father knew her. How could they, when she was so changed?

Every day the heifer would follow her sisters and her father, and they would stroke her gleaming sides and say, "How lovely!" Inachus picked grass and held it out for her to feed; she licked his hand with her rough cow's tongue, the only way she could kiss it. Tears rolled down her face. If only she could speak and tell them who she was, perhaps they could help her! But she had no words. There was just one hope: very slowly, with her hoof, she traced in the dust the letters of her name, first I and then O.

Instantly her father understood how his daughter had been changed, and cried, "Woe is me!" (The Greek word for *woe* is *io*.) Inachus put his arms around Io's horns and snow-white neck. "Are you really my daughter? I've been seeking you all through the world! But now that I've found you, I'm sadder than ever. You can't answer me except for a deep sigh out of your heart. And all it sounds like is mooing! All this time, in my ignorance, I have been planning for your marriage. I wanted a son-in-law and grandchildren, but now the only husband you can have must come from some herd! Oh, poor Io! Poor me! It hurts to be a god! I can't even die, but must go on sorrowing through all eternity!"

Even as father and daughter were lamenting together, Argus came and drove the heifer away to a far-distant pasture. From the top of a mountain, he watched over her. There was no escape from those hundred eyes.

But Zeus could no longer bear to see Io's great agony. He called for his son Hermes, the messenger of the gods, and commanded, "Kill Argus!" At once, Hermes fastened wings to his ankles, took up the wand that causes sleep, put on his magic cap, and leaped down to Earth. There he removed the cap and wings, keeping only his wand with him. Now he no longer looked like a god.

Disguised as a shepherd, he approached Argus, playing a little tune on the syrinx, the reed pipes. Argus was enchanted by the sound and invited him to come closer. "Whoever you are," he said warmly, "come and sit down beside me on this rock. There's plenty of lush grass in my pasture for your flock to feed on, and this cool shade is just made for a shepherd's comfort."

Hermes joined Argus on the rock, and they passed several hours while the god told stories and played softly on the pipes. His intention was to put the watchman to sleep by the drone of his voice and his lulling tunes, but Argus fought off drowsiness. Many of his eyes fell asleep, but more of them remained awake, on guard.

When Argus asked Hermes how the pipes had been invented, he began to tell the tale of Pan and Syrinx. It is not a particularly long story, and not a boring one, but this time, before Hermes had finished speaking, the last eyelids closed, and Argus was utterly lost in sleep. The god stopped talking and touched all hundred eyes with his magic wand, making the guard's slumber even deeper. Then, quick as lightning, Hermes took his curved blade and struck the sleeper at the spot where neck and head are joined, severing his head. He hurled it, dripping blood, over the cliff. The light of those bright eyes was extinguished forever.

But Io was still not free. In fact, an even greater agony awaited her.

Hera had seen everything. The jealous goddess flew down to Earth, where she picked up the eyes of Argus and fastened them among the feathers of her favorite bird, the peacock, covering its tail with starry jewels. Then, in her wrath, she sent a gadfly after Io to torment her endlessly with invisible and pitiless stings. Thus goaded, the heifer went almost mad with terror.

Io fled all over the world. From her passing, the Ionian Sea got its name, and also the Bosphorus, which means "Ford of the Cow." But no matter how far she ran, she could never escape the stinging of the gadfly. When she arrived at the River Nile, Io could endure no more. She sank to her knees and lifted her head toward the stars, groaning and weeping in anguish. Her tears and wild lowing reached Zeus, and seemed to plead with him to end her misery. He embraced his wife and begged her to cease tormenting Io. "I swear to you, she will never again be the cause of any grief to you," he said. And he called Styx to be a witness to his oath. Such a promise, Hera knew, could not be broken, even by a god.

Appeased at last, the goddess yielded. At once, the stiff hairs dropped from the heifer's snowy hide, her horns fell off, the great round eyes grew smaller, the wide mouth shrank. Then shoulders and hands appeared, and the black shiny hoofs turned back into toes and fingers. Every sign of the heifer had vanished, except for the whiteness of her fair skin. The happy nymph rose to stand erect and walk again on two feet. For a time she didn't dare to try her speech, afraid that she would still low like a cow, but little by little she gained confidence, and began to use human language.

Much later, Io became a goddess, who was famous and adored. Dressed in snowy linen robes, people from all the known world visited her shrine to worship her, along with her son Epaphus. In the years to come, one of her descendants would be Hercules, the greatest of the heroes.

Hera's Revenge: Callisto

THE LAND OF ARCADIA WAS THE PLACE ON EARTH THAT ZEUS loved most. Once, as he was wandering there, he chanced upon a nymph named Callisto. As too often happened when he saw a beautiful maiden, the god was consumed with love for her.

Callisto was not the type of girl to spend her time on feminine pursuits, spinning soft wool or trying out new hairstyles. She dressed in simple clothes, with just a buckle to fasten her dress, and tied her hair up with a plain white ribbon. Choosing to follow in the ways of the hunter goddess, Artemis, she went about always carrying her slender spear or curving bow. Of all the maidens who hunted with Artemis on the wooded mountain slopes, Callisto was the goddess's favorite. But alas, favorites often fall from that position.

On the day that would change her life, the sun shone bright and hot overhead, and Callisto entered the shade of a dense forest, which had never felt the blows of an ax, to find a secret glade she knew about. She slipped the shining quiver from her shoulder and unstrung her bow. Then she lay down on cool, velvety grass to rest, using her quiver for a pillow.

Just then, Zeus chanced to look down from Olympus. When he saw Callisto, so tired and beautiful, so unprotected, he thought, "Hera will never find me if I go down there, but even if she does, who cares?"

The god took on the form and dress of Artemis and entered the woods. Disguised as the goddess, he gently woke the nymph. "My dear," he said, "wake up and chat with me awhile. What mountains have you been hunting through today?"

Callisto rose to greet the false Artemis. "Ah, great goddess, welcome! I will always greet you with joy, you who are greater than Zeus himself! Yes, you are! Don't laugh—I would say that even if he could hear me!"

Zeus chuckled, amused and pleased at the idea of being greater than himself. He kissed the nymph, more than once, as she began to tell him about her day's hunting. When she felt those kisses and his embrace, the maiden knew that this was not Artemis. She fought him off as hard as she could, but she was not strong enough to withstand the mighty god.

After Zeus had gone back up to Olympus, Callisto hurriedly left the forest she now hated, so quickly that she almost forgot her bow and arrows. Just as she emerged, Artemis came by, surrounded by her followers and brimming with pleasure at the trophies they had taken in that day's hunt. She called out to Callisto, but the girl was frightened and shrank from her. This might be Zeus come back again in disguise! Then she saw the other maidens gathered around Artemis, and she knew it was indeed the goddess.

Callisto joined the others, but even though she was perfectly blameless, she was filled with shame. She could not raise her eyes from the ground to look at the goddess. Silent and blushing, she walked beside Artemis, who did not guess her secret. Some of the other girls, however, did.

Callisto could not hide forever what had happened to her. One day, after the moon had waxed and waned nine times, Artemis and her handmaids were hot and tired from hunting under the rays of the bright sun, the goddess's brother. They came upon a shaded grove of trees, where a murmuring stream gently ran over golden sands. When they took off their robes to swim in the cool water, Artemis discovered Callisto's secret. Angrily, she turned on her former favorite.

"Out of here!" she ordered in a voice like thunder. "You aren't worthy of being in our company. Don't let me see your face again—ever!" Callisto left, sadly weeping.

Now, Zeus might have thought he could successfully keep secrets from his wife, but he rarely could. Hera had known about the incident for a long time. The vengeful goddess was waiting for the most painful time to punish the innocent girl. When she learned that Callisto had given birth to a boy, she knew that time had come. Hera filled herself with wrath.

Appearing before Callisto, the goddess shouted at her. "This was all I needed! Don't think you'll escape my punishment! I'll fix you! That beauty of yours may have caught my husband's eye, but it is about to be spoiled forever!"

Hera grabbed Callisto by the hair and threw her down, hard, onto the ground. The nymph raised her arms to beg for mercy, but as she did, she saw her white limbs grow black and rough and covered with shaggy hair. Her hands curled inward into feet, and her fingernails lengthened into claws. The mouth that Zeus had found so lovely became snarling jaws and a hideous snout. And, just in case her piteous words and prayers might have the power to move some listening god, Hera made sure that out of Callisto's throat came only angry, menacing growls.

Her form had become that of a terrible bear, but Callisto still had the heart of a woman. She held up her hands—her paws, really—to Heaven, and wordlessly she blamed Zeus.

Now her life became one of constant terror. Although she herself was a beast, she feared wild beasts; she would hide from bears, forgetting that she too was a bear. Afraid to rest in the lonely woods, Callisto prowled back and forth in front of what had once been her home, her familiar fields. Often, she was pursued by hounds over steep crags: a huntress running in panic from the hunters! She lived in terror of wolves, although her own father had been transformed into a wolf, who hunted with the pack.

Fifteen years of this torment passed. Then, one day, Callisto's son Arcas was hunting in the woods of Arcadia. Suddenly, he came face–to–face with a huge black bear. The moment she saw him, the beast stopped and stood, frozen like a statue. She seemed to recognize the young man, but he had no idea that the creature was his mother, for nobody had ever told him about her terrible transformation. He shrank away, frightened at the sight of the bear that stared at him so, although he did not know why he felt such fear. Shyly, she inched nearer. Arcas drew back his arm and aimed his javelin at her heart, meaning to strike a fatal blow. But his arm was paralyzed; he could not throw the javelin. Just in time, Zeus had seen the incident, and he stopped the boy from committing the worst of all crimes.

Then Zeus came as a mighty wind and whirled both of them, mother and son, up through vacant space, up and up into the very dome of Heaven. There he fixed them against the sky as constellations. We know them as the Great and Little Bear.

When Hera saw Callisto shining in the sky, she was enraged all over again. That girl crowned with glory, indeed! The queen of Heaven flew down to the sea, to speak with the gray-headed sea goddess Tethys and old Oceanus himself, who had raised her when she was a girl. Why, they asked her, was she so angry? Hera replied, "Just wait until it's dark, and you'll see that another queen has taken my place in Heaven!

"There they are, new stars at the very peak of the sky, circling around the farthest pole! Look at them! This is an insult I cannot bear! Everyone is going to laugh at my power—look, I transform her from a human being, and what is she now? A goddess! Maybe Zeus will give her back her human features, as he did Io's. Maybe he'll divorce me and marry her. I am your foster daughter. If you have any love for me, the least you can do is forbid those two ever to enter your beautiful crystal and azure waters!"

Oceanus and sea agreed to do as she wished. Hera rode off back to Heaven in her feather-light chariot drawn by a team of peacocks, whose tails were bright with Argus's jeweled eyes. And because the sea and Oceanus would never allow them to dip down into their waters, as all the other constellations do, the Great and Little Bear are the only ones who move around the heavens and never set below the horizon.

The Singer: Canens

KING PICUS WAS THE SON OF SATURN, AND A MORE handsome young man you would have to go far to see. Imagine him as a statue, mounted on one of the war horses he loved to train and ride, the picture of perfection. In life, he was just that perfect. Inside he was as beautiful as he was outside, his soul as graceful and clean as his body.

Picus was just under twenty, and his handsome looks attracted all the nymphs from the woods, the fountains, the streams, the lakes—they all loved him the moment they saw him. But he had eyes for only one: the beautiful nymph Canens.

When the time was right for Canens to marry, her parents chose Picus. How happy he was! His bride was not only a nymph of unsurpassed beauty, she had a singing voice that delighted everyone who heard it. Perhaps that should be every *thing* that heard it. For when Canens sang, the rocks were moved to tears, trees kept time by swaying to her beat, wild beasts grew sentimental, the rivers stopped to listen, even the birds wandering through the sky almost forgot to fly. Her name itself meant "singing."

One day, as Canens was pouring out her voice in song, Picus rode into the woods to hunt wild boars. The young man sat easily on his charger, his scarlet cloak fastened at the neck with a golden clasp, his lances held in his left hand, ready to throw at any moment.

That very day, as it happened, the sorceress Circe, daughter of the sun, had chosen the same woods in which to gather herbs for her charms and potions. Deep in the underbrush she could not be seen, but she saw Picus, and just one look at him made her feel faint. The plants fell from her hands as a thrill ran through her veins like fire. When her mind had cleared, Circe wanted to tell Picus of her love. But he still did not see her, and each time she began to speak, he rode away before he heard her, or his servants got in her way.

"You won't escape me," she muttered, "not even on the wings of the wind, not if there is still magic in flowers and I still have voice to chant my powerful spells!" Out of her imagination, the goddess conjured up a phantom boar, so lifelike that Picus would have to think it was real. When she sent it running across his path, he immediately gave chase. The shadow-boar led the young king deeper into the woods, and then it seemed to dart into a thicket, where the trees and undergrowth grew so dense that he had to dismount to follow it. Soon he was lost in the depths of the woods.

Circe began to chant, singing all the charms she knew, the charms that hide the moon's white face in mist and cloud, that hide even the face of the sun, her father. As she sang, the woods darkened; daylight disappeared in a thick fog that rose from the forest floor. The hunting party could see nothing, and in the fog each one groped blindly and lost the trail, until they were all scattered in different directions.

Now Picus was alone. Circe approached him, saying, "Your bright eyes have captured mine; your beauty, most handsome of kings, has stolen even a goddess's heart. Love me, I beg you, favor me! Take me for your wife, become son-in-law to the sun. Don't harden your heart toward me!"

But he repulsed her violently. "Whoever you are, I cannot be yours. My heart is given away already, to one I hope will hold it forever. Canens is my wife, and I will be faithful to her for as long as the Fates keep her safe for me!"

Again and again Circe humbled herself to plead with him, but in vain. Picus would only repeat his love and loyalty to Canens. Then the goddess lost her temper. "You'll pay for this!" she exclaimed. "Canens has seen the last of you; you won't go home to her, ever again! Now you'll learn what a woman can do, a woman who's been wronged, one who loves and has been scorned, especially when that woman is Circe, daughter of the sun!"

Twice to the west she turned, and twice to the east; three times she touched Picus with her wand, three times she sang her magic spell. When he turned to flee, he found himself running faster and faster, more swiftly than he ever had before. Then he realized that he had grown wings; he was no longer running, but flying through the air. Outraged at this change, furious at the strange bird he had become, he began to strike at the oak trees with his hard beak, drilling holes through the boughs. His wings shone, as red as the cloak he had been wearing; the golden brooch that had pinned it became a ring of bright feathers around his throat. All that was left of Picus was his name, which means "woodpecker."

All this time, his comrades and servants had been looking for their friend and king, calling his name. But he was nowhere to be found. Instead, they found Circe, who had cleared the air by calling up the winds and sunshine. By her guilty look, they guessed what she had done. They drew their spears and threatened to use them against her. "Where is our king?" they demanded. "Bring him back at once, or ... "

But Circe was too quick for them. Before they could attack, she made her evil potions into a poisonous mist, while she called forth Night and the gods of Night out of Hell and Chaos, repeating the name of Hecate, queen of the witches. Then the whole forest seemed to leap into the air, the Earth groaned and rumbled, the trees grew white as frost. Where her magic mist dripped onto the grass, pools of blood stained the ground. Stones made bellowing sounds, dogs began to bark, and the forest floor swarmed with terrible black snakes and horned lizards. The air was filled with the souls of those long dead, fluttering silent phantoms. Stunned by the power of this sorcery, the hunting party stood aghast, paralyzed with fear. Circe moved among them, touching their faces with her wand, and as she touched each face, the young man dropped, changed into some wild beast—each one different, each one horrible.

Now the sun was dropping below the horizon, and Canens was worried. She searched the evening light, longing for the sight of her husband returning home. But he did not come. At last she sent her servants to search, and the townspeople joined in, spreading through the woods with torches in their hands, hoping to greet their king and lead him home.

Midnight came, but there was still no sign of Picus. Canens wept, and tore her hair, and rushed outside. Like a madwoman, she ran all across the countryside, through fields, over hills, and into the valleys. For six days and six nights she wandered, calling out the name of her husband. For six days and six nights she neither slept nor ate a morsel of food.

On the seventh day, she reached the banks of the river Tiber, who, as it turned out, was the last ever to look on her form. Exhausted from her travels, but even more from her grief, Canens sank down on the river's edge. There she lay, weeping uncontrollably and singing songs of woe. She sang until at last her frail body dissolved in misery and tears, leaving only a silver veil of water that, still singing, trembled into mist and disappeared.

That place remains as a memorial to her, the sorrowing wife. The Muses, who had heard her singing, named it Canens, to preserve her name and keep her story alive.

Consumed by Love: Semele

THE MOMENT ZEUS LOOKED DOWN FROM OLYMPUS AND spotted the Theban princess, Semele, he was in love again. She was the daughter of Cadmus and Harmonia, and the loveliest girl in all the city. Of course Zeus would be interested!

Disguised as a mortal man, the god presented himself at the palace and began to woo Semele. He was so persuasive that she could not help but love him back, and she agreed to marry him.

Poor Semele! Of all the girls Zeus loved, this princess was to be the most unfortunate. For Hera discovered the affair just at a time when she was already irritated with her husband. Instantly, she turned the full force of her anger upon Semele. The goddess began to curse and rage. Then she stopped herself.

"What good have curses ever done?" she asked. "What's the point of harsh words and threats? I'm going to have to go down to Earth myself and take care of that girl! She has to feel my anger, full force! If I am worthy of my name—mighty Hera, queen of Heaven—if I'm fit to hold my jeweled scepter, if I am truly the wife of Zeus himself, I must act. I'll destroy her!"

The goddess's wrath was fueled by her discovery that Semele was carrying Zeus's child. Hera imagined that the girl was showing off, preening herself on her beauty and on her conquest of the god.

"Arrogant, is she?" the goddess muttered. "I'll take care of that! She is about to go to the black marshes of Hell, and it will be Zeus himself who sends her there. That should be punishment for them both!"

Hera rose from her throne and wrapped herself in a bright cloud of gold, then descended to the home of Semele. Before anyone could see her, she put on a disguise, taking on the shape of an old, old woman. White hair fell down over her forehead, her skin was wrinkled and dry, her voice quavered. She walked with her back bent over, her steps shaky and feeble. By the time she appeared before the girl, she looked exactly like Semele's old nurse, Beroe, and talked like her, too.

In Beroe's voice she greeted the princess, who was delighted to see her. They began to chat and gossip happily together. After a time, the old woman sighed. "You know," she said, "I believe your husband may really be the great god Zeus himself!" Semele softly confessed: he had hinted that he was.

"Ah!" said the false nurse. "But that frightens me. Many men will tell you lies like that, you know, to win your love. I hope it's true, but if it's not, what then? Who is he? If he is indeed Zeus, he ought to prove his love. He appears before Hera in all his glory as a god. Can't he do as much for you? You see only the weak mortal form that he puts on to be with you!"

With these subtle wiles, the goddess tempted Semele and made her dissatisfied with her love. Such suspicions, once they are planted, can only grow like noxious weeds.

The next time Zeus visited the princess, she began to wheedle. Would he grant her a wish, any wish she could name? Would he prove his love by promising her anything she asked for? Anything?

His reply echoed her word. "Anything, my love! There's nothing I would deny you. Only ask, and I'll give it. If you doubt me, I promise in the name of the great, boiling River Styx!" Semele was thrilled. Alas, if she had only known it—the moment that gave her such delight was to be her undoing. She was doomed by the very promise her husband gave her. But the girl did not understand.

"Appear before me," she began, "as you do before Hera …" As soon as Zeus realized what she was about to say, he tried to stop her lips, but she spoke too quickly. The harm was done. Zeus foresaw at once the tragic ending, for no mortal can behold a god in his full glory and survive. But it had to be; even a god was powerless to break an oath sworn by the River Styx. He could not undo his promise, and she could not unsay what she had said.

In his grief, the god soared up to Olympus. He wrapped the clouds around him, the dew and fogs, called up the storms, unleashed the thunder, the lightning, the fire that no man can escape. Again and again he tried to weaken his tremendous power.

At last, try as he might to put it off, he had to fulfill his promise and visit Semele in all his godliness. Still, he tried to soften what was to happen. He left his heavy lightning bolts behind and took only the lighter ones the Cyclopes had made for him in their workshop, the ones the other gods made fun of when they teased him. Carrying the bolts, he crossed the threshold into the palace.

At the moment the princess saw him appear before her in dazzling light, her body flashed into fire, consumed by the glory that is death to mortals. But before she was entirely burnt in the flames, Zeus rescued her unborn child, and hid it from Hera, sewn into a gash in his thigh, until the time came for it to be born. Then he gave it to Semele's sister Ino to raise. That child was Dionysus, god of wine and freedom, the only Greek god who had a mortal parent.

It was said that in Thebes, Semele's tomb continued to smoke and smolder for years. But her son often thought of the mother he had never seen, and he longed for her. When he grew to manhood, Dionysus swore to rescue Semele from the Underworld. He dared to undertake that long and dangerous trip, and when he arrived in the realm of shadows, he confronted Death.

"I have more right to Semele than you do," her son challenged the ruler of that drear kingdom. "You cannot keep her from me!"

Death yielded to the superior claim. Then Dionysus took his mother away and carried her up to Olympus. The gods consented to let her stay. Although she was mortal, they agreed, she was the mother of one of the immortal gods, and worthy of dwelling among them.

One wonders what Hera thought.

The Most Beautiful Woman in the World: Helen

THE TROUBLE STARTED AT THE WEDDING OF KING PELEUS AND THE SEA NYMPH THETIS. ALL THE gods had gathered for a lavish banquet to celebrate the marriage—that is, all but one. The goddess Eris, whose name means "discord," had not been invited. Because of her quarrelsome nature, she was often left out of events among the gods, especially those in which peace and harmony would be important.

Eris was angry, and thought hard. She was determined to cause trouble. What could she do to set the gods against each other and spoil the fun of the wedding feast? Then she had an idea. Into the midst of the gods in the banqueting hall, she threw a golden apple that bore a label. "For the Fairest," it said. But which goddess was the fairest? Each of them claimed that the prize was obviously meant for her. They set up a great clamor and begged Zeus to decide which of them should get the golden apple.

But Zeus was too wise to let himself be drawn into a competition among goddesses. There were three most obviously in contention for the prize: Athena, Hera, and Aphrodite. Thinking fast, Zeus suggested that they ask a young man to act as judge. He knew just the one, he said: handsome Paris, who was a famous appreciator of feminine beauty.

Paris was a prince of Troy, the son of King Priam, but when he was a baby, an oracle had prophesied that he would bring ruin to his country and everyone who lived in it. To prevent this fate, his parents abandoned him on the slopes of Mount Ida, where shepherds found him and raised him as their own.

Now, as Paris tended his flocks, the three goddesses appeared before him and begged him to help them. They needed him to decide, they said, which of them was the fairest. Dazzled by their beauty and by their faith in his judgment, he agreed. Paris was a better judge of beauty than of wise behavior; it would have been far better if he, like Zeus, had found a way out. But he was happy to be chosen.

Now each of the goddesses took the young prince aside and offered him a reward if he chose her. Athena promised to help him lead the Trojans in a victorious war against Greece. Hera said that she would make him lord of both Europe and Asia. Aphrodite was the last to whisper in his ear, and she vowed that, if he named her the fairest, she would make sure that he could have the most beautiful woman in the world for his wife.

Paris awarded the golden apple to Aphrodite. He was more interested in love than in leadership, in beauty than in winning battles.

There was no question who the goddess meant by "the most beautiful woman in the world." Beyond dispute, that title belonged to Helen, the daughter of Zeus and Leda. Unfortunately, she was married already, to Menelaus, the king of Sparta.

Word of Helen's beauty had spread throughout Greece while she was still a young girl. Suitors came from all over the known world to compete for her hand. Helen's stepfather, Tyndareus, who was responsible for her, was worried. How could he choose among them? Most of the suitors were royal princes or the sons of very powerful families. As soon as he accepted one of them, he feared, the others would turn against the lucky young man and start a fight whose consequences might be huge.

At last Tyndareus found a solution. He asked each of the suitors to swear that he would uphold the honor of the man who was chosen, and would fight to protect that man's life and rights, if the need should ever arise. Each of them agreed, thinking that he might well be the lucky one to win Helen's hand. Gladly they all swore the oath.

The winner was Menelaus. His position as king of Sparta and his great wealth made him eminently suitable. What's more, he was brother to Agamemnon, king of Mycenae, who was married to Helen's sister, Clytemnestra. Never mind that Menelaus was much older than Helen and a rather boring man. That kind of thing didn't weigh very heavily in the mind of Tyndareus.

Helen's reputation for beauty did not end when she married. She was still known far and wide as the most beautiful woman in the world. And it was Helen whom Aphrodite had in mind when she gave Paris her promise. Marriage had never meant very much to the goddess of love.

Aphrodite wasted no time. She whisked the Trojan prince off to Sparta and introduced him to the royal couple, who made him welcome in their palace. During his visit, Menelaus was suddenly called away to Crete for the funeral of his grandfather. He left his wife to entertain Paris, secure in the inviolable rules of hospitality, which decreed that neither host nor guest should harm the other. But Menelaus didn't know about Aphrodite's promise to Paris, or the power that she would exert over his wife. Helpless to go against the goddess's will, Helen fell in love with Paris, just as he had fallen in love with her.

Menelaus returned from Crete to discover the terrible truth. Paris and Helen had run away together, taking with them much of the king's treasure. When they reached Troy, the lovers were formally married, in spite of strong opposition by many of the Trojan leaders. There they lived together happily as man and wife.

But Menelaus could not give up his wife so easily; he had to defend his honor. The king called on all the other Greek chiefs to help him, as they were bound by sacred oath to do, having sworn it while they were still suitors for Helen's hand. Before he started a war, Menelaus tried a diplomatic mission, headed by himself and Odysseus, but failed to make the Trojans return his wife. There was only one recourse now.

A thousand ships gathered and sailed to Troy to besiege the city and win Helen back for her husband. The battle that ensued, known as the Trojan War, was long and bloody. Both sides suffered terribly, losing almost all of their greatest heroes. Perhaps there would not have been such tremendous destruction if the gods hadn't involved themselves in the war. Angry with each other, they fought out a battle of their own, using the Greeks and Trojans as their weapons. Remember that Athena and Hera were both furious with Paris for his judgment in the beauty contest, and of course they sided with the Greeks. Naturally, Aphrodite stood with the Trojans, and so did Ares, the god of war, and Zeus himself. Ultimately, the Greeks won, and Troy was utterly destroyed, the city burned to the ground.

Now Aphrodite intervened once more. Just before Troy fell, she found Helen and swept her away from the city. Although Helen's beauty was still overwhelming, the goddess added to it just a little more. Then she led her to Menelaus, who was dazzled again by the force of such unearthly loveliness, and forgave Helen everything. At last Menelaus had regained his wife. He sailed back to Sparta with her, where they lived together for many more years.

And what should we think of Helen? There are those who call her a bad woman, faithless, vain, and utterly selfish, the cause of the greatest war of ancient times, which nearly destroyed two civilizations. But her husband willingly forgave her and took her back with no punishment. She lived out her days with him in peaceful harmony.

To Homer, the author of the great epic poem the *Iliad*, Helen is not to blame for anything that happened. It was not her fault that she was so beautiful; she couldn't help it that men fell in love with her beauty even before they knew her. And as a mortal, she was powerless against the will of the goddess Aphrodite, who used the woman to accomplish her own desire. Aphrodite did, after all, win the title she wanted, and she is still known as the most beautiful of the goddesses.

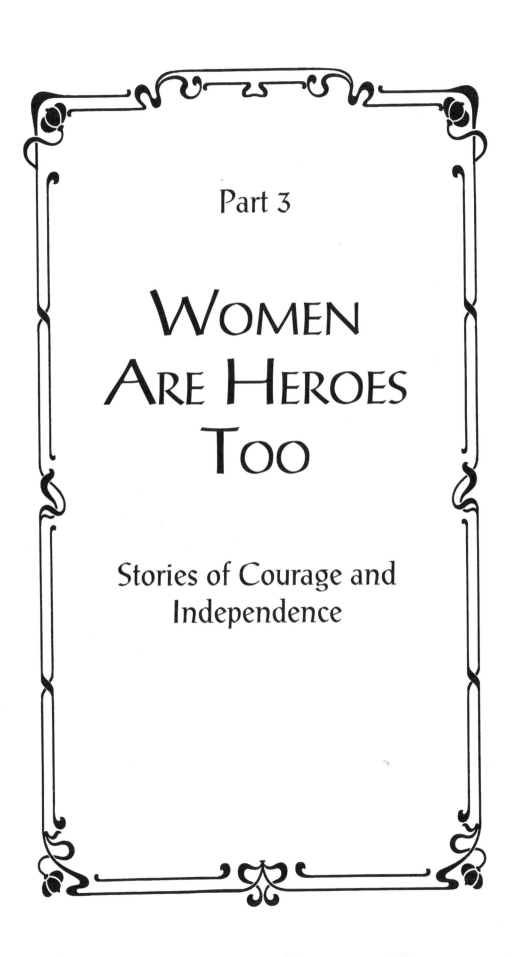

Part 3

WOMEN ARE HEROES TOO

Stories of Courage and
Independence

Women of Courage

The Wise Goddess:
Athena

O F ALL HIS CHILDREN, THE GRAY-EYED ATHENA WAS ZEUS'S FAVORITE. SHE ALONE WAS ALLOWED to carry her father's thunderbolt and his great breastplate, called the Aegis. Athena was the only Olympian who was not born of a mother, but sprang directly from the head of Zeus, fully grown and dressed in armor.

Athena was the most complex of the twelve great Olympian gods and goddesses. As the goddess of war, she could perform mighty deeds of battle; at least twice she defeated the war god Ares. Yet war gave her no pleasure. She preferred peace, and would rather settle disputes by wise judgment than by fighting. In this, she was most unlike the wild Ares, who loved battle for its own sake, and was never happier than when he was slaughtering enemies or destroying cities. It was probably Athena's superior intelligence and strategy in battle that made her stronger than the war god with his mindless fury and love of bloodshed. In peacetime, she put off her armor to dress in graceful flowing robes. Although many of the gods desired to marry her, Athena chose to remain single.

Like all of the other deities, Athena took a deep interest in the affairs of mortals. But unlike many of them, she tended to use her power to make life better for those humans she cared for.

This is a typical gesture: Athena competed with Poseidon, the god of the seas, over a new settlement of people, which was destined to be one of the greatest cities in the history of the world. Which of them should become the patron of the city, to be named after the winner? With the other gods and goddesses sitting as judges, Poseidon and Athena each performed a miraculous act on the heights of the Acropolis, overlooking the new city.

First the sea god struck the rock with his trident, and immediately a great fountain of water burst forth. Everyone was amazed: even though the water was salty, it was a wonder to see a spring rising from the top of a mountain. Then Athena struck the rock with her spear. From the rocky soil grew a tall olive tree, loaded with fruit. How much more useful that was than a flow of brackish water!

The goddess was made the patroness of the great city, now named Athens in her honor. Ever since that time, the olive tree has been her special tree, and the owl, the symbol of wisdom, her special bird.

It was not only Athens that this goddess protected, but all of civilized life. Think of the innumerable gifts she brought to Earth for the benefit of mortals! She invented the flute and the trumpet for our pleasure, the earthenware bowl for our convenience, and taught all the women's arts, especially weaving. But she also worked to improve farming, inventing the plough and rake, the yoke to harness oxen, and the bridle for horses. She gave us the chariot and the ship; she first taught us the science of mathematics.

During the Trojan War, many of the Olympians took sides; in fact, it was as much a war among the gods and goddesses as between the Greeks and Trojans. Athena took the side of the Greeks, and long after they had won the war, she continued to help them. She watched after Odysseus during his ten-year journey home from the war, offering him advice and assistance when he most needed it. Among her other favorites, to whom she offered help and comfort during their ordeals, were Heracles, Perseus, Jason, Bellerophon, and Orestes and Iphigenia.

Athena, called Minerva by the Romans, was unique among the deities. She defines heroism in a new way: courage does not necessarily mean fighting, but standing firm for what is right. She can serve as a model for women everywhere. The divine protector of human civilization, the goddess of war who preferred peace, the judge who believed in mercy—this was indeed a gracious goddess, and a wise one.

The Princess with the Golden Thread: Ariadne

CRETE AND ATHENS WERE ENEMIES, AND THEIR HATRED LAY deep. It had begun long ago, when Minos, the king of Crete, sent his son Androgeus to visit Athens. The boy died there, but nobody in Crete knew why. Perhaps he had been killed over envy of his athletic skill, or perhaps, as some said, Aegeus, the Athenian king, had done a terrible thing, a thing no host should do. Rumor whispered that he had sent the youth on a dangerous expedition to kill a vicious bull, but the bull was too strong and killed Androgeus instead. Whichever was true, Minos was enraged by his son's death. Seeking revenge, he invaded Athens and defeated Aegeus. Then imposed a dreadful punishment on the city.

For Minos had a fearsome weapon hidden away, deep inside his island kingdom. Some years earlier, his wife had given birth to a monster, a hideous creature, half human and half bull. The Minotaur, as he was called, was a giant of a beast, violent and cruel. Minos kept him closed up inside an elaborate structure called the labyrinth, from which escape was impossible. Designed by the brilliant architect Daedalus, this labyrinth wound its intricate way through the rock deep beneath Minos's palace.

After his victory over Athens, Minos threatened to raze the city to the ground unless Aegeus sent, every year, seven of the handsomest young men and seven of the most beautiful young women of the city to be thrown into the labyrinth as a sacrifice to the blood-craving Minotaur. In the labyrinth's twisting passages, the youths and maidens had only two choices: they could stay where they were until the Minotaur discovered them, or they could wander around in the darkness until they stumbled upon him. Either way, the outcome would be the same. They were doomed to be slaughtered and devoured by the beast.

Theseus, the son of Aegeus, had been away from Athens, adventuring around the world. As fate would have it, he arrived home just as the lottery to choose that year's victims was to be held. At once, Theseus went to his father.

"Let me be the first man chosen!" he entreated. "I believe the gods sent me back to Athens just at this time so that I can rid the country of its terrible curse. Let the Minotaur taste death at my hands instead of feeding on Athenian youth!"

Aegeus was most reluctant to let his son go, and begged him not to risk his life in such a hazardous undertaking. But Theseus was determined. Finally, the father agreed, asking only one thing: if he succeeded, Theseus must promise to change his ship's black sails to white ones when he returned, so that his father could know in advance whether to mourn his son's death or rejoice in his triumph. Then the lottery was held, and Aegeus blessed all the young women and men who were doomed by the chance of the draw.

When the Athenians arrived at Crete, they were paraded to the king's palace through throngs of hooting and laughing Cretans, celebrating, as usual, the day of the sacrifice, which was a festival for them. In his throne room, King Minos began to examine the victims. He wanted to make sure that each of them was beautiful or handsome enough to fulfill his purpose. Theseus stepped forward and spoke to the king.

"I am the royal prince of Athens, the son of Aegeus. I ask as my right the privilege of meeting the Minotaur alone, first of all the Athenian youth." Minos was astonished at such a request. Faced with confronting the Minotaur, his victims usually were reluctant, to say the least.

"Think carefully before you ask such a thing!" the king answered. "The Minotaur has torn to pieces everyone who has entered his terrible lair. Even if you were to defeat him, you would find it impossible to make your way back out of the labyrinth. You would simply stay there in the dark until you died of hunger and thirst."

"If it must be so, let it be so," came the reply. "I only ask that you give me the chance to try my skill." Minos, uncertain whether he should admire the prince's courage or laugh at his cockiness, agreed that on the next day he could meet the Minotaur alone. Theseus did not brag that he would kill the beast, for that would be hubris, the sin of pride, nor did he beg for mercy, for that would be cowardice.

But Theseus had already made one conquest, although he did not yet know it. Ariadne, King Minos's daughter, had noticed the prince among the victims while they were being displayed before the Cretan crowd, and she was entranced by his appearance. In the throne room, she worked her way up to the front where she could see him better. Before he finished speaking, she had fallen deeply in love with him, not just because he was so handsome, but for his courage and his princely bearing.

That night, when everyone was asleep, Ariadne stole into the chamber where Theseus lay. She whispered in his ear: "Listen to what I tell you, prince. I have the means to help you escape from the labyrinth."

Theseus awoke, and when he saw Ariadne, he too fell in love.

"Because I love you," the princess confided, "I must help you, even though it means betraying my father and the people of Crete. I know the secret of the labyrinth; Daedalus himself told it to me. All the passages lead finally to the lair of the Minotaur, and nobody has ever been able to find the way back. But I know how you can reach the center and still make your way out of the maze."

From her pocket Ariadne pulled a ball of golden silk thread, tightly wound. "Daedalus gave this to me," she said. "It is long enough to reach the very heart of the labyrinth. When you go in, you must tie one end to the entryway, and unroll the ball as you move into the depths. Then you need only follow the thread back, and you will come out where you started. If you kill the Minotaur and make your way back, I'll help you get home safely, with the other Athenians. All I ask is that you take me with you and marry me— my father will be terribly angry with me."

Theseus was happy to give her his promise, for he was enamored of Ariadne's bright eyes and lovely ways. Gratefully, he took the thread from her and hid it among his clothes.

The next morning, a group of soldiers marched Theseus to the entryway of the labyrinth. He waited until their backs were turned, and tied the end of the thread securely, down low on the gatepost, where it would not be spotted. Then he slowly made his way into the labyrinth, unwinding the golden thread as he went.

All the other sacrificial youths and maidens of Athens gathered at the entry, and watched breathless as Theseus disappeared into the blackness. For a very long time, there was no sound. Peering into the dark passages, they could see nothing. Suddenly they heard a fearsome roaring, as of a beast joyfully spotting its prey, followed by a tremendous clashing and rattling and banging, louder than any thunderstorm. Then all was silent again. Looking at each other in anguish, the Athenians waited. They had almost given up hope for their prince and their own lives when Theseus burst forth from the doorway covered with blood.

What had gone on in that dark maze? Of course, there were no witnesses, so it isn't surprising that accounts of the battle varied. Some maintained that Ariadne had given Theseus a magic sword, the only weapon that could kill the Minotaur. Others said the Athenian prince used his own sword. Still others swore that he had no weapon at all, but slew the beast with his bare hands, battering the Minotaur to death, or tearing off one of his horns and stabbing him with it through the forehead. Who could know the truth? Theseus never said.

However it had happened, one thing was perfectly clear: the Athenian prince had won. He threw his arms around Ariadne and thanked her from the depths of his heart. She had saved not only his life, but the lives of countless young men and women of Athens.

Ariadne begged her lover not to linger. The princess had drugged the watchmen, but any moment now, they would awake and discover that the Minotaur was dead. Minos would be furious! She urged the Athenians to make haste to the harbor, where their ship was ready to sail, only awaiting their arrival. For good measure, Ariadne had drilled holes in the hulls of the Cretan ships, so that her countrymen could not pursue them. The Athenians hurried on board and quickly set sail. By the time King Minos heard the news, their ship had almost disappeared over the horizon; all that could be seen was the very top of the highest mast. Ariadne and Theseus were safe, and turned toward Athens, planning a brilliant and happy marriage.

Now, what happened next is also unclear. This is certain: the Athenian ship put in to harbor at the island of Naxos, and Theseus sailed away, leaving Ariadne asleep on the island, with not even a word of farewell.

Had he so quickly ceased to love the princess and stranded her deliberately? Again, the stories differ. According to some, Theseus had been warned by Athena in a dream that Ariadne was destined to become the bride of a god, not a mortal, and that he must leave her. Others maintain that Ariadne had become terribly seasick on the voyage, and Theseus set her down on Naxos to rest. Then his ship was blown away in a violent storm. By the time he was able to return to the island, Ariadne had died from grief.

Crueler tales say that he had fallen in love with her sister, Phaedra, and abandoned Ariadne to flee with her. It is true that later Theseus and Phaedra married.

But many of the stories—which you might prefer, as I do—provide a happier ending for Ariadne, who had given up her country, home, and family to help Theseus triumph over the Minotaur.

These accounts begin sadly. They tell of Ariadne awakening to find herself alone, and wandering, distraught, along the beach, her hair streaming down and her clothes all disheveled. As she was crying out in anguish to ask Theseus why he had left her stranded on the island, she heard the sound of drums and cymbals. All at once, into her sight there came a parade of satyrs and Bacchanals, led by Silenus, and at last appeared the god Dionysus, driving a chariot drawn by brilliantly striped tigers and decorated with clusters of green and red grapes.

Three times Ariadne tried to flee from the god's presence; three times she could not move. Dionysus took her up into his chariot and set a crown on her head. He kissed her tenderly, saying, "Ariadne, you will be my wife, and I will be far more faithful to you than your former lover was!"

To seal his pledge, the god swept off her crown; then, changing its gems to fiery stars, he tossed it into the heavens to become a constellation, the Corona Borealis. He embraced Ariadne, and they departed together to live in happiness as god and wife.

As for Theseus, he quite forgot his promise to his father, and neglected to change the sails of his ship. From his lookout, Aegeus spotted the black sails and, believing his son dead, leapt into the ocean and drowned. That sea is called the Aegean after the sorrowing king and father.

The Girl Who Rescued a Hero: Nausicaa

NAUSICAA, THE DAUGHTER OF KING ALCINOUS, LAY FAST ASLEEP IN HER BRIGHTLY PAINTED bedroom, with two of her handmaids sleeping nearby. The princess was so beautiful, an onlooker might have taken her for one of the goddesses of Olympus; her maids were as lovely as the Graces.

Into the room Athena drifted like the wind and took on the form of Nausicaa's best friend. Naturally, the grey-eyed goddess had a motive for this appearance. She had decided that it was time for the wandering hero Odysseus to reach home at last. He had just been shipwrecked on the island kingdom of Phaeacia, ruled by the good Alcinous, a land of kind and generous people, fine sailors all. After swimming for two days and two nights to reach the island, Odysseus was exhausted. Naked and cold, he had dug a hollow place in the sand to rest, and covered himself with warm dry leaves. Now, as he slept, Athena was determined to help him.

In the friend's voice, she scolded, "Shame on you, Nausicaa! Look at the careless way you've scattered your clothes around. I can't believe you're your mother's daughter! Pretty soon you'll be married, and you'll need a fine supply of clothes, for yourself to wear and to give to the wedding party. That's the way a bride is judged, you know.

"Come on, let's go and wash these clothes. I'll go with you and we can scrub them together. We'll have fun—the time will fly! You have so many men from all over the country courting you, it won't be long until your wedding day. First thing in the morning, go to your father and beg for the mule-cart to take everything to the washing pool, your dresses and scarves and bed linen, too. It's much nicer to ride than to walk when you have so many things to carry." Once she had planted this idea in the sleeping girl's head, Athena flew back up to Olympus.

As soon as dawn came, Nausicaa awoke. Rapt in the spell of her dream, she went, still dressed in her beautiful nightclothes, to find her parents. Queen Arete, her mother, was seated by the hearth with several of her waiting-women, spinning yarn of a vibrant, deep-sea blue. Her father was just leaving the palace to join a council of the noblemen from the island.

Nausicaa came up close to the king and softly said, "Dear Papa, could you have the mule-cart sent around for me, the high one with the pretty wheels? I want to take our clothes down to the river pools and give them a good washing. All our things could use it—and there you are, going to a council meeting—you should be wearing spotless clothing! And my brothers! Two of them may be married, but the other three are bachelors, and they always want clean shirts when they go out dancing. There's so much I must think of!"

The princess didn't mention her own wedding, but her father saw her blush. "Of course you can have the mules and cart," he quickly assured her. "Anything you want! Go on, now. The grooms will bring the wagon around right away!"

As soon as the cart came, Nausicaa filled it up with things to be washed. Meanwhile, her mother packed a picnic hamper full of wonderful treats, and handed her daughter a bottle of golden olive oil to rub on after bathing, to make her skin soft and supple.

Nausicaa took up the reins and the wagon moved off, carrying the princess, the linens, and her attendant maids. Soon they reached the washing pools by the river, where the water always flows fresh and clear. The girls unhitched the mules and sent them along to graze on the lush grasses that grew along the riverbanks. Then they lifted down great armloads of clothes, plunged them into the pools, and danced on them, making a race of it to see who could finish first. Before long, everything was spotless, and they spread it all out on clean pebbles to dry in the noonday sun.

Now the girls themselves bathed in the cool water and smoothed the golden oil over their skins. On the riverbank they ate their picnic lunch as they waited for the clothes to dry. When they had eaten their fill, they threw off their veils and began to play a game of ball. All were lithe and beautiful, but Nausicaa stood out among them with her graceful, tall figure, and her white arms that flashed in the sun as she ran.

At last the princess declared that it was time to end the game, fold the laundry, and return home. But once again, Athena intervened: Odysseus had to meet the princess so that she could lead him into town. And so the last time Nausicaa threw the ball to one of her maids, it missed, splashing into a whirling stream. They all shouted, and their cries woke Odysseus from his long sleep.

"Who are these people?" he asked himself. "Are they savages or are they kind? I hear women's voices. Nymphs are they, or human? Do they speak my language?"

Covering himself as best he could with a branch he tore from an olive tree, he came out from the bushes. What a sight he was! Encrusted with salt from the sea, uncombed, his eyes burning like a hungry lion, he terrified the girls, and they fled in all directions. All, that is, except Nausicaa. Her heart was filled with courage, and she stood fearless, waiting for him.

How should he speak to her? Odysseus wondered. He chose a gentle voice, calm and charming. "Here I am, at your mercy. Are you divine or human? If you are a goddess, you must be Artemis; you look just like her in your grace and bearing. But if you are a mortal, your father and mother are blessed, and your brothers, too. It must give them such joy to look at you! And the luckiest one of all is the man you will marry. I've never seen anyone like you."

With such soft words he spoke. Then he told her about the storm that had brought him to this island, and begged her to give him some bit of cloth to cover his nakedness.

"Stranger," the princess replied, "I can't see anything wicked or foolish about you. I know it's Zeus who hands out the fortunes of men, both good and bad, and he seems to have given you plenty of hardship! You've borne it well. But now you've come to our land, and we will treat you kindly. I am the daughter of King Alcinous. I'll give you clothing, and show you the way to town, too."

Then she called out to her maids: "Girls, stop! Does the sight of a man scare you? Do you take this one for an enemy? You know the gods love our land too much to let anyone come here and destroy it. No, this man is a castaway, and we must take good care of him. Quick, get him food and drink, but first take him down to the river, somewhere out of the wind, to cleanse himself."

They led Odysseus to a sheltered spot, laid out a tunic and cloak for him, and gave him the flask of golden olive oil. Then they hurried back to their mistress, leaving him to bathe alone.

When he had scrubbed himself well, getting rid of all the brine and dirt on his skin, and had rubbed his body with oil, Odysseus put on the clothes the princess had given him. Now Athena made him taller and more massive, his hair crisp and curly as the petals of wild hyacinth. She lavished beauty all over his head and shoulders, so that when he went down to the beach again, he was covered with splendor.

When Nausicaa saw him, she turned to her maids. "The gods can't be all against this man. He seemed so wild and terrible before, but now he looks almost like a god himself. I wish my husband could be as fine as that! But never mind—give him something to eat."

Odysseus ate ravenously; it felt like years since he had touched food. Meanwhile, Nausicaa busied herself with folding the linens and stowing them in the cart, then hitched up the mules again. Taking the reins, she turned to Odysseus and said, "Up with you now, my friend. We'll go back to town, to my father's house, where you will meet the noble Phaeacians."

Then she had second thoughts. "No. If you go with me, there'll be gossip. Everyone will wonder where I picked you up, a shipwrecked stranger. There's a quiet grove near the road, sacred to Athena. You can wait there until we have time to get home. Then you can walk into the city and ask the way to my father's palace.

"Once you have reached the palace, go straight across the hall, and find my mother. You'll see a lovely sight! She'll be sitting there in the firelight, spinning sea-blue wool, with her women behind her. My father's throne is right beside her, and he sits before the fire, drinking his wine, looking more like a god than a mortal. Go past him, and on your knees before my mother. If she looks on you kindly, you will be sure to see your friends and loved ones, your own country, again." She raised her whip and touched the mules, who trotted on quickly. Odysseus stayed in the grove, praying to Athena for her continued help.

When Nausicaa reached home, she went quietly to her bedroom, where her old nurse lit a fire for her. Now Odysseus made his way into the city, and asked directions of a little girl. Although he did not know it, the child was Athena in disguise. Eagerly, she led him to the palace.

"Queen Arete answers all our prayers," the child said, "and the king loves her. She is honored more than any woman on Earth, by her husband and by her children and all the people of the land, too. They look on her as a goddess. Her grace and wisdom are so great that men come to her seeking wise judgment. If she favors you, you will get home again."

Odysseus looked at the palace, marveling at its beauty and richness. Then he entered and, following Nausicaa's directions, he found the queen. Falling on his knees among the ashes of the hearth, he threw himself on her mercy to beg for passage home. The king and the queen lifted him up and begged him to sit, offering him food and wine.

Their visitor's manners impressed them favorably. Still, Arete had one question. "You said you came here from the sea," she said, "but where did you get those clothes?" For she had recognized the tunic and cloak he wore as ones she herself had made.

Now Odysseus told the king and queen how he had been saved by the princess Nausicaa, how delicately she had behaved, and how generously. "Your daughter is flawless," he concluded.

There was no question that the generous islanders, so skilled as seamen, would help the wanderer make his way home. For several days he stayed, getting back his strength; he ate and drank his fill, and at night he slept on the softest of beds. Telling stories of his adventures, he held everyone spellbound.

Alcinous invited his guest to stay in Phaeacia forever, to marry Nausicaa and receive lands, houses, and wealth. But he was married already, Odysseus replied, and must go home to his wife.

When the day came for his departure, Nausicaa, looking more beautiful than any woman ever had, stood beside a column as he passed. "Goodbye, my friend!" the princess said. "When you are at home in your own land, remember me sometimes."

Odysseus replied, "If Zeus wills that I make it home, I will think of you every day of my life. You are like a goddess to me, you must know. Dear girl, how could I forget you? You have saved my life!"

Standing Up for the Right: Antigone

WITH ALL HER HEART, ANTIGONE BELIEVED IN TWO PRINCIPLES: FAMILY LOYALTY AND OBEDIENCE TO the moral laws set down by the gods. When her father, Oedipus, the great king of Thebes, was forced to leave his city, she knew that his exile was just. He had transgressed the laws of the gods, and even though he had done it unknowingly, eternal laws must be upheld.

But Antigone would not let him suffer alone. She was determined to stay with her blind father, to act as his guide and comfort. Together they wandered from city to city, begging for food, until they found refuge at Colonus, near Athens. At last Oedipus was safe, and he could die in peace.

After her father's death, Antigone returned to Thebes. There she found the city in turmoil. Her sister, Ismene, who had stayed behind, told her what had happened.

When Oedipus went into exile, his twin sons, Polynices and Eteocles, had agreed that it would be fairest not to choose one of them to succeed their father, but to share the kingdom. They would alternate as kings; each would hold the position for a year, then hand it over to his brother. They drew lots to choose who would be first, and Eteocles won.

But when Eteocles had ruled for his year, he refused to give up the kingship. Creon, Oedipus's brother, took his side, hoping that there would be open conflict between the twins, because he himself burned with ambition to rule Thebes. And conflict there was.

Polynices had fled for refuge to Argos, where he won the support of the king. Now, at the head of seven armies, Polynices hurled a mighty force at Thebes, once his home, now his enemy. The battle raged fiercely, and it seemed it would never end. The two sides were evenly matched, the invaders led by one of the sons of Oedipus, and the defenders by the other. Each of the seven captains attacked one of the doors in the city walls, but on the other side of each door was an equally strong force ready to repel them. Inside the besieged city, the people were starving; outside, the invaders were weakened by hunger and disease. But neither the attackers nor the defenders would surrender.

The situation appeared hopeless until both sides agreed to resolve the conflict by a single combat between the two brothers. If Eteocles won, the attacking army would withdraw, and he would become sole king. If Polynices won, Eteocles would go into exile, leaving him to rule alone.

The brothers met outside the city walls. Glaring at each other, they closed in and began to fight. Their struggle would determine the fate of Thebes, and it was made fierce by the anger each harbored against the other. Onlookers from both sides were covered with drops of sweat just from watching the strenuous conflict. Cheers rang out, now from inside the walls, now from outside, as one brother seemed to have the edge, then the other.

Again and again, the two men struck at each other, until the ground was slippery with royal blood. At last, both of them were exhausted; their blows fell more and more weakly, and they sank to their knees at the same time. Polynices knew he was dying. With his last breath, he spoke.

"Eteocles, will you grant me one last wish? In justice, will you bury my body in Thebes? Let me always be part of the land I love!"

The wounded Eteocles could only nod his agreement. At the next moment, he fell dead beside the body of his brother.

Now the battle was over, and there was only one winner. Creon had his wish: he had become king of Thebes. For his first act, the new ruler decreed that Eteocles should be buried and honored, as the defender of Thebes and the rightful successor to Oedipus. Polynices, he declared, was a vicious rebel who had attacked the kingdom, and he must lie unburied, exposed to the sun and wind, outside the city walls. There his body would be devoured by wild dogs and vultures. That would be a just punishment for his crime, the king declared.

Antigone was appalled. What was her uncle thinking? This order not only went against family loyalty, it contradicted all moral law. The unburied dead, everyone knew, were punished eternally. Their souls could not cross the River Styx into the Underworld, but were condemned to wander forever, desolate and without rest. The gods had commanded that the dead must be committed to earth. Why, it was a sacred duty to bury even the body of a stranger! Now Creon's law made it a crime for anyone to bury her brother. Which laws were stronger, those of morality or politics? For Antigone, there was no question.

The day of Eteocles's burial was declared a time of mourning for the whole land. A huge funeral pyre rose toward Heaven for the cremation of a great hero. Cattle were sacrificed before the altars as an offering to the gods, and the smell of incense filled the air. No aspect of royal ritual was overlooked. At the same time, the king ordered a guard to be set, day and night, over the body of Polynices. Nobody must attempt to bury him, Creon decreed, on pain of death.

Antigone went to find her sister. They had to talk about the king's unjust ruling.

"This is no idle threat, Ismene. He means to enforce his law. Anyone who buries Polynices will be stoned to death. Now it's time for us to show our royal blood. Will you help me, sister?"

"Help you do what?" Ismene replied, bewildered. "What are you talking about?"

"Will you help me lift him, carry him away, bury him?"

"But, Antigone!" her sister protested. "You can't do that! It would be against the law!"

"He is our brother, Ismene. How can we desert him?"

Ismene was afraid. "We're only women, Antigone, weak women. How can we fight against men? The law is more powerful than we are! We have no choice but to accept it! I loved my brother too, but to disobey our uncle's order—the king's order—that would be madness!"

Antigone drew herself up. Quietly she replied, "Very well, Ismene, I won't ask you to help—no, I wouldn't welcome your help even if you offered it. Do what you have to do. I will bury him alone. If I die for it, so what? I'll be happy to have died for doing what is right. Live, if that's your choice, and defy the dictates of the gods!"

Ismene wept. "I'm not defying them, but I can't act against the law. I'm not strong enough to do that! But if you're set on committing this terrible act, I promise I won't tell a soul; I'll keep your secret."

"Tell anyone you want!" Antigone scoffed. "Publish it to the whole world! I will do what I have to do."

The next morning, one of the sentries who had been set to guard the body of Polynices approached the palace, trembling with fear. "King Creon," he muttered, "there is something I must tell you, though I can't find the words to say it—something very strange."

"Out with it!" shouted the king. Halting and stumbling over the words, the sentry told his story.

"Last night there was no moon," he said, "and when the night was at its darkest point, someone managed to get past our guard and bury the body. The covering wasn't very deep, but there was dust scattered all over, like a holy burial."

Creon was outraged. "Unbury him!" he ordered. "Double the watch! I want to find out who dared to disobey me. That person will die and become an example to the whole kingdom."

It was late afternoon of the same day when Creon saw, far off, a group of sentries marching up to the palace. They seemed to have someone else with them. As they drew nearer, he realized that the figure they surrounded was his niece, Antigone.

The guard saluted. "Here she is, sir," he said triumphantly. "This is the one who buried him. We caught her in the very act! We had uncovered the body, swept off all the dirt, and left only the naked corpse, just as you told us to. We were watching very closely, and then, around noon, a tremendous dust storm came up. We had to shut our eyes tight for a few minutes. When we opened them again, we saw her, this girl, screaming over the body and pouring sand out of a bronze urn. Three times she made her offering to the dead. And then we rushed down and caught her. She wasn't at all afraid; in fact, she seemed proud of what she was doing!"

Creon turned to Antigone, his face pale. "Was it really you who did this?" he demanded, unbelieving. "Do you admit it?"

"Yes," she answered quietly, "I do not deny it."

"Didn't you know that I gave an order forbidding anyone to bury Polynices? And that the penalty for breaking that law is death?"

"Yes, of course I knew." Antigone looked at him with disdain. "That order didn't come from the Gods. There is no justice in such a law! The order I obeyed is stronger. Heaven's laws are eternal; men's laws are around for only a brief moment."

Creon was shocked. Now he faced a dilemma. This defiant person—this criminal—was his own niece, the girl who was betrothed to his son, Haemon! How could he put her to death? And yet he must. If he weakened now, why should anyone obey any law he made in the future? But it would look equally bad in the eyes of the people if he killed a princess of the royal family.

The king found a compromise. Instead of stoning Antigone to death, he ordered her to be walled up inside a cave, with a certain amount of food and water. Then, he thought, when she died, it would not be as if he had killed her himself.

At Creon's words, Ismene threw herself forward, fell to her knees, and begged to be allowed to share Antigone's fate. "I helped her do it!" she sobbed. But Antigone refused to let her share the blame.

"She did nothing to help me," she said scornfully. Turning to her sister, she added, "You chose life, Ismene. I chose death. Please, go away and let what must happen, happen."

Haemon, Creon's son, came to plead for the life of Antigone, whom he loved. Vainly he argued with his father, telling him that the people would turn against him if he carried out such a harsh sentence against a girl, a member of his family at that. Furious, Creon lashed out at his son. "You shall never have my enemy for your wife! She has to learn that it's better to obey the living than the dead!"

Now the blind prophet Tiresias appeared before the king. He had been warned that new calamities were in store for Thebes because the king was intent on punishing the innocent Antigone, and because of the sacrilege committed against the body of Polynices. He warned Creon, "The gods are angry at what you have done to King Oedipus's children."

Creon's only reply was to insult the old man. "Who has bribed you to frighten me with such lies?" he shouted.

Tiresias answered him: "Before the sun sets this day, you shall pay twice. Yes, there will be two more corpses in return for one! And their blood will be on your hands, Creon."

Although the king had seemed to stand firm, this pronouncement frightened him; one should not take lightly the words of such a seer. Creon called together his council and asked them what they thought he ought to do. They answered as one. "Bury the body of Polynices and let Antigone free," they chorused.

Reluctantly, Creon agreed to do as they advised, and gave the order. Then he set off for Antigone's cave, accompanied by a crowd carrying axes and crowbars to tear it open. His son, who had run ahead of the rest, began to strike at the wall. He made a crack in it and peered into the cave.

Haemon uttered an awful cry. Frantically, he tore the rest of the wall down and entered the cave. In a moment he emerged, carrying in his arms the body of his beloved Antigone. Alone in the darkness, she had twisted her veil into a noose and strangled herself. Gently, Haemon laid her on the ground and arranged her dress, his face streaming with tears. Then, before his father could stop him, he pulled out his sword and threw himself upon it, falling dead across the body of his betrothed.

When Creon's queen heard all that had happened, how her son and Antigone had died, she too despaired, and killed herself. So it was that what Tiresias had foretold came true. Before the sun had set, two of the king's house lay dead beside Antigone—two corpses for one. The whole of Thebes mourned, and Creon was forced to bury the bodies of all the dead from the battle.

Antigone had stood up for the right. The price was a terrible one to pay, but principle had triumphed. That was what really mattered.

A Daughter's Vengeance: Electra

A FEUD IS A FRIGHTFUL THING, whether it is carried on between countries or between neighbors. It's worst of all when members of a family begin to hate each other and swear to take revenge for someone's actions. And that is just what happened in the family of Agamemnon, the king of Mycenae.

It all began when Agamemnon was trying to reach Troy to fight for his brother Menelaus in the Trojan War. He had collected an army together at Aulis, but the ships could not set sail because a mighty wind was blowing onshore, preventing anything from leaving the harbor. For days and days it blew, and the men were beginning to despair. Then the prophet Calchas had a vision. The wind, he said, had been sent by the goddess

Artemis, who was angry at Agamemnon for neglecting a duty to her. She would never let them go unless the king sacrificed his oldest daughter, Iphigenia, to the goddess.

Of course, Agamemnon refused to commit such an act; of course, the wind continued to blow. The army was becoming angry and frustrated, and at last turned hostile. They demanded that Agamemnon perform the sacrifice, threatening violence if he did not. The reluctant king was forced to agree.

He sent for his wife, Clytemnestra, and his daughter, telling them that the girl was to be married to Achilles. Joyfully, the women arrived at Aulis, and Iphigenia put on her bridal dress. But when she approached the altar, she realized that the real reason she had been summoned to Aulis was quite different from a wedding. Saying that it would be easier for both of them to bear if she went alone, the girl sent her mother away, and bravely stepped forward to her death.

Mourning for her daughter, Clytemnestra returned to Mycenae. But sorrow was not her only emotion. The queen was horrified by her daughter's sacrifice, and infuriated at her husband for permitting—no, ordering—it.

"How could a father commit such an act?" she asked herself. "I have been married to him for many years—I should have been able to see what kind of man he was! If I'd suspected such treachery, I might have been able to save Iphigenia's life."

The seeds of violent hatred had been planted, and during the ten years that Agamemnon was away at the Trojan War, those seeds grew and flourished. In the end, they would bear bitter fruit.

Clytemnestra's first act of vengeance was to bring another man to live in the palace. Aegisthus, who had reasons of his own to hate Agamemnon, accepted her offer gladly. Clytemnestra and Aegisthus now ruled over the country together, as king and queen.

But they were not destined to rule comfortably. Iphigenia had not been an only child; she had two sisters and a brother, and Electra, the older of the two remaining girls, loved her father deeply. Although she too mourned her sister's death, she knew that Agamemnon could not have committed such a terrible deed unless he had been forced to do it.

Electra refused to accept Clytemnestra's new arrangement. Outraged by her mother's behavior, she made no pretense of going along with it. Daily she heaped scorn on the queen, telling her outright that she was an immoral woman.

Soon Clytemnestra and Aegisthus had had enough of Electra's defiant behavior. The girl must be punished! Determined to make her life miserable, they sent Electra away, giving her a filthy hovel outside the palace gates. There she lived, dressed in rags, forced to do the lowest, most menial work, while her sister Chrysothemis continued to live the life of a princess.

All Electra had left was her beloved younger brother, Orestes. But she feared for his life, knowing that Aegisthus's hatred for their father put her brother in danger. Secretly, she arranged for Orestes to be taken in by a trusted family friend, who agreed to watch over the boy and keep him safe until he grew to manhood.

And so the years went on, long years for Electra. Long for Clytemnestra, too, whose hatred for her husband continued to grow, along with her sorrow for the death of Iphigenia.

Often the queen would go off by herself to stare in the direction of Troy and pray to the gods that Agamemnon would be killed in battle.

Finally, after ten years, the war was over. Agamemnon was on his way home. Now the queen's prayers changed; this time she begged the gods to raise a violent storm that would sink her husband's ship and drown him. But none of her prayers were answered. If Clytemnestra wanted revenge, she would have to get it by her own act.

From her usual lookout point on the palace walls, the queen saw Agamemnon arrive home in triumph. The people crowded the streets to greet their king joyfully and welcome him back. But there was an uneasy edge to their rejoicing, for they all knew the family history—how the gods had put a curse on all the descendants of Tantalus, of whom the king was one. They knew, too, that the queen had not been faithful to him, and had still not sent Aegisthus away. What was being plotted behind the walls of the palace? They sensed that there was trouble ahead.

When the king's carriage stopped in front of the door, Clytemnestra came out of the palace. She held her head high as she greeted her husband. "Even though we are not alone, I have to tell you how much I love you," she said, looking around defiantly at the gathered crowd, all of whom knew what had been going on while he was gone.

"Every minute that you have been away has been torture for me," she continued. "Seeing you is pure joy, like cool water to a thirsty traveler. Please, come into the palace where we can rejoice together."

Agamemnon responded to his wife's words rather coldly. He pointed to a lovely woman who was seated next to him in his carriage. This was one of the spoils of war he had brought back from defeated Troy: the prophetess Cassandra, whose destiny it was to utter truths that nobody would ever believe. The sight of the young and beautiful woman kindled Clytemnestra's anger into new flames. Her husband had never really loved her, and now he was bringing this woman into the house! She swore to herself that he would be dead by nightfall.

Now Agamemnon and Clytemnestra turned and entered the palace, walking on the red carpets that the queen had ordered her attendants to spread before the king. The door closed behind them.

Cassandra was left outside. "Whose house is this?" she asked wildly. When she was told it was the house of Agamemnon, she cried, "No! This is a house God hates, where men are killed, and the floor is red with blood."

The older men in the crowd looked around uneasily, for they too had misgivings about what might happen. But the younger ones jeered and laughed at Cassandra's words. At last she said, "Today there will be two more deaths, and one of them will be mine. But I can bear to die." Then she too entered the palace, and the door closed once again.

That night, Clytemnestra prepared a great victory feast for her husband and his generals. The people were still gathered in the street, waiting for the king to come out onto the balcony and say a few words to them. Instead, they heard a shout from within. It was the king's voice, crying out in agony: "I've been struck! God! It is my death blow!" Then they heard another cry, this time the voice of Cassandra.

Outside, the people stood stunned, trying to decide what to do. Should they break into the palace? Before they could make up their minds to act, the door opened, and Clytemnestra stood before them, her dress and her hands and face stained red with blood. She stood proudly, confidently, holding a bloody sword in her hand.

"I have killed my husband," she announced boldly, "and nobody can say I did wrong! This deed was a just deed, for at last I have punished the murderer of my child." Aegisthus came out to stand beside her, and he too was stained with blood. The people accepted the queen's words; they went home, quietly talking among themselves.

Now Clytemnestra was free to marry Aegisthus, and they continued to rule with ever-increasing power.

During all the years that her brother was growing up, Electra had sent him letters to remind him of his father's death and his duty as a son. Now Orestes had grown to manhood, and the time had come for him to confront the terrible problem the gods had placed before him. Honor decreed that he must take vengeance on his father's murderer. But that murderer was his own mother, and the eternal laws forbade matricide. Where did justice lie?

Torn between these conflicting moral demands, Orestes went to Delphi to lay his problem before Apollo's oracle. The god's answer was very clear. Because he was the only male relative, it rested on Orestes to restore honor to his family. Even if it brought ruin on him, he must kill his mother, and her new husband as well.

So Orestes, with his cousin Pylades for company, set out for the home he had not seen since he was a small child. Hoping to keep his presence in Mycenae a secret, Orestes sent a messenger to the queen to tell her that her son was dead. Then he went to visit his father's grave, to offer a sacrifice: libations of wine and milk and his own hair.

Each day during all those long years, Electra had gone to mourn at the grave of Agamemnon, praying that her brother would soon return and avenge her father's death. Once she met a friend there, who begged her not to spend all her time in hatred. "You shouldn't forget your enemies, but you shouldn't hold on to excessive anger, either. You're the one who will be hurt—such self-torture will destroy you!"

Electra replied, "I know that I'm consumed by my grief and anger. But remember, I have nothing else in my life: no husband to fight for me, no children. My mother hates me as I hate her; I am treated like a slave, starved and beaten. And my brother, for all his promises, does not come!

"Just think, every month my mother celebrates her happy day—the day she killed my father—with music and sacrifice, to thank the gods for his death! And I have to stand by and watch. Then she yells at me when there's a rumor that Orestes is on his way home. How can I be calm and dutiful? With evil all around me, there is nothing I can do that is not evil!" Her friend left, shaking her head sadly.

On the day Orestes secretly returned, their sister Chrysothemis, who still lived in the palace, went to Agamemnon's grave. There she met Electra, mourning as usual.

"Why are you here again?" Chrysothemis asked. "Can't you learn to hide your anger instead of showing it off? I hate our position just as much as you do, and if I had the strength, I'd let them know what my real feelings are. But my policy is to bow before the storm, not to make a show of defiance, when I have no power to strike a blow!"

"You ought to be ashamed, if you're our father's daughter!" Electra replied. "You support our mother's side by keeping silent! You say you'd like to show how much you hate her, but you do nothing to defy her. You can't have it both ways!"

Chrysothemis stared hard at her sister. Then she said, "The only reason I've come out here and brought this whole thing up is that I've heard our mother and Aegisthus talking about a terrible punishment to keep you quiet."

Electra laughed. "Punishment? What could be worse than what I suffer now?"

"Aegisthus is away right now, but when he returns, they plan to banish you, to throw you into a dungeon, where you will never again see the light of day."

"Well, then," Electra replied, "let it happen soon! At least I'll never have to look at any of you again! But what are you holding?"

"Our mother's libations for our father's grave," answered her sister. Electra was horrified. How did her mother dare to offer libations for the man she had killed?

"She has had a frightening dream," Chrysothemis confided. "She dreamed that our father returned to life and grabbed the scepter that Aegisthus carries. He planted it near the altar, where it sprouted and grew, casting a shadow over all Mycenae."

Electra answered, "You must not let any offering from our mother touch our father's tomb! Throw those things away, and then give him a lock of your own bright hair, and this dull lock of my hair. Kneel and pray that Orestes will come soon to crush his father's enemies under his foot!" Chrysothemis left.

Almost at once Clytemnestra appeared, and began once more the constant quarrel between mother and daughter. "I had justice on my side when I killed your father, and if you believed in justice, you would agree that my act was right. He did something no other Greek has ever dared to do, sacrificing his own child to the gods!"

As they stood arguing, the messenger Orestes had sent arrived with his false story. Vividly, he described how the young man had died in a chariot race.

Clytemnestra was silent for a moment, torn between a mother's grief at the loss of her child and relief that the threat of vengeance was lifted from her. She turned to go back to the palace, leaving Electra in agony.

"Orestes, if you are dead, how can I go on living? Your death has torn the last shred of hope from my heart!" Sinking to the ground, Electra sobbed, "Let them come and kill me! It would be kindness! Life is nothing but pain to me, and I want to die!"

Just then Chrysothemis reappeared, wreathed in smiles. "Oh, Electra!" she cried. "Such good news! Orestes is here! I know he is, because when I went to the tomb, there were fresh libations, milk and garlands of flowers, and a lock of hair newly cut off. It has to be Orestes! Nobody else could have brought that offering."

"No, you're wrong," Electra answered her bitterly. "Orestes is dead. It must be someone who did that act for him, in his memory. Only we are left to avenge our father's death. Are you brave enough to help me kill Aegisthus? Now think! You'd be doing your duty to our father and brother, and afterwards you could live proudly, in honor, and make a good marriage. All men admire courage, and think of the courage you will have shown! Come, join me, it's up to us now to put an end to our shame."

But Chrysothemis replied, "Do you forget that you are only a woman, weaker than your enemy? We couldn't possibly set a snare for such a man and not be caught ourselves in the net of doom! Please, be careful! What if somebody heard you talking this way? Think what you do before you destroy us all!"

Electra only replied, dryly, "I admire your caution, but I despise your spirit. So, I will have to do it myself."

Seeing that it was impossible to change her sister's mind, Chrysothemis left sadly, promising that she would not tell anyone what Electra was planning.

As soon as she had gone, Orestes and Pylades arrived, carrying an urn that they pretended held the ashes of Orestes. At last brother and sister stood face-to-face. It had been so long since they had seen each other that neither of them recognized the other. But when the two young men handed Electra the urn, she was so stricken with sorrow that her brother guessed who she was. He showed her a sign, the cloak she had made for him to wear when she sent him away, and she understood. Electra and Orestes were at last reunited, and they embraced each other in joy.

The three young people wasted no time in making their plan for vengeance. They would enter the palace together, with Electra carrying the urn. "Now don't forget your part," Orestes cautioned. "Don't let our mother see you with a smile upon your face! She must not suspect anything."

"Don't worry," his sister replied. "She will never see me smile; hatred has burned in me too long for that. I'll be weeping, but it will be for joy that you have come home at last."

At the palace, they presented Clytemnestra with the urn, and Electra went out again, to watch for the arrival of Aegisthus. From inside, she heard Clytemnestra cry, "Help!" and then, "Have mercy on your mother!"

"You had no mercy for my father!" Electra shouted through the closed doors.

When Orestes and Pylades came out of the house, their hands were red. "Is everything all right?" Electra asked anxiously.

"Yes," said her brother. "It's all right if Apollo was right in commanding me to do this deed!"

At that moment, Electra saw Aegisthus coming down the street. "Quick, back into the house!" she exclaimed. The men went in, and in a moment, Aegisthus too entered the doors of the palace, never to come out alive again.

The door opened, and a shaken Orestes emerged. Nobody needed to be told what he had done. But he was not triumphant. "I know Aegisthus's death was just," he muttered. "He was an adulterer as well as a murderer. But my mother? It's true she was a vile woman, and she killed my father. But she was my mother! It was only because of Apollo that I could do such a deed."

Although Apollo had ordered it, some of the gods could not accept this revenge. To kill a mother, they argued, for whatever reason, was unforgivable. They sent the terrible

Furies after the young man, and he left, tortured by their wrath. Electra was once more left alone in Mycenae.

Orestes wandered for years without rest, pursued by the Furies. At last he went to Athens to plead his case before Athena, the goddess of justice. She heard him, but was undecided: had his action been justified? Suddenly Apollo appeared and said, "It was I who ordered Orestes to commit that murder. Therefore, I alone am responsible for her death."

Orestes drew himself up. "No," he said, "I cannot accept that excuse. It is true that Apollo told me what to do, but I knew right from wrong, and I must take responsibility for my own actions."

Athena accepted the young man's brave statement. She admired his strength. His long suffering, she declared, had cleared him of guilt. And now, for the first time in generations, the curse that had plagued this family was lifted.

Orestes, the goddess declared, was free to go wherever he wanted. Electra married Pylades, and they lived out the rest of their days in peace.

Iphigenia in Tauris

O N THE SHORES OF THE UNFRIENDLY SEA, BEYOND the Clashing Rocks, lived a fierce and cruel people. Any foreigner unlucky enough to be found on the land of Tauris was doomed to die. The Taurians beheaded prisoners of war and impaled the heads on long stakes, then set them up to watch over the house of their captors. Shipwrecked sailors were sacrificed publicly to Artemis, their headless bodies tossed into the sea from her magnificent temple. Greeks of noble blood were given to the temple's virgin priestess, who prepared them for the sacrifice. Then she handed them over to others, to be killed in the inmost chamber, and their bodies burned in the sacred fire there.

Now there was a new priestess at the temple. She was Iphigenia, the daughter of Agamemnon and Clytemnestra—alive, not dead, as everyone believed. Years ago, Agamemnon had vowed to give Artemis the loveliest creature born within a year. He did not fulfill his vow, for that beautiful thing was his firstborn daughter. When Iphigenia was grown up, the angry goddess refused to let a thousand of the king's ships sail off to the Trojan War unless he sacrificed his daughter, and he was forced to agree. Summoned to her father on the pretense that she was to marry Achilles, Iphigenia was led to the altar. There she was held high over the fire, and the sword fell.

But it did not fall on Iphigenia. Artemis was the protector of small creatures, and she would never have allowed the sacrifice of an innocent girl. At the last moment, she came, invisible, to the altar, where she made all the witnesses bow their heads while she wrapped the girl in a cloud and carried her away. When the men looked up again, they saw, instead of a girl, a young deer with its throat cut. "Iphigenia must have been carried off to Heaven!" they marveled.

It was not Heaven to which Artemis had taken her, however, but to Tauris, where the goddess made her the priestess of her temple. And now it was to Tauris that Iphigenia's brother Orestes and cousin Pylades also made their way. Even though Athena had absolved Orestes from guilt for killing his mother and her new husband, some of the Furies had continued to persecute him. At last he went to seek counsel from Apollo at Delphi. There the oracle ordered him to take the statue of Artemis from Tauris and set it up in Athens. When he had done so, the oracle said, he would be free of punishment, finally healed of his guilt, and at peace.

Orestes and Pylades knew what would happen to Greeks who were found on Tauris. They waited until it was dark to land their ship, then secretly made their way to the temple. Nearby, they found a hiding spot, but in the morning they were discovered by some herdsmen, who captured them and led them, bound with ropes, to Thoas, the king of Tauris. He ordered them to be taken to the temple at once to be prepared for sacrifice.

Orestes was brought first before the priestess. Brother and sister had not seen each other since he was an infant, so of course neither of them had any idea who the other was. He was suprised to find that the priestess seemed genuinely sorrowful about his death, even more that she spoke Greek and was strangely interested in his country. She wanted to hear about everything that had happened there; in particular, she asked about the royal family. Now Iphigenia learned for the first time of the deaths of her father and mother, and the part Electra and Orestes had played in the tragedy.

Iphigenia was overjoyed to hear that her brother Orestes was still alive. She thought for a moment. "I have an idea that will help both of us," she finally said. "If you will carry a letter for me to Mycenae, I will save your life. Let your friend alone be sacrificed to Artemis, since the law demands a victim."

But Orestes could not agree to that. "Pylades is here only because he wanted to help me. I would be a terrible coward if I let him die, and lived myself."

"Very well," the priestess replied. "I see that your heart is noble! Let him take the letter, then, and you will be the victim." Orestes agreed.

"Who will offer me for sacrifice?" he asked.

"Alas, that's my dreadful duty! I have no choice but to obey. But I do not wield the sword; I only sprinkle water on your head for purification."

For the first time, Orestes fully understood what he faced. He groaned. "O gods! If only my sister could be here to compose my body for burial!"

"A hopeless prayer," Iphigenia replied. "But I will do everything for you that a sister could. I'll pile gifts on your burial-place, pour golden olive oil over the fire to quench your ashes, and anoint your pyre with honey. Now you must wait here while I go and fetch the letter from the temple."

When Orestes joined Pylades and told him of the plan, his cousin bluntly refused to save his own life at such a cost. "The very idea is shameful!" he exclaimed.

Orestes hastened to persuade him. "I accept my own fate," he said. "But I cannot accept being responsible for your death. If you hadn't tried to help me, you would be home now, safe and happy. You have no blood taint on you, as I have. You must escape, and marry my sister Electra, as you had planned. You will have children and will carry on my name that way."

As Pylades reluctantly agreed, Iphigenia returned with the letter. She handed it to him. "How can I be sure that you will deliver it as I ask you to?" she said. "Swear by Zeus that you will, and I will swear by Artemis that I will see you alive and safe out of the country."

"What if I should be shipwrecked," Pylades worried, "and the letter lost? That would make me break my oath!"

"To make doubly sure my message gets through," Iphigenia answered, "I will tell you the contents of the letter. Say to Orestes, the son of Agamemnon, that the message is from Iphigenia, who was not sacrificed after all, but lives in Tauris as the priestess of Artemis."

When he heard these words, Orestes leapt up amazed. "Sister, you're alive! I am Orestes!" he cried. Iphigenia could not believe such wonderful news. But her brother told her things only he could know. He described the tapestry she had woven for him when he was an infant, the lock of hair she had sent to her mother, the ancestral spear she kept in her room at the palace. At last she was convinced, and embraced both the men, laughing and crying at the same time.

Now Iphigenia had to make a new plan, one that would save her brother as well as Pylades. When Orestes told her that Apollo had ordered him to take the statue of Artemis back to Athens, she thought carefully.

"I must rescue you from this terrible situation," she said. "If I can, I'll help you take the statue and get on board the ship. I'll try to go with you, but if that's not possible, you must carry it off without me, and I will die. It's worth the risk. I'm not afraid to die if I can get you away safely."

"Now I see Apollo's plan," her brother mused. "He meant me to find you here! I think we'll reach home safely, if we are bold enough. Perhaps we could kill the king and escape in the confusion."

"No, that would be wrong," Iphigenia answered. "I am a foreigner, and he is my host. But I think I begin to see a way. I can use your misfortune to deceive the king. A sacrificial victim must be pure. I'll tell him that you murdered your mother; you are unclean and unfit for the sacrifice. And that Pylades helped you, so he too is unfit.

"I'll say that I need to purify your bodies in the sea, and that the statue must be cleansed too, because you have defiled it by touching it. Then we'll go to the headland where your ship is anchored. I'll carry the image; nobody else is allowed to touch it."

She turned and sent a prayer to Artemis. "O goddess, you saved me from my father's murderous hand. Now protect me once again, and bring us safely out of this savage land, with your statue. In Athens, you will be more joyfully served."

When King Thoas came to the temple to make sure that the men had been readied for sacrifice, Iphigenia told him the story she had prepared. "How did you know they were unclean?" he asked, and she replied, "The statue itself let me know. When they came near, it shook and closed its eyes, shrinking back on its pedestal."

Thoas was horrified when he heard that the men had killed Orestes' mother. "Even a savage would shrink from such a deed!" he exclaimed. And he agreed to let her take them to the sea for cleansing, along with the goddess's image. The guards, he said, would cover their faces, and he himself would stay in the temple until the ceremony was completed, to make sure that nobody else was defiled by contact with guilty blood.

After a time, King Thoas, still hidden in the temple, heard one of the guards shouting. "Come out! That priestess has gone, has fled with the two strangers, and they have taken the statue of Artemis as well!"

The guard went on breathlessly, "She took the cord that bound the men in her own hands, and told us to stay back so that she could light the holy flame and perform the purification. They went out of sight, then we heard her singing incantations and uttering strange cries. We were suspicious, but still we sat in silence, for fear of seeing what is forbidden to us.

"But after a while, we got up and went over the rocks, and there was a Greek ship, with her rows of oars lifted, fifty rowers ready to take her away, and the men and the priestess about to board. We grabbed hold of Iphigenia and tried to drag her away, but we were badly beaten up by the men. None of us had swords, so we retreated and began to throw stones, when archers appeared on the deck and shot arrows at us.

"Just then, a huge wave lifted the ship, foam swirled around Iphigenia's feet, and Orestes picked her up, strode into the sea, and caught the ladder. They all boarded safely, with the statue. But as the rowers set to, a wind came up and began to blow them back to shore. The priestess started praying to Artemis, but the ship has still not been able to get away. I think we can catch them if we hurry!"

As Thoas gave his soldiers the order to run to the seashore, he was stunned to see the goddess Athena appear above the porch of the temple. She began to speak.

"Do not go after them. It was Apollo that sent Orestes here. By taking his sister home and carrying the holy statue safely to Athens, Orestes will be released from all his torment. Poseidon is even now calming the winds, at my request, to give the ship a smooth passage. I myself will accompany them to Athens, keeping watch over the holy treasure in honor of my sister Artemis."

Thoas called back his men. "To hear a god's command and disobey it would be madness. I take back my anger. I will let them go, and may they speed their way home."

And so they did. When the ship touched land in Greece, they built a new shrine to Artemis and set up the image there. In gratitude for the goddess's help, Iphigenia continued to serve as her priestess and keeper of the sacred keys.

RUNNING FREE

The Hunter Goddess:
Artemis

T HE GODDESS LETO WAS ABOUT TO GIVE BIRTH, BUT NOWHERE ON EARTH COULD SHE FIND A PLACE
to have her baby. Hera had seen to that. Once again she was furious with Zeus and
with his new love—this time Leto, who wandered the world, begging every country and
island for help. Alas, they were all afraid of Hera and her terrible temper. Everywhere,
Leto was denied refuge.

At last she came to a tiny wisp of a place, a floating island named Delos. "We are
both wanderers," the island replied to her request. "I will happily shelter you." But Hera
refused to let Ilithyia, the goddess of childbirth, help the mother-to-be. For nine days and
nine nights she suffered the pains of birth. Finally, the other goddesses took pity on her
and offered Hera a beautiful necklace of gold and amber, nine yards long, if she would
only let Leto give birth. The queen of Heaven could not resist, and Iris whisked Ilithyia
down her rainbow to Delos.

Standing in the middle of the island, Leto put her arms around a palm tree, and her first child was born. It was the goddess Artemis. At once, the infant grew into a beautiful young girl, tall and dark, surrounded by a silvery glow. She demanded to have a brother, so Leto gave birth to a twin for her, named Apollo. At the same time, Zeus made pillars grow from the seafloor to anchor the island so that Leto and her children would have a permanent place to live.

Zeus was proud of his new children: Apollo, golden as the sun, and Artemis, silver as the moon. When Artemis turned three, her father told her that he would grant her anything she wished. She was quick to reply. First, she said, she wished never to marry, but to remain single forever, free to roam the hills and woodlands, hunting and living a life of total independence. Zeus agreed, only adding that if she should ever fall in love, she could change her mind.

Next, Artemis asked for a silver bow and arrows and the best pack of hunting dogs to be found anywhere in the world. The Cyclopes were happy to forge for her a beautiful bow and a quiver that had special powers: whenever it was empty, it would instantly fill up again with swift silver arrows. The god Pan gave her his ten very best dogs. Then the child asked to have the office of bringing light to the world, as many names as her brother Apollo, a beautiful hunting tunic, all the mountains in the world, and sixty ocean nymphs and twenty river nymphs to attend her. All this her father granted. Now Artemis was ready to begin her new life as huntress.

Around her, the goddess gathered a group of like-minded nymphs and maidens, women who had also sworn to live a life of independence from men. They spent their days in carefree hunting, running lightly over the mountains and through the trees. But woe betide any of her girls who fell in love. Such a one was banished at once from the goddess's company, or worse, severely punished. Young women who were being forced into unwanted marriages would pray to Artemis to save them. Usually she did, although sometimes she had to do so by changing them into something else: a tree, a flower, a deer.

The chaste goddess of the moon was a somewhat contradictory character. Although she herself had nothing to do with men, she brought fertility to other women. The greatest huntress, she was also the tender protector of little children and all small animals. She would do anything to defend her band of women, so long as they remained loyal to their vows, but she could take terrible vengeance on them if the vows were broken. The goddess who stood up for women was also responsible for their natural deaths, just as Apollo was responsible for the deaths of men. She had the power either to inflict plagues and death on mortals or to heal them. Both gentle and fierce, Artemis was a warrior, whose fighting skill helped the gods win their war against the giants.

If someone failed to give the goddess the honor she deserved, her vengeance could be terrible. When Oeneus, king of Calydon, neglected her during his harvest sacrifices, Artemis sent a monstrous boar to ravage his land. An act of the Mycenean king Agamemnon—perhaps he boasted that he was a better hunter than Artemis, perhaps he had broken a vow to her—caused the goddess to demand that he sacrifice his daughter, Iphigenia. Some stories claim that the goddess was too tender-hearted to carry out this vengeance, and saved the girl at the very last minute.

Men who threatened the chaste Artemis were usually treated roughly. Such a man was the great hunter Actaeon, son of King Cadmus. One day, when he had spent the morning on the mountain hunting stags, Actaeon suggested to his companions that they rest from the hot noonday sun. As he wandered off alone, Fate led his feet into a grove of cypress and pines, sacred to Artemis. In this grove there was a cave, as beautifully arched as if the hand of man had made it, but the artist was nature alone. From the side of the cave sprang a fountain of clear water. It was here that the goddess came to bathe when she was hot and tired from the chase. Now she had just handed her bow, quiver, and javelin to one of her nymphs and her robe to another. While a third bent to remove her sandals and a fourth arranged her hair, still others drew pitchers of the sparkling water to pour over her body.

Onto this scene burst Actaeon. The nymphs all screamed and rushed to hide Artemis from his sight, but she was taller than the rest. Her face turned as pink as the clouds at sunset—with surprise, embarrassment, or anger, who can say? She reached for her arrows, but they were not there. The goddess snatched up a pitcher of water and threw it into the young man's face, saying, "Tell everyone, if you can, that you have seen Artemis at her bath."

Suddenly, a huge pair of branching stag's antlers sprouted from his head. Actaeon's neck grew long, his ears sharp and pointed, and his whole body became covered with a hairy hide. He stumbled back and caught sight of himself reflected in the water of a pool—he was now a magnificent stag. At the same moment, his dogs spotted him and gave chase. Not knowing who it was, Actaeon's companions cheered them on, until at last his own dogs brought him down and tore out his life.

Another time, two giants named Otus and Ephialtes fell in love with Artemis and Hera, and planned to capture them. They drew lots to see which goddess would be their first victim; the chance fell on Artemis. The brothers began to hunt through the woods and mountains, but could catch no sight of the goddess. At last they spotted her on the seashore and followed her all the way to the island of Naxos. There she disappeared, but—lo and behold!—in her place stood a beautiful white deer. At once, the giants forgot their original intention and began to hunt the deer. As they approached a clearing, they saw it grazing quietly, and split up to approach it from two different sides. When it lifted its head, each of the brothers hurled his spear, but the deer leaped aside, and the spears found a different target. The two brothers had killed the only things they really loved: each other.

Zeus's promises to his daughter were fulfilled. She lived the life she had asked for, unmarried, with the best of everything for the hunt. She brought light to the nighttime world. And she had many names. As goddess of the moon, Artemis was called Phoebe and sometimes Semele. The Romans knew her as Diana.

Daphne and Apollo

THE RIVER GOD PENEUS WAS CRAZY ABOUT HIS DAUGHTER, AND NO WONDER, FOR SHE WAS THE unsurpassable Daphne. No nymph had ever been lovelier than she, more charming, or more natural. She was blissfully happy, but her life was soon to change.

For Daphne was destined to become the first love of the sun god Apollo of Delos, the god of music, poetry, and medicine. His love for her was not accidental—no, it was Cupid, spiteful Cupid, who brought it about.

One day Apollo saw Cupid draw his tiny bow, and teased him. "Little boy, what are you doing with a weapon like that? A bow is not meant for children, but for grown-ups, for someone like me.

"Now I," he boasted, "I never miss my aim, whether I'm shooting at my enemies or at wild beasts. Why, just now I killed the serpent, Python, whose nasty bloated body has been spoiling acres and acres of land. A torch is the proper toy for a child like you! You can get the flames of love burning hot enough with that. Go play with fire, and leave the glory of the bow to me."

Saucy Cupid only laughed. "Ha! We'll see whose glory is greater! You may conquer the whole world with your great bow, but I can still conquer you with my little one!" And Cupid shook his wings and flew up to the top of Parnassus, Apollo's own sacred mountain.

From his quiver he drew forth two arrows, the one that kindles love and the one that repels it. The first of these is golden and needle-sharp, the second blunt and tipped with lead. With the leaden arrow Cupid pierced Daphne's heart, but with the golden one he shot Apollo, straight through his bones and marrow. In that instant, Apollo felt the stabbing pain of love, although he didn't yet know who the object of that love would be.

But Daphne was horrified by the very idea of love. Though many men adored her and would have courted her, she scorned them all. Love, husband, marriage—none of this interested her. She preferred to spend her days wandering in the forest. She knew its secrets: the most private and shadowed spots, the hiding places of animals. Like Artemis, the hunter goddess, Daphne loved the chase, but despised the joys of love.

Her father Peneus grieved over her unmarried state, and often reproached her. "Dear daughter, it's high time I had a son-in-law!" he would say. Another time he might begin "Dearest daughter, you really should give me a grandchild to be the joy of my old age!"

But to Daphne marriage seemed repulsive, even criminal. She would blush and put her arms around Peneus, saying, "Father, dear Father, let me spend my days forever unmarried. You know Artemis's father granted her that wish. Can't you do the same for me?" Her father loved her, and reluctantly agreed.

Still, Daphne's beauty was her enemy. Against her deepest feelings, she attracted every man who saw her. And, like those mortals, the god Apollo had only to look at her to feel the fire of love. It flamed in his heart like stubble blazing in the grainfields after harvest, or like a dry hedge that burns bright if someone brushes against it with a torch.

Daphne, who disdained her beauty, wasted no time on her clothing, and caught her hair up carelessly with a length of ribbon. When Apollo saw her long tresses falling in tangled waves against her neck, he thought, "How beautiful she is! How much more beautiful she'd be if that hair were combed and tamed!" He gazed at her eyes, sparkling like fiery stars, at her lips, her fingers, hands, wrists, arms, at her shoulders, white as ivory. His love only deepened.

But Daphne was terrified by his attentions. She turned and ran from him, faster than the wind can run, and would not stop to listen as he begged: "Wait for me, nymph! Please wait! I'm not your enemy; you mustn't be afraid of me! I know a lamb runs away from the wolf, and a fawn runs from the lion. All creatures must escape their foes, but I am not your foe. It's love that sends me chasing after you."

Then he began to worry: she might fall down, running so fast. What if she scratched her face, or briars tore at her legs? It would be his fault. "Do be careful!" he cried. "Watch where you're going! The ground is so rough here! I promise, if you will only slow down a little, I'll follow more slowly, too.

"You know," he went on, "you haven't even asked who I am that loves you so. If you knew, you madcap girl, you'd stop running! I'm not some peasant or a mountain cave-dweller. I am the son of Zeus, the lord of Delphi. I am the one who reveals past, present, and future through my sacred oracles. With my lyre I make the music poets borrow when they praise the gods. My arrows always find their mark. But someone else's arrow has pierced my heart, which was once so carefree! I invented medicine, and know the power of herbs, but still there is no herb that can cure my love. My own arts have failed their master!"

There was even more the god wanted to say, but Daphne was too frightened to listen. She ran on and on. In flight she was even more beautiful than before, her slim legs bare in the soft wind, her dress blown back, hair streaming behind her as she ran.

And Apollo, made swift by love, flew after her, but now he ran silently. Their chase was like the greyhound running after a rabbit across a field. He runs to catch the prey, she runs for safety, and now he's almost sure he has her—yes, she's in his reach, and she too thinks she's caught, but then she finds a sudden surge of strength. So ran the god and the girl, he on the wings of love, she on the wings of fear. She had no moment to rest, and slowly he gained on her, until at last she could feel his breath warm in her hair.

Worn out by the long flight, her strength was gone, and she was pale as death. But at that moment, she realized that she had reached the banks of her father, the River Peneus. Daphne cried out: "Father, help me! Help! If there is any power in your waters, destroy my body, this beauty that has caused me so much anguish!"

She had hardly finished speaking when she felt her limbs grow languid, heavy and numb. A thin, smooth layer of bark began to close around her bosom; her hair became leaves, fluttering in the gentle wind. Her slender arms turned into branches, and her feet, which had been so swift, sent roots deep into the ground. Her face was hidden by a circle of leaves. Everything was gone except her grace, her slender form, her shining loveliness.

Apollo loved her still.

He put his hand on the bark, and could feel the warm heart beating beneath it. He embraced the branches as if they were still her arms; he clung to the trunk and kissed it, but even the wood shrank from his embrace.

The god exclaimed, "You can never be my bride, but you can still be my chosen tree. Laurel! your gleaming leaves will crown my hair and twine around my lyre and quiver. In times to come, all the heroes will wear your wreath as a sign of triumph and praise. And just as I cannot age, but will be forever young, let my laurel tree be forever green and shining."

The god stopped speaking, and the laurel moved her newly made branches gracefully. It seemed to him that the leafy crown bowed and nodded *Yes.*

The Warrior Women: The Amazons

O N THE COAST OF THE BLACK SEA LIVED A nation of women famous for their warlike qualities. The Amazons, as they were called, excluded men entirely from their society. In their country, which had many rich cities, they raised only female children, sending the boys away to neighboring lands or putting them to death.

Amazons were warriors who could, and did, compete against the best male soldiers, and usually won. Their mother was Harmony, a nymph who loved peace, but their father was the fierce god Ares, and his descendants took after him. They worshiped Ares as the god of war, and Artemis as the virgin goddess of female strength and hunting.

How strange it must have seemed to male warriors to see these women, bows in hand, riding into battle! How unlike their picture of female beauty! And yet the Amazons were beautiful as well as warlike. But they did not go to war just for the fun of it. They only fought when they had good reason to.

In their encounters with the Greek heroes, the women warriors were treated very shabbily. The first to behave badly was the great hero Heracles. One of the twelve difficult labors he had to perform led him to a tragic confrontation with the Amazons. Admete, the daughter of the man who imposed these labors on the hero, was pining to have the splendid waistband, called a girdle, that belonged to the Amazon queen Hippolyta, a gift from Ares himself. Heracles set sail, and after many difficulties he reached the Amazons' land.

All might have gone well except for the interference of the goddess Hera. Hippolyta greeted Heracles kindly, and welcomed him. The queen found the hero very attractive; she would gladly give him the girdle, she said, as a love token. Then she accompanied him back to his ship, which was anchored in the harbor.

But Hera, who hated Heracles, did not want this mission to succeed. The goddess disguised herself as an Amazon warrior and ran through the street, crying, "Watch out! The strangers are stealing our queen away!"

Of course, such an act could not be tolerated. The outraged Amazons at once mounted their splendid horses and rode down to the harbor to charge the ship. Suspecting treachery, Heracles ignored the kindness and generosity Hippolyta had shown him, and killed the queen in an instant, without a second thought.

Because he was aboard his ship, Heracles was in the position of advantage for a fight. As the Amazons attacked, he slew each of their leaders one by one, until finally the rest of their army was forced to turn and flee. Then he removed Hippolyta's ornate belt, and picked up her axe and bow, along with other weapons and rich robes that he took from the defeated women. All these things he stowed aboard the ship, and set sail for home, leaving behind him a terrible devastation among the slaughtered Amazonian warriors.

The next of the Amazons' tragic encounters was with Theseus, the greatest of the Athenian heroes. This time a Greek man captured their queen, Antiope, the sister of Hippolyta.

Some say Theseus was part of Heracles's expedition and won Antiope as his share of the booty. Others say that he arrived at the land of the Amazons some time later. Whichever is true, there is a certain unhappy similarity to the two men's actions, a similar betrayal of trust on the part of the so-called hero. Again, a Greek was given a warm welcome by the Amazons, and was offered no violence. Indeed, the women seemed to find the presence of so many handsome men a pleasant diversion, and sent tokens of friendship to them. Antiope herself boarded the ship to give Theseus their gifts, but as soon as she was aboard, he ordered the anchor to be raised, and simply sailed off with her.

Again, the Amazons would not take such a treacherous action lightly. Led by Antiope's sister Oreithyia, they pursued Theseus and his men. When they reached Athens, they besieged the Acropolis, and a great battle ensued. At length, after four months of hard fighting, Theseus emerged victorious. He married Antiope, and they had a son, whom they named Hippolytus.

During the Trojan War, the Amazons fought on the side of the Trojans, under the leadership of Queen Penthesilea. In these battles, they distinguished themselves greatly, winning praise for their valor and skill. Penthesilea herself accounted for many deaths, but at last she was overcome and killed by Achilles. When the hero removed her armor and saw her body lying in death, he was overcome by grief. In tears, he mourned for the loss of such youth, beauty, and courage.

But mourning could not alter the fact: Greek men had always proven the downfall of the Amazons, the otherwise invincible warrior women.

The Swiftest Runner: Atalanta

WHEN ATALANTA WAS BORN, HER FATHER flew into a rage. "A girl!" he shouted bitterly. "What use is a girl-child? I wanted a boy who would become my heir and rule over this kingdom after me. I don't want to see this wretched creature again! Take it and put it out on the mountaintop!"

His servants were afraid to disobey their master's orders, even though they were reluctant to do as he bade. Sadly, they carried the little girl up deep into the hills, and left her there to die of hunger and cold.

But the baby was a sturdy child, and strong, with good healthy lungs. She began to squall angrily. A she-bear was attracted by the noise, and came to investigate the source of such a din. She found a strange little animal with a rosy body, furless and vulnerable. Her motherly instincts aroused, the bear carefully lifted Atalanta in her mouth, and carried her back to her own den. There she warmed the baby, fed her, and kept her safe.

One day, while the bear was out, a group of hunters chanced to enter her cave. When they found the little girl, they marveled. "Let's take her back to our families and raise her as one of our own. She is certain to bring us good luck!"

So it was that young Atalanta grew up strong and fearless, and wonderfully skilled in the hunt. No one was better than she at handling bow or spear; no one could run so fast. People said of her that she was more like a boy than a girl, although she was surpassingly beautiful.

Whatever the weather, Atalanta could be found roaming the hillsides and forests in pursuit of game. It was her only passion. Boys interested her merely as companions in the hunt, or as competitors in sport. She would rather face the fiercest beast than listen to soft words of love. Although many men were attracted by her strength and courage as well as her beauty, if they were so foolhardy as to try to woo her, they got only rough words and anger in reply.

Now it happened that the kingdom of Calydon was being ravaged by a terrible beast. When the king, Oeneus, made sacrifices to the other gods in thanks for a fruitful year, he neglected to pay honor to Artemis. The vengeful goddess sent into the land a boar, huge as a bull, its eyes glowing fire and blood, with spear-sharp bristles and tusks as big as an elephant's. This monster trampled down the growing grain, destroyed vines and olive trees, and terrified the farm animals into stampedes. No one dared go out, so whatever crops remained undamaged rotted in the fields, and flocks wandered the countryside aimlessly.

Oeneus's son, Meleager, called for the greatest heroes of Greece to hunt the boar. Among them came Atalanta, a shining brooch pinned to her cloak, her hair pulled back in a simple knot. Her limbs were suntanned and sturdy, and she carried her spear lightly. On her left shoulder hung an ivory quiver, whose arrows rang together like a bell as she walked, and her left hand held a bow. She seemed to combine the best of feminine beauty with the grace of an athletic youth.

Meleager had only to look at her to feel the flames of love. "Whoever wins her love will be a happy man!" he thought. But this was not the moment to declare himself. There was a job to do.

First, Meleager had to persuade the heroes, who grumbled at letting Atalanta join their expedition. It demeaned them, they muttered, to hunt with a woman. But as it turned out, it was lucky for them that she had come.

When the hunters found the boar, the battle that followed was long and bloody. Rushing at his pursuers, the beast killed two of them immediately; a third was stabbed by a misthrown spear. One climbed a tree for safety, while another tripped on a root and fell flat. Atalanta kept her head and, seeing the proper moment, sent one of her arrows flying at the boar. It flashed through the bristles on his back and lodged just below his ear, drawing blood. Swiftly, Meleager fell on the wounded boar and delivered a fatal thrust with his spear.

Placing his foot on the beast's head, Meleager turned to Atalanta and offered her the prize of victory, the head and the boar skin. But envy and resentment of the maiden caused some of the men to cry out in anger.

"This isn't women's work!" they shouted. "She doesn't deserve a prize!" And they grabbed the head and skin from her. Chief among the protesters were two of Meleager's uncles. In a rage at this insult to the one he loved, the youth forgot the ties of kinship and put his mother's brothers to the sword. Alas, this deed was to be his own death as well.

At his birth, Meleager's mother, Althea, had been visited by the Fates, who placed a log on the fire, saying, "Just as long as this log burns, so long shall your son live." The moment they left, Althea snatched the log out of the flames and locked it away in a chest for safekeeping.

Now, distraught at hearing of her brothers' deaths, she opened the chest and took out the log. Four times she began to throw it into the fire, four times she drew back. The claims of motherhood and sisterhood warred in her breast. At last, weeping with sorrow, she placed the log in the hearth. The fire greeted it hungrily, flaring up at once.

At that same moment, Meleager, without knowing why, felt a cruel pang as if his body were in flames. He sank to the ground in agony, calling out the names of his father, brothers, and sisters, then at last "Mother!" As the fire died away, gradually his pains began to diminish, and as the glowing embers turned to ash, his spirit went out into the air.

Meanwhile, Atalanta's father was still without an heir for his kingdom. When the story of her victory over the Calydonian boar reached his ears, he discovered who she was. He sent for her. Perhaps this daughter was as good as a son!

Atalanta was now of marriageable age, and her father thought it was time for her to wed. The girl's reputation for swiftness and sureness of foot spread throughout the land. Nobody could win a race against her, it was said, not even the fastest runner among men. Suitors came from far and near, drawn by her beauty and her athletic skill.

But Atalanta was determined not to marry. Had she not consulted an oracle and received a reply as puzzling as it was frightening? "Atalanta," the oracle had said, "run from the very idea of marriage! Refuse a husband. But you will not refuse, and while you still live, you will lose yourself and never get away!" Puzzled by this mysterious threat, she vowed to remain unwed.

So when suitors arrived to ask for her hand in marriage, Atalanta answered them, "I will marry only the man who can run faster than I can." (For she knew there was no man alive who could.) "If you want to woo me, run against me in a race. If you win, your prize will be to have me for your wife, but if you lose, the penalty is death."

As hard as these conditions were, her beauty was irresistible, and young men thronged to try their skill against Atalanta's.

Among the watchers one day sat young Hippomenes. "Just look at those silly sheep!" he laughed. "Who would be so foolish as to risk his life in such a gamble?" But when the race began, he was dazzled by Atalanta's grace as she flew past him like an arrow, the ribbons at her feet and knees blown backward by her speed, her hair spreading like wings across her shoulders, her body glowing, rosy as the sunrise.

"Now I understand why men are willing to die for the chance of marrying such a divine creature!" he said to himself. "Well, why shouldn't I try, too? But I know I can't run as fast as she can. I will have to ask for heavenly help."

The young man approached Atalanta and challenged her. "Why waste your time with these slow-footed fools? It's too easy! Try me, Hippomenes the undefeated! If I win, it would be no shame to marry me; I am the great-grandson of Neptune himself. And think how great your glory will be if you win!"

Atalanta looked at him with softened eyes, and for a moment she wondered which would be better, to win or to lose in such a race. Her thoughts grew confused.

"What god," she asked herself, "is so envious of men that he tempts them to risk their lives for me? I'm not worth it! Now, any girl would be happy to have this man—not me, of course! It's not his beauty that moves me, although it could—he has charm, but no—it's only because he is so young, so very young—and so fearless—of good family—and says he loves me so much that death means nothing to him. Why should I care if he dies when so many others have? I'll be hated if I win. I don't care—it's not my fault! He's crazy, but since he is, I wish he were a faster runner!"

Poor confused Atalanta! She was unschooled in love, an emotion so new to her. She loved, but did not know it.

Now Hippomenes appealed to Aphrodite to take his side and help him win not just the race, but the woman who had inspired his love. The goddess of love was moved by his prayer, but there was no time for elaborate plans. In her hand she held three golden apples, which she had just picked at her temple in Cyprus, and quickly she gave them to the young man, telling him how to use them.

The race was about to begin. When the starting bell rang, both runners shot forward, barely touching the sand with their feet, running so lightly they might have run over the sea and never gotten their sandals wet. Hippomenes heard the crowd cheering him on.

It would be hard to say which racer the cheers pleased more, Hippomenes or Atalanta. She was running as slowly as she dared. So many times she could have sprinted faster, but lingered a moment to steal another look at his face. Then, remembering herself, she would speed up and pull ahead.

Hippomenes was beginning to tire. Catching his breath in great sobbing gasps, he saw the finish line still far ahead. Now he tossed one of the shining apples down, just in front of Atalanta and a little to one side. She looked at it in wonder, then veered slightly off her course to pick it up as it was still rolling. Recovering her lost momentum, she passed him and heard the crowd cheer.

Down went the second apple, a little farther away this time, and once again she fell behind in order to pick it up, but sprinted and passed him again.

"Oh, blessed goddess, gift-giver, be with me now!" the youth prayed, and threw the third of the apples far off to one side.

When Atalanta saw the golden fruit flash through the air, she seemed to hesitate for a moment, drawing her breath. But Aphrodite exerted her will, and Atalanta ran to pick up the last apple. At that moment, Hippomenes put on a burst of speed and crossed the finish line.

The winner led off his prize, who was no longer reluctant. But alas, he neglected one very important thing: Hippomenes was so thrilled by his victory that he completely forgot to give thanks to Aphrodite by burning incense and offering prayers. Instead, when he and Atalanta came to the goddess's temple, he took his bride in his arms and told her how he loved her.

At once, their necks began to roughen, as tawny manes grew there. Their fingers hooked into sharp claws, their arms changed into legs, their chests grew heavy, and they swept the sandy ground with their tails. When they talked, only growls came forth; anger blazed from their eyes. The lovers had been changed into lions.

The Naiad Who Became Music:
Syrinx

ON THE COOL MOUNTAIN SLOPES OF ARCADIA LIVED A BEAUTIFUL NAIAD NAMED SYRINX. MANY satyrs and gods of the woodlands and fields loved her, but she would have nothing to do with them. She swore she would remain unmarried, like the goddess Artemis, whom she worshiped. Syrinx strove to be like her heroine in every way; she dressed like Artemis and learned the art of hunting. And though her bow was made of horn, not of silver, it would have been easy to mistake her for the goddess, so swift and sure of foot was she, so beautiful.

One day the god Pan was coming home, with a wreath of pine bound about his brow, when he saw Syrinx. He praised her and began to speak of love. But the naiad refused to hear his flattering words and fled from him.

She ran through the pathless woodland until she reached the quiet, sandy waters of the River Ladon, which stopped her in her flight. Syrinx could go no farther, and Pan was close behind her. She begged her sister water nymphs to change her form, to save her from the unwanted attentions of the god.

As he ran up to the riverbank, Pan believed he had caught the naiad at last. He reached out to gather her in his embrace. But what he gathered was not Syrinx; instead, he found his arms full of tall marsh reeds.

The nymphs, Syrinx's sisters, had heard her plea for help and had changed her slender, lithe form into swaying, hollow grass.

Pan sighed in sorrow, and as he sighed, the soft wind of his breath stirred the reeds he held in his arms, making a thin and tender music. The sound was so sweet, so magical, that Pan was enchanted. He exclaimed, "Syrinx, this is our music! It will hold us together in harmony forever!"

As he spoke, he took up reeds of different lengths, fastened them together with wax, and began to play on them. And ever after, people have imitated the god, making beautiful music on the reeds. Some call this instrument the Pan pipes, but those who know the story call it Syrinx.

The Nymph of the Spring: Arethusa

THE WOOD NYMPH ARETHUSA LED A LIFE THAT SUITED HER PERFECTLY. The keenest hunter in all the land of Achaea, she spent every day roaming the hillsides and valleys, setting her nets or following the tracks of woodland animals. She could hunt all day without exhaustion, braving any part of the forest unafraid. Soon the nymph became famous for her courage and strength.

Although Arethusa gloried in her reputation, she felt only contempt for something else that people had begun to talk about: her quite astonishing beauty. Some girls like to be praised for their looks, but Arethusa took no pleasure in that kind of compliment. When she was offered one, she would blush, perhaps embarrassed or perhaps angry. It seemed wrong to her to attract men by something as superficial as mere physical beauty.

One day, Arethusa was making her way home through the woods, tired from the exertions of a long chase. The sun shone bright; it was very warm, and she felt doubly hot because she had been running hard all day. Suddenly she came to the edge of a lovely stream, deep but flowing so softly that it hardly made a sound, and no ripples disturbed its placid surface. The water was as clear as glass: she could have counted the smallest pebbles lying in its bed. Along the gently sloping banks grew poplars and silver willows, leaning over to make a green and inviting shade.

Arethusa could not resist. First she dipped her feet into the cool water, then waded in up to her knees. How wonderful it felt! At last, she laid her dress on the bank and dived into the clear depths. She began to swim, stroking out boldly and turning somersaults in sheer joy.

But as she swam, the nymph thought she heard something, a strange sound. Perhaps it was not heard, really, so much as felt, a rumbling that arose from far down underneath her. Terrified, she leapt onto the nearby bank. Out of the water sounded a deep voice. It was the River Alpheus himself, and he was speaking to her.

"Arethusa!" he boomed. "Where are you going? Why are you in such a hurry to get away from me?"

Twice the river called to her in his rough voice, and twice was enough. The nymph didn't wait to hear any more, but turned and ran as fast as she could. And not a moment too soon! Alpheus took on human form and followed after her, as fierce as a hawk when it pursues a fluttering dove. They ran and ran, through fields, through thickets of trees, across rocks, and down steep cliffs. The blue waters of a gulf flashed by, cold snowcapped mountains, and still they sped.

Arethusa ran with all her strength, and Alpheus could not catch up with her. She was faster than he, but he had greater endurance. At last the nymph began to tire. The day was growing late, and the sun cast long shadows; the river's shadow lengthened until it seemed that he was getting closer and closer to her. She could hear his feet pounding behind her, feel his breath blowing the hair on the back of her head. The nymph was terrified.

"Artemis!" she cried out. "Dearest goddess! Please help me! If you don't, I'm lost! Remember all the times we hunted together and I carried your bow and your quiver of bright arrows!"

The goddess was moved by her young friend's plea. She gathered together dew-drops and raindrops, and wove a dense, white fog-cloud around the nymph to obscure her form. Alpheus could no longer see her; still, he knew she had to be hidden somewhere inside that mist! He stalked around the edges of the cloud, calling to her: "Arethusa! Arethusa!" Twice he came so close she thought that surely he must see her.

Arethusa was terribly afraid. She felt like a lamb who hears wolves howling around outside the sheepfold, or like a little rabbit who hides under a berry bush, watching the jaws of the hounds snapping as they come closer and closer.

Alpheus waited. He could see her footprints leading into the cloud, but not coming out. He knew she was still in there—and a river can wait for a very long time. Now cold sweat was pouring off the terrified nymph. It ran down her body, and everywhere she stepped there was a little pool. A silvery stream began to run from her hair down to her feet, faster and faster.

More quickly than words can say it, Arethusa had turned to water. But she was still not out of danger. When he saw the stream flowing out of the cloud, Alpheus recognized it; he knew it was the nymph. Swiftly, he changed his own form again, from human back into his watery shape. Of course, now that he had become a river once more, he could flow even faster and more tirelessly. He continued to pursue her.

Once more, Artemis came to the nymph's rescue. She broke into the solid ground and opened a passageway for her fellow huntress and worshiper to escape. Arethusa slipped into the crack and plunged downward into the vast caverns that lie below the earth. She traveled a long way through these dark underground regions, until she reached Ortygia in Sicily, an island sacred to the hunter goddess. There Arethusa burst forth at last into the open air. She had become a spring of pure, crystalline water.

In Greece today, people will tell you that Alpheus was not in the least daunted by this, but followed after Arethusa, and that his waters flow under the sea, reaching as far as Sicily. At Ortygia they emerge and mingle with the waters of his beloved nymph. Often, people say, you can see Greek flowers growing in the heart of the fountain, and if you stand on the banks of the River Alpheus, in Greece, and throw a cup into the water, it will come up in Sicily, at the spring still called by the name Arethusa.

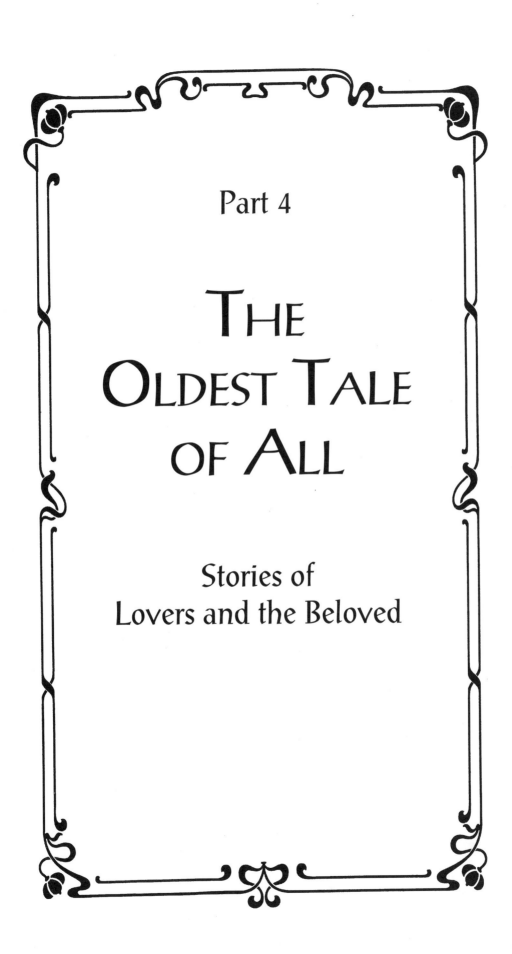

Part 4

THE
OLDEST TALE
OF ALL

Stories of
Lovers and the Beloved

WOMEN WHO LOVE

The Goddess
of Love:
Aphrodite

S HE ROSE FROM THE SEA IN A SWIRL OF FOAM, AND WHEN SHE WALKED ON THE LAND, FLOWERS sprang out of her footprints. She is the symbol of beauty and of love, the most exquisite of the goddesses.

Aphrodite, called Venus by the Romans, was, of course, incomparably beautiful, and irresistible to mortals and gods alike. She loved laughter, and usually you can see a smile on her face. But that smile, like love, can be of different kinds: sweet and gentle, looking lovingly on the successful suitor; or mocking and cruel, taunting the one who loves in vain.

And, like love, Aphrodite was very powerful. The Greek poets speak not only of her golden beauty, but also of the qualities of love she brought to life: girls whispering together, smiles and deceptions, flattery, delight, and sweetness. To the Romans, wherever Venus appeared, wreathed in light, the ocean waves laughed in joy, storm clouds flew away, and sweet-scented flowers appeared over the Earth.

Although she was married to Hephaestus, the ugly but peace-loving god of fire, Aphrodite is not known for her faithfulness. In fact, she loved many men, gods and mortals alike. One of her most famous loves was Adonis, about whom she quarreled fiercely with Persephone, goddess of the Underworld. So keen was their rivalry over this man that Zeus intervened. He judged that Adonis should spend the fall and winter with Persephone and the spring and summer with Aphrodite. We know he has returned to

Aphrodite when we see the anemone blooming, the red flower that sprang up from drops of Adonis's blood after he was killed by a boar.

The Judgment of Paris, one of the most famous contests in Greek mythology, established Aphrodite as the goddess who surpassed all others in beauty. One day, Eris, the goddess of discord, was furious because she had not been invited to an important wedding in Olympus. She threw into the feasting hall a golden apple marked with the words "For the Fairest."

At once a quarrel arose among Aphrodite, Hera, and Athena. Which of them deserved the apple, and—much more important—the title of most beautiful of all the goddesses? The three appealed to Zeus to judge their beauty, but he was too smart to involve himself in a contest that would inevitably make two goddesses angry. Instead, he suggested that they ask Paris, the young prince of Troy, to name the fairest goddess.

Paris, who was known as a great lover of feminine beauty, was not as wise as Zeus. He agreed at once. Before the judging, each goddess took the young man aside and offered him a reward if he would choose her. Hera said she would make him lord of all Europe and Asia; Athena pledged a great victory for Troy over Greece. Then Aphrodite promised him that the most beautiful woman in the world would become his. Paris was more interested in women than in leadership, and he awarded the apple to Aphrodite. The goddess was faithful to her promise, but there would be enormous consequences for the ancient world. When she arranged for Paris and Helen to meet, the devastating Trojan War was destined to begin.

Stories about Aphrodite depict the goddess of love and beauty in many different ways. Perhaps that's because love itself can take so many forms. Sometimes it is joyful, sometimes sad; lovers may be faithful or inconstant; both parties may love equally, or one person's love may not be returned. Aphrodite is the goddess of all the kinds of love that mortals can experience.

Dido, the Queen of Carthage

DIDO, THE BEAUTIFUL DAUGHTER OF THE king of Tyre, was more than just another lovely face. She was a woman of great intelligence, courage, and resource. After her husband was murdered, Dido managed to escape from Tyre, taking with her her sister, Anna, and a band of followers. They landed on the coast of North Africa, where Dido began to bargain with the local king for land. Her demands were modest: she just wanted, she said, as much land as a bull's hide could contain. The king agreed. Dido had the hide cut into thread-thin strips, and when the strips were laid out, they enclosed enough land to build a citadel.

Dido called her splendid new city Carthage, and she ruled there wisely for some time. But not even the queen, clever as she was, could withstand the will of the gods, who once again were quarreling and plotting behind the backs of mortals.

Juno had never gotten over the beauty contest young Paris had judged, when he named Venus the most beautiful of the goddesses. Ever since that day, she had hated all Trojans, and none more than the hero Aeneas, who had escaped from Troy as the city burned. The Fates had decreed that he would become the father of a people who would ultimately rule the world, and Juno did not want that to happen.

Accompanied by a number of men from the destroyed city, Aeneas put to sea in search of a new home. Juno, seeing her chance to destroy this mortal, persuaded the god of the winds to cause a tremendous storm. The sailors nearly perished, but just in time, Neptune, the sea god, chose to calm the sea. When it became clear that Aeneas was about to land safely on the African coast, Juno had another idea.

What if Dido and Aeneas were to fall in love? After all, she was a beautiful widow and the ruler of Carthage; he was a widower and a great hero. If he loved Dido, he would stay in Carthage, happily settle down, and never find a place to begin his new kingdom.

The plan might have succeeded if it had not been for Venus, who was Aeneas's mother, and who was keeping a watchful eye on him. The goddess of love always liked to thwart Juno's plots, and besides, she wanted her son to reach Italy and become the ancestor of a powerful race of people. But she had no objection to his having a safe and pleasant stay in Carthage while he repaired his ships and gave his men some rest.

Venus went to plead with Jupiter, her lovely eyes brimming with tears. "You promised me that Aeneas would start a great dynasty!" she sobbed. "And look what Juno is doing!" Chuckling, the god kissed away her tears and told her not to worry, that everything would be as he had foretold. Nothing, not even the gods, could change the future once it had been decided by the Fates.

Venus wanted Aeneas to fall in love with Dido just enough to enjoy himself while he was in Carthage. The queen was beautiful and accomplished enough, the goddess knew, to catch his interest. But what if she did not love him in return? She was known far and wide as one who had turned down dozens of offers for her hand, as one who was not susceptible to the flattery of men. So Venus enlisted the aid of her son Cupid, and the result was inevitable.

When Aeneas landed, Venus, disguised as a huntress, met him and told him to go to Carthage and ask to see the queen. Then she caused him to appear radiant as a god, handsome as Apollo. Dido, looking as lovely as Diana herself, received him more than graciously.

"I know what it is to be alone in a strange land," she said. "I too was once cast on these shores in misery with just a few friends. It's a pleasure for me to be able to help those who are suffering the same misfortune I endured."

That night, Dido gave a great banquet for the hero. She invited him to tell the story of the fall of Troy and what had happened to him since. As he spoke eloquently of battle and his lonely wanderings, she grew more and more intrigued with this man. Was it Cupid's presence that set her heart aglow, or would she have fallen for him so passionately anyway? Although she had sworn never to marry again, Dido confided to her sister Anna that she was in love, and was thinking of Aeneas as a husband.

Generously, the queen offered him an equal share in everything she had. Her wealth, her palace, her throne—all were his, too. Aeneas was more than satisfied with this arrangement. At last he seemed to have found a home, a kingdom, and a wife—a happy place where he could at last rest from his wanderings. While his fleet was being repaired, he was lavishly entertained. Every day there were hunting parties; every night there were banquets with a beautiful woman at his side, listening to his stories with admiration. Dido gave him jeweled swords, the finest horses, and clothes of gold and purple, some of them made by her own hands. As the months went on, Aeneas became more and more content, and at last he thought that he would marry Dido and settle in Carthage forever.

But of course, the Fates had promised a different ending to this story. Jupiter sent his messenger, Mercury, to warn Aeneas that he must set sail again. "You're wasting your time here,". Mercury whispered in his ear. "You're growing soft from all this luxury! Remember that it is your destiny to found a new kingdom. Jupiter himself has sent me to tell you that it's time for you to leave. You must go immediately!"

But how could Aeneas tell Dido that he was going away? It was impossible. The only thing to do, he thought, was to leave secretly. He told his men to outfit the ships and prepare everything for departure without letting anyone know what they were doing. Inevitably, though, Dido got wind of what was going on, and called Aeneas to her.

At first she could not believe that he really meant to leave her. She spoke to him quietly, reminding him of her love and her faithfulness. But he became more adamant, reminding her that they were not married, and that he was free to leave any time he wanted. She began to weep and to reprimand him.

"I've given you everything I had!" she said angrily. "You came here broken, miserable, starving, and I helped you. Now you can just walk away like that? You weren't even going to tell me, but planned to sneak off like a thief! That's inexcusable!" She begged him to change his mind.

Aeneas would have liked to comfort her, to ease her pain and hurt, but what was there to say? The gods had ordered him to leave, and he must obey. Weeping, Dido fled from him.

The Trojans set sail that night. Aeneas, standing in the stern of his ship, watched sadly as the walls of Carthage receded. Suddenly they seemed to glow with a bright light, and he saw the flames of a huge fire leap into the air. Then the flames died down and all was darkness. What, he wondered, had that been about?

He could not know the answer to his question, which was this: Dido had ordered an enormous pyre to be built, saying that she wanted to destroy everything that reminded her of Aeneas. But when the pyre was lit, she took out a sword he had given her, threw herself upon it, and then leaped into the heart of the flames.

Later, Aeneas was to learn that even in death Dido did not forgive him. The Sibyl of Cumae had agreed to take him into the Underworld so that he could speak with his dead father. There he walked beneath the myrtle trees that dotted the Fields of Mourning, the place where wander those unhappy lovers who have killed themselves for love. When he saw the pale shade of Dido, he began to weep.

"Did you kill yourself for love of me?" he asked, trembling. "I swear to you that I always loved you, and that I left you against my will!"

But she might as well have been made of marble. She never looked at him, nor gave him an answer. She only walked away, as he had done to her.

The Lovers of the Sun: Clytie and Leucothoe

THE SUN SHOULD LOOK ON ALL THINGS EQUALLY, but he had eyes for only one girl, Leucothoe. Just so that he could see her longer, he would rise too early in the eastern sky and sink into the western waves too late. Lingering to look at her, he lengthened the winter days. Sometimes the darkness in his heart turned outward and dimmed his rays, so that people moved terrified through an unnatural dark. And the cause of his pallor was not an eclipse, as often happens when the moon comes between him and Earth. It was simply love.

Now that he had seen Leucothoe, the Sun scorned all the other girls for whom he had once felt a fondness. Clytie, especially, suffered the anguish of rejection. She had been devoted to the god for a long, long time, and ached for him to return her love as he used to do. But he had forgotten everyone except Leucothoe. She was the daughter of Eurynome, who in her girlhood had been the most beautiful maiden in all the perfumed lands of Arabia. As Leucothoe grew up, she became even more lovely than her mother.

The sun god's horses graze in the far meadows that lie beneath the western skies. It's not ordinary grass they eat, but ambrosia, which gives them the power to pull the Sun's chariot through the skies each day. Every evening, when they are put to pasture, they are exhausted. Every morning, their strength is renewed.

One night, while his horses were feeding and darkness had taken over the heavens, the Sun disguised himself as Eurynome and went to Leucothoe's room. The girl sat among a dozen handmaids, spinning smooth, fine threads with her wooden spindle. The sun god kissed her like a mother and said to her girls, "Please leave us alone for a while. I have something private to discuss with my daughter."

As soon as the maids had left, the god said, "I must confess, I am not your mother. I only dressed up like her so that I could get into your room. Really, I am the Sun, the god who measures out the year. I see everything, and it's because of me that the whole world can see, too. I am the glowing eye of the universe. And, Leucothoe, I have to tell you—I love you dearly."

Shocked, the girl dropped her spindle and distaff. In her fright, Leucothoe was even more beautiful than ever. The Sun delayed no longer; he took on his true form and stood before her in all his glory. The girl's eyes were dazzled by the sight. In that instant, the god's splendor and beauty won her love. How could it be otherwise?

Poor Clytie—she was utterly rejected. Her jealousy of Leucothoe burned as hot as her love for the sun god. Goaded by anger at her rival, Clytie decided to tell the world of the love between those two. She spread the news far and wide, taking particular care that Leucothoe's father should learn about it.

When he heard the gossip, the father was furious. Brutally, he turned against his daughter. He was relentless in his harsh judgment of her, and would not listen to anything she had to say. He would never forgive her for such terrible behavior, he asserted. The girl begged for his forgiveness, pleading with her arms stretched toward the Sun. "He made me love him against my will!" she cried.

But her father would not soften toward Leucothoe. In his wrath, he decided on a horrible punishment. He buried his daughter deep in the earth and heaped her tomb with a high mound of heavy sand. "Try to get out of that!" he exclaimed.

The Sun was anguished at the father's cruel act. He sent his powerful beams to scatter the sand so that Leucothoe might lift up her smothered head and breathe again. Alas, it was too late. When the sand had burned away, all that remained was her lifeless body, crushed under the terrible weight that had been piled upon her. Nothing so grievous had happened to sadden the god for a long time. Try as he might to revive her death-cold limbs with his warm rays, it was hopeless. Fate was more powerful even than the Sun; death was her destiny.

Then the Sun, in mourning, sprinkled fragrant nectar over Leucothoe's body and her grave, saying, "My love, I cannot bring you back to life, but I can make sure that you reach Heaven!"

At once, her body melted away under the touch of the nectar, and from the ground a sweet scent drifted up, filling the air. Slowly there arose a beautiful shrub of frankincense, its roots deep in earth, its shoots breaking through the burial mound.

And what became of Clytie? Her overpowering love might be said to excuse her grief, and grief might excuse her telling tales, but never again did the light-giver come to her with words of love. From that time, she who had made the sweetness of the Sun's love turn sour began to pine away. She had grown used to love, and was driven to madness by the lack of it. Now Clytie hated and envied all her sister nymphs, and for days she sat alone under the empty sky on the hard, rocky ground. Her head was unadorned, bared to the cold breeze, her hair tangled and disheveled.

Nine days and nine nights she passed this way, touching neither food nor drink except for the dew and her own salt tears. She never moved from the earth on which she sat. Her eyes were fixed on the Sun's bright face, following his path as he moved across the heavens.

After a little while, they say, her limbs began to take root in the soil. Her color, already pale with suffering, changed to a pearly whiteness, as she became a bloodless plant. Here and there appeared a bright blushing color, and where her face had been, a flower—something like a violet—hid her features. And though she is rooted fast in the ground, the Heliotrope still turns her face toward the Sun all day as he crosses the sky. Her shape is changed, but her passionate love burns untransformed.

The Last Word: Echo

O N MOUNT HELICON THERE LIVED A BEAUTIFUL WOOD NYMPH, whose name was Echo. She was a favorite of Artemis, and loved nothing more than to run through the woods, hunting with the goddess. No, to be honest, there was one thing she loved more. She loved to talk. Echo was one of those girls who always had to have the last word.

One day Hera, jealous as usual over the exploits of her husband Zeus, came down from Olympus to find out what he was up to. She suspected that he was in love with one of the nymphs, and she was trying to discover which one, when Echo began to chatter away to her. Amused by the gossip in spite of herself, Hera forgot for a moment what she had come for. By the time she remembered, the nymphs had fled, and the mountain was deserted. It was too late for Hera to learn who had caught her husband's eye this time.

As always happened when she suspected Zeus of straying, the goddess was furious. She turned on Echo, blaming the nymph for the failure of her mission. "You and your gabbing! Look what you've done with all your pointless talking! That tongue of yours made a fool of me, but it will have to learn to speak more briefly. You like to have the last word? Very well, you shall have it—but only the last word!"

With a snap of her fingers, Hera made it impossible for Echo ever to start a conversation. The only words the nymph could utter would be the ones she had just heard coming from somebody else's lips.

Nearby, there lived a youth named Narcissus, the most handsome young man anyone had ever seen. He had just reached the age of sixteen, and wherever he went, girls followed, adoring him for his beauty. But the admiration Narcissus continually received had gone to his head, and he had grown very vain. He took as natural all the sighs and blushes and loving looks his handsomeness inspired. Admiring himself more than anyone else, he spurned all the maidens, and would have nothing to do with them.

Echo was among those who had seen Narcissus and fallen under the spell of his beauty. But how could she attract his attention? She could follow him, but she could not speak to him unless he spoke first—and he never did. The situation seemed hopeless to her. She was doomed to follow him, and sigh with longing, and remain silent.

Then, one sunny day, Narcissus came up the mountain to hunt. Hidden behind a tree, Echo watched him, her eyes soft with love. Perhaps she made a slight noise as her foot slipped, or started up some rustling in the leaves of the trees. For whatever reason, the youth seemed to sense he was not alone.

"Is anyone here?" he called out, and from her hiding place Echo joyfully answered, "Here!"

"Come to me!" cried Narcissus. Echo replied, "To me!"

"Why do you run from me?" he asked, bewildered because he could see nobody. "You run from me!" came back from the woods.

"Come, join me here!" he called, and Echo, her heart bursting with happiness, ran into the clearing, her arms outstretched to throw around his neck. "Join me here!" she cried with delight.

But Narcissus jumped back. "Keep away from me! Don't touch me! I'll die before I let you have me!"

"Have me!" Echo replied longingly. But he only turned away and fled.

She said no more, but went to hide her sadness and shame among the trees of the forest. From that time on, Echo dwelt alone on the mountain cliffs and in the caves that dot their steep sides.

Her love for Narcissus lived on; in fact, it deepened with her suffering. In her grief, Echo could not sleep, but sorrowed day and night. She grew thinner and thinner, until at last her flesh withered away and her bones turned into stones. Nothing of her remained but her voice.

Now no one could see her, although she still dwelt in the mountains, still eager to reply to those who would speak to her. One thing was left to Echo: she always had the last word.

Before long, Narcissus was to pay for his cruelty to Echo and all the other maidens who loved him in vain. One of his rejected lovers begged Nemesis, the goddess of revenge, to repay him for all the hurt he had caused.

"Let Narcissus find out what it is to love and be disdained! Make him fall desperately in love with someone he can't win over!" she cried. The goddess heard the prayer and understood. She granted the girl's request.

So it was that one day Narcissus, hot and thirsty from hunting, found a pool deep in the woods, where no shepherd had ever brought his flocks to muddy its silver waters. When he leaned over to drink, he saw an image so beautiful it took his breath away. He gazed at the shining eyes, the hair gleaming and curly as Apollo's, the smooth cheeks and neck, the rosy color that spread across ivory skin. At once, Narcissus was hopelessly in love.

In vain the youth reached out his arms to embrace the figure in the pool, and leaned down to kiss its lips. Every time he touched the water, the image disappeared, only to come back when he withdrew. He begged it to speak, to return his love, but it said nothing.

At last, it dawned on Narcissus that this beautiful person was his own image. He had fallen in love with himself! But even when he knew this, he could not tear himself away from gazing at his own beauty, and grieved because he could not get love back from the reflection in the water. He yearned, he sighed, he beat his breast in anguish.

The young man's vivid color began to fade. His beauty dwindled and his body wasted away. But Echo still loved him. When he cried out, "Alas!" he could hear a sighing reply from the forest, "Alas!" And when he said, "You whom I loved in vain, farewell," her heart echoed the words. "Farewell!"

Narcissus pined away and died. The nymphs, in mourning, built a towering funeral pyre and searched for his body. But all they found was a flower, white petals arranged around a cup of gold. And a faint voice from the woods seemed to breathe *Farewell!*

A Daughter's Betrayal: Scylla

MINOS, THE KING OF CRETE, HAD BECOME A MIGHTY ruler, whose influence was known far beyond the ninety cities of his own island. After clearing the Mediterranean of pirates, he sought to make his power felt by many of the lands that bordered the sea.

Now Minos was laying siege to the city of Megara, where King Nisus reigned—he who had the lovely young daughter named Scylla. For six months the Cretan army had been battering at the walls of the city, but in vain. Although they did not know it, all their efforts were doomed to failure. Nisus had a peculiar feature: in his gleaming silver hair, there grew one purple tress, and in that single lock of hair lay the future of the city. For the Fates had decreed that his realm could never be overcome so long as the purple hair grew on the king's head.

A tall tower stood above the walls of Megara, built, the legends said, by Apollo. The god had once rested his golden lyre on the walls at the foot of the tower, and the stones had kept his music inside. Now, if pebbles were dropped from the top of the tower, the walls would play a beautiful tune that sounded like songs from a lyre itself.

Scylla loved to make music on the singing walls, and every day the girl would climb up with a handful of pebbles to set the stones ringing. That was during peacetime, but when the war began, her attention was drawn to something new. She was fascinated by looking out from the tower, where she could watch the enemy army preparing for battle on the broad plain beyond the walls. Soon she had become familiar with all the Cretan captains; she knew their names, their horses, their insignia, and their armor.

Most of all, Scylla's eyes were drawn to their general, Minos. He seemed hand-some to her, even though his face was covered by a shining helmet with waving plumes. In his armor, carrying his shield, his figure delighted her, and if he drew back his arm to throw the heavy spear, she was dazzled by his strength and skill. When he bent his bow to shoot, she thought that the god Apollo himself must look exactly like that. But oh! when he took off his helmet and rode bareheaded, wearing royal purple, on a milk-white steed, the girl went almost mad with love. She wanted to leap off the tower to greet him, rush through the enemy lines and look at him, throw open the great bronze gates of the city and welcome him in, do anything he wished, this wonderful man, Minos.

As Scylla sat in the tower, looking out at the white tents of the enemy, she began a long debate with herself. "What shall I do?" she asked. "I don't even know how I feel about the war, whether to cry or smile. War is a terrible thing, of course, and it's worse to be the enemy of the man I love. Yet, if it hadn't been for this siege, I would never even have seen him, never have known his face or his wonderful ways.

"I wonder—if I were his hostage, he would have to end the fighting. I would be both his pledge of peace and his comrade! If only I had wings so that I could fly through the air, land in the Cretan camp, and tell this king how truly I love him! I would say, 'If you will have me, I'll give you anything you ask for.'

"But what if he asked for my father's city? Of course, I'd say no—marriage at the price of treachery would be unthinkable. Still, there have been times in history when losing was all to the good, when the victor was generous and lenient, and the defeated ended up better off than before.

"Besides, Minos does have justice on his side; the cause of his war is honest, and those who fight for him are strong. Yes, awfully strong. I'm afraid we are sure to lose! And if our city is doomed already, why should we go down to bloody defeat when my love could unlock the city gates as surely as his weapons can? It would be far better for him to win without all that killing and bloodshed! Especially his own blood—I wouldn't have to worry that some blunderer would send an arrow or a spear into him."

Her own arguments convinced Scylla. She would be doing everyone a favor if she could end the war! She would offer herself to Minos and bring, as her dowry, her country. The only thing that stood in her way was her father, the keeper of the keys to the city gates.

That night, as darkness stole over the city, Scylla's courage grew. In the early hours of slumber, when she knew her father would be deeply asleep, she crept into his chamber. There she spotted the purple tress, glowing among his silver hairs, and softly, softly, she drew out her shears and cut it off. Taking the key, she opened the city gate and slipped out. Then she walked boldly through the Cretan lines, carrying the lock of hair like a shield, sure of her welcome. She reached the startled Minos and stood before him proudly.

"My name is Scylla," she said, "and I am the daughter of King Nisus. Love has brought me here to you, and here is my pledge of love, and my dowry." She held out the purple lock. "This is my heritage, my country's wealth and honor, and I give it all to you freely—myself, my land, my home. Take this, and know that with it goes my father's life. All I ask as reward is yourself, your love."

But now the scene became very different from the one she had imagined up in the tower, lost in her love dreams. Minos was not overjoyed by her offer— far from it. In fact, he was appalled. No gift of this sort had ever come his way before, no such deed of love! He drew back in horror and answered harshly.

"Get away from me! May all the gods reject you! May both land and sea curse you! You—you are a disgrace to our time! I would never let my island of Crete feel the touch of your feet. A monster like you would contaminate the land, the sacred land that took in the infant Zeus and raised him to manhood."

Minos was a man of honor, and a just man. How could anyone imagine that he would gain victory through such treachery? Horrified at the thought, he chose instead to offer Nisus terms of peace. Now Megara lay at his mercy, but Minos did not destroy the city. He only imposed some new laws that they must obey. Then he ordered his fleet to raise anchor and prepared to sail away to Crete.

When Scylla saw the ships being launched, she knew that the king had truly refused the reward of her crime, and that her prayers would not be answered. Anger filled her heart. With her hair streaming and her arms stretched upward in a passionate rage, she cried out.

"Are you really going to leave me here alone? I gave you everything, success and victory, I put you above my country, even my father! Does that mean nothing to you? Aren't you at all moved by my plight?

"Where can I go, abandoned as I am? To my country? But I have betrayed it; its gates are closed to me. To my father? I have betrayed him even more horribly! My countrymen all hate me, and with good reason. All the other cities are afraid of me. I'm banished from the whole world—I've made myself an exile, all for the sake of Crete, and now you deny me Crete!

"Father, Nisus, punish me! City that I betrayed, take your revenge! Rejoice in my anguish; I know that I deserve to die. But I'd rather die at the hands of those I've wronged than yours, Minos. You're a hypocrite! Why should you scorn me for having done the act that brought you triumph?

"Oh, my heart is breaking! I hear his voice ordering the sailors to hurry, and the oars are beating fast. They're leaving the land behind—and me as well. But you can't get away from me that easily, Minos! I'll follow you, even against your will. Look, I'll cling to the stern of your ship and be pulled behind you through the long swell of the sea, all the way to Crete!"

Passion—love and anger mixed—had given Scylla strength, and as she spoke she dived through the waves and swam out to the ship. There she clung with all her might, like an evil spirit, unwanted and hateful to the crew.

Suddenly an eagle plunged out of the sky and began to attack her with its beak and claws. It was her father, Nisus, who had been transformed into the regal bird. In terror, Scylla dropped her hold on the ship. She would have drowned, but as she fell, she seemed to feel a light breeze bearing her up, safe above the sea. She felt light as a feather; in fact, she was covered with feathers. Some god had taken pity on the girl, perhaps because her crime had been committed out of love, not hatred. She had become a seabird. From this time on, she would be known as Ciris, or Shearer, named for that shorn lock of hair.

The sea eagle is still angry with her, and whenever in his flight high above the waves he spots the smaller bird, he swoops down on her and attacks, seeking vengeance for her treachery so long ago.

Many may not know that the fruit of the mulberry tree was once white. This is the story of how a stain of blood turned the berry forever red.

Forbidden Love: Pyramus and Thisbe

IN A CITY OF HIGH BRICK WALLS, THE CITY BUILT BY QUEEN Semiramis, lived a boy and girl named Pyramus and Thisbe. He was the handsomest of all the young men in town; she was the most beautiful girl in all the East. As it happened, they were next-door neighbors, and because they saw each other so often when they were children, they became good friends. In time, their friendship changed to love. They wanted nothing more than to be married, but both sets of parents said no, they would never give permission for such a match. The lovers were told they could not even see each other again.

Of course, the disapproval of parents cannot put out the fires of love. In fact, as often happens, the young couple's love burned even brighter because it was forbidden. But they were sad to be so separated. They could communicate only by distant gestures—a nod here, a smile there. They couldn't even persuade the servants to carry messages for them.

As luck would have it, the houses in which Pyramus and Thisbe lived shared one wall, and nobody had ever noticed that in the wall there was a tiny chink, a flaw that had been there since it was built. Nobody, that is, until the young couple discovered it—for love will always find a way. This little chink became their dearest friend: through it they could whisper sweet words of love. Each day they would go to the wall and listen for the sound of the other's breath.

Sometimes the wall seemed to be their enemy instead of their friend. "Oh, wall, why do you stand in our way?" Thisbe would exclaim. "Are you jealous?"

"Why do you keep us from being together in body as we are in spirit?" Pyramus would add.

Then, hastily, they would go on, "But don't think we are ungrateful. If it weren't for you, we wouldn't be able to meet at all!" And each day they would end their futile talking with a whispered "Goodnight," pressing their lips against the wall in kisses that could never reach the other side.

Early one morning, Pyramus and Thisbe came as usual to their places at the wall. But this day was different, for they decided that at last they must do something to end their impossible situation.

After much discussion, the young couple made a plan. That very evening, as soon as night fell and all was quiet and dark, they would steal away from the eyes that guarded them so closely, slip out of doors, and leave the city altogether.

Only one thing worried them. How could they make sure they would find each other in the dark? If they just wandered through the fields, it would be so easy to miss the other! Then Thisbe remembered that alongside the tomb of Ninus there stood a tall mulberry tree heavy with snow-white fruit, close by a spring of clear, fresh water. If they met there, they would have a landmark to guide them.

The plan seemed excellent to them both, and they agreed. Now that they were waiting impatiently for the evening, day crawled by more slowly than they had ever known. At long last, the sun dipped into the ocean, and night came on, when they would be together at last.

The moment it turned dark, Thisbe put on her silken veil. Softly, she turned the lock; slowly, she opened the door, and she was out. Guided by the white fruit of the mulberry tree, she made her way to the tomb and sat down to wait for Pyramus. Although she felt nervous being out there alone at night, her love gave her the courage to stay.

But suddenly, by the soft light of the moon, she saw something terrifying. A lioness, her jaws all bloody from a fresh kill, came up to drink from the spring. The frightened girl fled swiftly to the safety of a dark cave nearby. In her haste, Thisbe didn't notice that she had dropped her veil. The beast, her thirst quenched, had just turned to go back into the forest when she spotted the veil lying on the ground and went over to sniff at it. She picked it up in her bloody jaws and shook it a few times; then, losing interest, she let it fall.

It was only a moment later that Pyramus arrived, eager to see Thisbe face-to-face at last. As he looked around for her, his eyes fell on the footprints of the lioness, and he turned pale with fear. He turned even paler when he discovered Thisbe's veil, all torn and stained with blood. How could he guess it was not his lover's blood? Alas, he leaped to the logical—but very wrong—conclusion.

Holding the veil to his heart, he sobbed, "Oh, Thisbe! Have you come to meet me and found only death? Will we never be together?

"She should have lived," he mourned. "She deserved a long and happy life! I've killed her by asking her to come alone, at night, to this frightful place. It's my fault! I should have been here first; then I could have protected her. Now there is only one way to be with her. This night will see the end of us both, two lovers joined in death.

"Oh, come for me, too, all you lions who have your lairs here! Tear me to pieces with your terrible fangs! Devour me!" Then he drew himself together. "But I'm acting like a coward, only wishing for death, doing nothing to hurry it along."

Under the shadow of the mulberry tree, Pyramus kissed the soft silk of Thisbe's veil, and his tears ran into the folds of the fabric. Suddenly he cried, "Veil, drink my blood, too!" He drew his sword, plunged it deep into his side, and withdrew it.

As he fell to the ground, his bright blood spurted up and reddened the white fruit that hung lowest on the tree. The tree's roots soaked up the blood and dyed every berry the same crimson hue.

All this time, Thisbe had been hiding in the cave. She was still frightened, but now she grew even more worried about disappointing her lover, and eager to tell him of her close brush with danger. When she emerged timidly from her shelter, the place seemed different somehow. The tree had the right shape, but there was something strange about its color. Could this be the same tree?

As she stood in confusion, she saw something stir on the ground, ground that was now dark and wet with blood. Thisbe jumped back, turning pale and shivering as water does when the wind blows across it. The shape on the ground was her lover, Pyramus! She rushed to where he was lying, and took him in her arms, bathing his face with hot tears that mingled with his still-flowing blood. Kissing his cold lips, she sobbed, "Pyramus, what has happened? Answer me! It's Thisbe calling you! Listen to me! Lift your head!" And for an instant, hearing her name, he opened his eyes, already heavy with the weight of death, and looked into her dear face. Then his eyes closed forever.

When she saw the veil and the empty ivory scabbard that had held his sword, she understood what had happened. "Poor boy!" she cried. "It was your own hand, your own love, that killed you. Well, my hand has courage too, and my heart holds enough love to give me strength. I will follow you in your fate! I know people will say I was the cause of your death, but I was also your companion at the end. Death was the only thing that could take you from me, but he won't have the power to keep us apart any longer!"

Thisbe sent prayers to Heaven. First she prayed that their unhappy parents would forgive them and grant a final wish: that she and Pyramus should share a tomb and be together in death. She begged the tree to keep forever the color of its dark fruit, so that they would never be forgotten. Then she placed the point of her lover's sword under her breast and threw herself forward onto the blade, which was still warm with his blood.

Thisbe's prayers had reached the gods. The parents' hearts were deeply moved by their children's tragic death, and a single urn holds the ashes of both true lovers, Pyramus and Thisbe. And to this day, the mulberry fruit still keeps its deep red hue as a memorial of their love.

The story of Pyramus and Thisbe will be familiar to anyone who knows Shakespeare's A Midsummer Night's Dream. *It may also suggest another Shakespearean play,* Romeo and Juliet.

Hero and Leander

SESTOS IS IN EUROPE AND ABYDOS IN ASIA, TWO CITIES LYING ON OPPOSITE sides of the water that separates them. Yet they are not that far apart, for the water is the Hellespont, and at that point it is at its narrowest, only a mile and a half wide. In spite of its powerful currents, a determined swimmer can cross it in an hour or so. And that was no distance at all for the swift arrows of the love god, Eros. They could, and did, fly easily from Sestos, where they struck the lovely maiden Hero, to Abydos, to find a young man named Leander.

Love was forbidden to Hero, for she was a priestess of Aphrodite, but Eros never pays attention to such things. He wanted them to love, so of course they must. The god saw to it that the two young people should meet at the festival of Adonis. Struck by Eros's darts, they stood together as the evening light deepened, talking and talking, graceful figures posed like marble statues against the setting sun.

Leander's talk was all of love, and he was very persuasive. He had a plan—a way to bring the lovers together so that no one would know. She lived in a high tower above the rocks where the waves broke, with only one old servant; Leander was a strong swimmer. If, at night, she sent him a signal to show him the direction, he could swim right up to her tower. Hero could find no objection to this plan.

At last it was time for them to go home and put that barrier between them again, the water that separated them. But it seemed a trifle now that love had found the means for them to meet.

Each evening of the long and beautiful summer that followed, Hero climbed to the very top of her tower and set out a lighted lamp. And each evening, Leander was waiting on the shore just across the Hellespont. As soon as he saw her signal light, he would plunge into the waves and strike out across the current with powerful strokes. When he arrived at the tower, Hero would anoint his skin with oil of roses to wash away the salt tang of the seawater. Just before dawn light broke, he would swim back to his home in Abydos.

So the happy summer passed. Then winter came on, its bitter winds whipping the waves high and rough. It was time to stop their meetings. But love made them both unwise, and when Hero put up the lamp, Leander entered the water. He struggled through waves that tossed him around as if he were a toy. First he would sink into a deep trough of black water, then rise with the crest to see the beacon flickering in the distance. Then all at once, a particularly strong gust of wind blew out the lamp. All was darkness.

Hero waited through the long black night, hoping and praying that Leander had not made the attempt to cross the Hellespont. But when dawn came with its icy winter light, she looked out from the tower and saw his body washed up on the rocks, broken and bleeding. With one terrible cry, she flung herself into the water below, to die beside her lover, united with him forever in death.

WOMEN WHO ARE LOVED

The Invisible Lover: Psyche and Cupid

ONCE THERE LIVED A KING AND QUEEN WHO HAD THREE DAUGHTERS, ALL FAMOUS FOR THEIR beauty. The older two were quite out of the ordinary, but the youngest, whose name was Psyche, was far more beautiful still. People came from miles around just to see her, and they strewed rose petals in her path when she walked by.

It began to be whispered that Psyche was as beautiful as Venus. Some said she was even more lovely, and men began to adore the girl instead of the goddess. They neglected their worship of Venus; her temples and towns were abandoned and decaying. Of course, she was outraged. No mere mortal could outshine the goddess of beauty and love!

Venus called on her son, Cupid, to help her. "Go down to Earth," she commanded, "and make this upstart fall in love with the vilest and most loathsome creature you can find!" Cupid did go down, but when he beheld Psyche, something wonderful happened.

The god who had made so many fall in love—deities and mortals alike—was pricked by his own arrow. He loved Psyche. Instead of obeying his mother's request, he played a trick of his own. Psyche did not fall in love with a beast; she fell in love with nobody at all.

Soon Psyche's sisters were both married to kings, but the girl who attracted the attention of so many men was not asked to become a wife. She was ardently admired, but never loved. Her father became concerned. What was wrong? Had they aroused the anger of one of the gods? He determined to seek advice from the oracle of Apollo at Delphi.

But Cupid had told Apollo the whole story and suggested the answer the king should receive. Accordingly, the oracle proclaimed that his daughter's husband would be a terrible winged serpent, and that the king must take her to the summit of a steep mountain and leave her alone there, where her husband would come for her.

The procession that led Psyche to the lonely mountaintop looked more like a funeral than a wedding. Weeping, the girl's parents left her and made their slow way home to mourn their daughter's fate. Psyche was terrified, but determined not to break down. Then, as she sat in the dark, alone and shivering with fear, she felt herself lifted gently from the mountain by the soft west wind, and set down in a meadow fragrant with flowers and soft grass. There she fell asleep. When she awoke, she saw a crystalline stream, and beside it a splendid palace, gleaming in gold and silver, inlaid with precious gems. The door stood open wide.

Psyche went up the steps and looked inside. She heard voices that welcomed her, though she could see no one. "Come in," the voices said. "This is your home, and we are your servants. Look, here is your bedchamber. Rest for a while. Then, when you have bathed and dressed, there will be food on the table." Psyche lay down on the deliciously soft bed and slept a little, then entered the bath, which was already drawn for her. Invisible attendants washed her as she lay in the scented warm water; unseen hands anointed her with perfumes, and dressed her in the loveliest of bridal garments.

The table was empty when Psyche entered the dining room, but as soon as she sat down, a sumptuous banquet was set before her. Delectable food appeared from nowhere; wine was poured. As she ate, a sweet voice began to sing, and then it was joined by a chorus of invisible singers, making the most beautiful music she had ever heard. And all this time she saw no one.

After she had finished eating, Psyche went up to bed. Around midnight, she felt a presence in the chamber and became frightened. But a tender voice said to her, "You have no need to fear me. I am your husband. We will be happy forever, if only you will promise never to try to look at me."

As soon as she heard him speak, Psyche knew that this was not a horrible monster, but the husband she had always dreamed of, one she could love forever. She gladly gave her promise. In the morning when she awoke, he was gone.

The next nights followed the same pattern. Her husband came to her in the darkness and was gone by morning. She never saw him. After a time, Psyche felt a little lonely, spending her days as she did in solitude, seeing nobody. She asked her husband if she might invite her sisters for a visit.

"That's not a good idea," he replied. "In fact, it would be dangerous to talk with them." But he could deny his wife nothing. Reluctantly he agreed, after making her promise that no matter what her sisters said, she would not try to find out what he looked like.

The west wind brought the sisters to Psyche's palace. When they looked around at the gold, jewels, and rich wood with which it was decorated, they burned with envy. They asked their sister what her husband was like, and she answered, "He is a very young man, just starting to get his first beard. He's out hunting now, that's why you can't meet him." The sisters left, whispering to each other jealously. Their husbands were old and ugly, they muttered, sick and miserly. Why should Psyche have all the luck?

Again, Psyche wanted to see her sisters; again, her husband warned her of danger. This time, he added, she was going to have a baby, who would be immortal if she kept her husband's secret, but human if she told her sisters that she had never seen him. Still, once again, he agreed.

But careless Psyche had forgotten what she had told her sisters on the first visit, and now she said that her husband was a rich, middle-aged merchant, away from home on business. After a time, she gave them gifts of gold and jewels and sent them on their way.

"What do you think of these lies she is telling us?" asked the oldest sister as they went. "Monstrous!" replied the second. "It's obvious she has no idea what he looks like. But we can use that to our advantage."

In a rage of jealousy, the sisters determined to ruin Psyche. They returned to the palace, pretending to care for her safety. In urgent tones, they warned her that her husband was indeed the loathsome winged serpent the oracle had foretold.

"Is the oracle ever wrong?" hissed one.

"He may seem kind now, but one night he will devour you," nodded the other. "But there is a way to make yourself safe. Here's what you must do … ."

Her sisters terrified Psyche so much that she agreed to do what they urged. They left, satisfied in their mission of ill will. All day she argued with herself, and the argument went back and forth: "He is so good to me … I cannot break my promise to him … No, they're right, he must be a monster. I must kill him or be killed … But … But … ."

That night when she retired to her chamber, Psyche hid a lamp and a sharp knife under the bed. As soon as her husband fell sleep, she quietly slipped from the covers, grabbed the knife, and lit the lamp, prepared to stab the monster who lay there. But instead of a monster, her dazzled eyes beheld the most beautiful being she had ever seen. She was too thrilled to put out the lamp; indeed, she leaned over for a closer look, and as she did, her hand trembled with joy and spilled a few drops of hot oil on his shoulder.

He awoke with a roar of pain and rage. Leaping from the bed, he ran out of the palace without a word. When Psyche followed him into the night, he flew to the top of a cypress tree and spoke to her angrily. At last, he told her who he was: Cupid, the god of love himself. Because of her faithlessness, he sputtered, he must leave her forever. "Love cannot live in a home where there is no trust!" And he was gone.

Psyche wept, scolding herself. "Here I was, the luckiest woman alive, married to the god of love, and I couldn't keep my promise to him. I have lost my only happiness!" In despair, she flung herself into the river, but instead of drowning her, the river set her gently back on the shore. Since she could not die, Psyche determined to search for her husband. "I will spend my whole life looking for him," she thought. "If he cannot love me, at least he will see how much I love him."

Meanwhile Cupid lay, groaning with pain, in his mother's house in the heavens. When Venus heard his story and learned that it was her enemy Psyche whom he had married, she was furious. She left him to his pain and went out to find Psyche to punish her.

Wandering miserably, Psyche looked everywhere for Cupid. She went from temple to temple, pleading for help from the gods, but none of them was willing to risk the anger of Venus. At last, the girl decided that her only hope was to go to the goddess and throw herself on her mercy. She would offer herself as a servant, begging for forgiveness and a chance to see her husband.

When they found each other, Venus vented her rage at the girl. She had Psyche whipped, and then lashed out at her, shaking her, ripping her clothes, and tearing out handfuls of hair. "Are you looking for a husband," she sneered, "since the one you have wishes never to see you again? You are so ugly and stupid that nobody will ever love you! You'd better learn to be a servant. I'll be generous and train you myself."

Venus led the girl into a room filled knee-deep with seeds of all kinds: millet and barley, oats, wheat, lentils, and poppy. "Here's your first job," the goddess said. "Sort these by midnight, or you'll be very sorry!" Then she swept out. She had a party to attend.

Psyche looked around her in despair. This task was impossible, she knew, and she wept a little out of fear. But as she did, an ant chanced by and saw her tears. Taking pity on her misery, he went and fetched his whole colony, who busily got to work separating the grains. By the time Venus returned, perfumed and a little drunk, she found neat piles of seeds, each of one kind.

The goddess was enraged. She hurled a crust of bread at Psyche and told her to sleep on the floor. "You've only begun your labors!" Venus snarled. The only way to destroy the girl's hateful beauty, she knew, was to keep her hard at work and short of food and rest. Meanwhile, she would see to it that her son was locked in his room so that he could not set eyes on his wife.

In the morning, Venus gave Psyche her next task. "Down by the river," she said, "there is a flock of sheep with golden wool. I want an armful of that wool for my knitting. Go and fetch it for me."

Reluctantly, the girl set out. She knew that those sheep were fierce and violent animals, and would kill her sooner than give her any wool. Sinking down at the edge of the river, she sighed. Perhaps this time she could really drown herself. But the reeds that grew along the banks began to whisper to her.

"Wait until the sheep have gone to sleep," they murmured, "and then go around that bend in the river. You will find plenty of wool there, brushed off onto the sharp grasses that grow along the bank." Psyche did as the reeds suggested, and returned to Venus with her arms full of the shining wool.

"You had help!" shouted the irate goddess. "I know you haven't done this by your-self! All right—I have yet another job for you, one that will really test your wisdom and courage. Do you see that mountain over there? Up near the top, you will find a river of dark water bursting out of the cliff. That water comes from the River Styx. I want you to fill this flagon full and bring it to me, ice-cold and foaming. And be sure you draw it from the very middle of the stream as it gushes from the rocks."

Taking the flagon, Psyche set out. When she arrived at its foot, she saw that the mountain was impossible to climb, so steep were its sides, so mossy and wet and slippery, so sharp the crags. And the stream, far above her, was guarded by vicious dragons. As she stood looking upward in despair, help came to her once more. Jupiter's eagle, who owed Cupid a favor, swooped down, snatched the bottle, and returned it to her full of the icy black water.

"You must be a witch!" snapped Venus when Psyche presented her with the brim-ming flagon. "Very well, then, you should be able to do another simple task. My beauty has worn out a little with worry over my poor son and tending to his terrible wound. Take this casket to the Underworld, and ask Proserpina to fill it with some of her beauty. I need it for a party tonight."

Mortals cannot enter the realm of the dead and return alive, Psyche well knew. In despair, she climbed to the top of a high tower. Perhaps if she threw herself off and died, she could enter the Underworld that way. But the tower began to speak to her.

"Take two golden coins in your mouth, and in each hand carry a cake soaked in honey and wine. At the River Styx, give one of the coins to Charon, the ferryman. He will not take you across unless he is paid. Then, when you reach the Underworld, give one of the sweetsops to Cerberus, the three-headed dog who guards the door. The other cake and coin are for your return trip." The tower also warned her to beware of three traps that Venus had set for her. She must ignore the pleas for help she would hear from an old man with a lame donkey, from a body that would be floating in the river, and from three women weaving on the other side. And most of all, when she received the box of beauty, she must not open it.

Psyche followed this excellent advice, or at least most of it. Charon and Cerberus were satisfied with their payments; she avoided the snares set by the goddess; Proserpina was happy to share her beauty with Venus. But on her way back with the prize, the girl was overcome by a desire to open the casket. She knew that worry and her hard life had taken away some of her beauty. What if she were to meet her husband now? Would he find her attractive, or would she disgust him? It was so important that she look her best! Surely it would not hurt to take just a little of the beauty for herself!

Cautiously, she lifted the lid. Nothing! The box seemed to be empty. But it wasn't. Instead of beauty, Proserpina had filled the casket with sleep. Psyche opened it wider, and at once she fell down, overcome by a sleep so deep it was like death.

Now Cupid had recovered from his wound, and he found himself missing his wife dreadfully. Venus might have locked his door, but there is no way to keep love a prisoner. All he had to do was fly out the window, and the moment he did, he saw Psyche lying at the roadside in her sleep of death. He swept down and knelt beside her, waking her with a little prick from one of his arrows. Then he sent her on her way to present the casket to Venus.

Meanwhile, Cupid flew up to Olympus. He begged Jupiter to let him bring his wife there to live among the gods.

"You have caused me a lot of trouble with your arrows," Jupiter replied, "but I have a lingering fondness for you, and I will grant your request." He called a council of the gods and explained his decision to them. Cupid and Psyche, he announced, were formally married. It would be better, he added, if Cupid were to settle down and stop roaming around.

So Mercury was sent to carry Psyche to Olympus, where a great wedding feast was held. Jupiter himself gave her a cup of ambrosia to drink, making her immortal. Now Venus could find no reason to object to the marriage. Besides, the goddess no doubt realized that if Psyche were living on Olympus, she would not be around on Earth to compete with her in the matter of beauty.

And from that day on, Cupid and Psyche—love and the soul—have dwelt together in joy and happiness. Their daughter's name is Pleasure.

Loved by a Monster: Galatea

WAS EVER A MAIDEN MORE EXTRAVAGANTLY wooed than Galatea was by the Cyclops Polyphemus? From the day he fell in love with her, he was a changed monster. Forgotten was his taste for blood, his violence. Ships that once would have been in great danger when they passed his rocks and sandbars now sailed by unthreatened and unharmed.

Polyphemus had only to cast his single eye on the beautiful Nereid, Galatea, to adore her. The Cyclops was so in love that he even began to care about his personal appearance for the first time in his life. He combed his matted hair with a rake and trimmed his shaggy beard with a sickle, using a pool for a mirror. Watching his reflection in the water, Polyphemus tried out all kinds of expressions to make his fierce face look softer, so that the nymph would understand how much he loved her.

But Galatea only scorned the giant. She would have nothing to do with him, for she was in love already. Her heart had room for Acis, only Acis.

This was a good and beautiful youth, whose parents adored him. Their son gave them joy, but he made Galatea even happier, for he declared that he loved her beyond anything in the world. Acis was sixteen, and just beginning to grow his first beard; a more handsome young man could not be found. To say that Galatea returned his love would be an understatement.

Everything should have been perfect, but the young lovers had a problem. Polyphemus loved Galatea just as much as she loved Acis. Day and night the giant pursued her. Her love for the one was equally matched by her hatred for the other.

Poor Polyphemus! He had never been in love before. Dazzled by this new state, he neglected all his usual duties. He forgot to guard the coastline, and let his flocks wander at will. Each day, when he climbed his mountain, the sheep trailed behind him, disheveled and unnoticed. At the topmost peak, he dropped his walking stick, an enormous pine tree, tall as the mast of a ship. Then he sat down on a rock to play on his shepherd's pipes, made of a hundred reeds, and sent his song of love across the Earth and waters. The very mountains trembled at the noise. These are the words he sang:

"Galatea, my love, you are so beautiful! Whiter than the flowering evergreen, more graceful than the alder tree, your bloom outshines the meadow. Brighter than crystal you are, livelier than a young kid, smoother than polished shells, more welcome than sun in winter and green shade in the summer. You are lovelier than apples, slenderer than the plane tree. My love, you are purer than ice, sweeter than ripe grapes, softer than swan's down, and more fragrant than a garden watered by cool streams—or would be, if only you'd accept my love.

"But there's my problem!" the song went on. "That Galatea who spurns me is more stubborn than a wild heifer, tougher than a knotty oak, falser than the waves, sharper than the briars that grow along the roadside, harder to move than rock, more violent than the mountain torrents.

"Yes—you know it, too! You're vainer than any peacock, crueler than the bite of fire, deafer than the sea, more savage than a she-bear guarding her cubs, more pitiless than a stepped-on snake, and worst of all—oh, I wish it weren't true—swifter than a deer when it is fleeing the hounds, swifter than the wind itself.

"But, Galatea, if you really knew me, you wouldn't run away like this! Instead of hiding, you'd seek me out. I own this whole mountainside and all its caves, where neither midsummer sun nor winter's cold can find their way inside. My apple trees hang heavy with fruit on every bough; my grapes, both green and purple, are waiting just for you to come and gather them. With your own hands you can pick wild strawberries in the shade of my woods; in autumn you can gather cherries and plums, not only the juicy purple-black ones, but new kinds, yellow and fat. Chestnuts and tart berries grow in my woods just for you. All of this can be yours if only you will take me for your husband!

"I have even more riches to offer you. This huge flock of sheep, for example—all mine! I own twice as many as you see here, wandering through the valleys or sheltering in the woods, still others stabled in my caves. I don't even know how many head of cattle I have; only the poor man counts his flocks. You don't have to trust my words. Just look for yourself. See how much milk they give! I have younger animals, too, young lambs, young goats, young calves, all of them put up in warm stables. In my house there is always snow-white milk to drink, and plenty more for making cheese.

"Oh, and you can have pets, too, if you want. I'll get you the rarest kind, not the usual ones, deer or rabbits or doves. Just the other day, up on the mountaintop I found two black bear cubs for you to play with, so much alike you can't tell them apart. As soon as I caught them, I thought, 'These are for my lady'!"

Now the giant tried a softer tone. "Come on, Galatea, raise your head out of those deep blue waters, don't spurn my gifts. I'll tell you something else," he went on. "I've seen myself reflected in a pool, and I liked what I saw. It must please you to look at me. Just see how big I am! Jove himself up there in the clouds doesn't have a bigger body, and you always talk about him with admiration.

"Look at my hair, how long it is, hanging over my face in the front and tumbling down my back. In fact, my whole body bristles with good, thick, coarse hair! Beautiful, don't you think? Like nature: a tree is ugly only when it's bare of leaves; a horse is ugly when it doesn't have a mane! Don't birds have feathers and sheep have wool to make them more attractive? Just so, beard and bristles are becoming on a man!

"True, I have just one eye, in the middle of my forehead, but it's a huge eye, as big as a shield. And so what? The sun looks down from the sky and sees everything on Earth, and the sun has only one eye!

"What's more, my father Neptune rules over your sea, and he will be your father-in-law, if only you will pity me and listen to my pleas! No other girl in all the world could ever conquer me. I laugh at Jove, and his sky, and his thunderbolts. It's only you I fear, Galatea, your anger more deadly than lightning.

"I could stand anything—even your not loving me—if only you felt scorn for other men. But how can you turn me down and fall in love with Acis, that little twerp? I wish I could get my hands on him. He'd learn that I'm as strong as I am big! Just give me the chance and I'll tear him apart, rip out his guts and pull off an arm or two, and scatter the pieces all across the fields and the sea. Look, the fire of love you lit burns even hotter because you scorn me. I have a volcano inside me, and you don't care at all!"

A mile away, Galatea sat in the shade of a rock, resting in the arms of Acis. She heard the giant's song, and thought Polyphemus was only bragging. But suddenly he rose and stalked across the fields and woodlands until he faced the lovers. He shouted, "So there you are! This is the last time you two will ever see each other!"

The voice of Polyphemus was a roar that shook Mount Etna itself. Galatea panicked and leapt into the sea. Acis turned to run away, screaming, "Help, Galatea! Help, Father and Mother! Save me, I am going to die!" He ran his fastest, but the Cyclops was close behind. Suddenly the giant tore off the top of the mountain and hurled it at Acis. Although just the very tip reached the youth, it was enough to bury him.

Galatea watched in horror, powerless to save her lover. But the Fates gave her one last chance. There was a magic formula that could call up the supernatural power of Acis's own ancestors. The Fates let her pronounce the words. At once, crimson blood began to trickle out from under the huge rock; then it faded and turned the color of a mountain stream swollen by melting snow and spring rains. At last it cleared entirely. The ground split, and out of the fissure grew a tall green reed. From beneath the rock and clay came the sound of running water. Suddenly, miraculously, a youth was standing there, waist deep in the water. His newly formed horns were crowned with twisted rushes.

It was Acis, changed into a river god by the magic of his ancestors—with help from his beloved Galatea.

Orpheus and Eurydice

IN THE VERY EARLY TIME OF THE WORLD, GODS mingled more freely with mortals than they do in these later days. So it was not surprising that the Muse Calliope, she who inspires epic poetry, gave birth to a son whose father was a mortal man. He was the king of Thrace, the most musical of all the people of Greece. Calliope named her son Orpheus, and from his infancy, she and her sister Muses were his teachers. Even before he reached manhood, he was accomplished in all the arts, but especially in poetry and music.

When Orpheus made music, all the world stopped to listen. Wild beasts drew near him, so entranced they put aside their fierceness. Trees gathered around to hear his beautiful notes. Rivers stopped flowing along their banks so that they could hear Orpheus, whose music was more harmonious than theirs. The very rocks softened when he touched his lyre.

Orpheus drew the most wonderful music from his instrument. With his gift he could embolden people to do deeds they didn't dream they had in them. When he sailed on the Argo with Jason to search for the Golden Fleece, it was his lyre that heartened the men on those nights when they lost courage and despaired of reaching their goal. It was his lyre that soothed and calmed them when quarrels threatened to sow disharmony. It was his lyre, singing louder than the sultry song of the Sirens, that saved the Argonauts, who might have left their bones on that dangerous island as so many other sailors had.

But music was not enough. Something was missing in Orpheus's life. He knew what it was when he met the wood nymph Eurydice and for the first time felt the joy of love. She returned his feelings, and happily agreed to become his wife.

Orpheus invited Hymen, the god of marriage, to bless the wedding with his presence. Hymen came, but his words were not auspicious, and the omens he brought with him were not happy ones. The torch smoked, bringing tears to the eyes of the wedding party. When it was swung, it would not blaze into flame.

And the omens proved true. The loving couple's happiness was all too brief. Their marriage was not an hour old when Eurydice, walking across the meadow with her brides-maids, innocently trod upon a viper, who struck out at her and stung her on the foot. At once, she was carried away to the Underworld, the dark region of the dead.

Orpheus was distraught. Grieving, he bore the young body of his beloved Eurydice to the grave, and the music he played tore at the hearts of everyone who followed. It was whispered among their friends that the gods were jealous and would not let a mortal man and woman live together in immortal happiness. Whether that is true or not, the bereft husband was inconsolable. How could he live without his wife, the other half of his soul? Orpheus determined to perform an unthinkable act, an act no mortal man had ever at-tempted. He would do this for his love: he would follow her into the Underworld, and there he would beg the dark powers to give her back to him.

So Orpheus set out, taking with him only his songs and the lyre with which he would accompany his plea. He found the crack in the dark cave that leads to Hades, the realm of death, and he followed it down, deeper and deeper. Soon he saw the River Styx, which separates the Underworld from the world of the living. As he approached, he played on his lyre, and hearing his sweet song, the boatman Charon could not resist it. He agreed to ferry Orpheus to the other side of the river, even though the living should not be allowed to cross.

Then, at the mouth of Hades, Orpheus played and sang to Cerberus, the three-headed dog who guards the entryway to keep away those who have not died. Cerberus drooped his three heads low, ceased snarling for a moment, and let him pass. Once inside, Orpheus searched through the long dark passageways, calling for Eurydice and plucking the strings of his lyre. The shades of the dead, among whom he searched for his wife, drew just out of sight as he went by.

Frightened but determined, Orpheus continued, winning his way by the beauty of his music. As the dark passages opened up for him, his music gave a moment of relief to many of the souls who suffer eternally to pay for the sins they have committed in the upper world.

Over there was Sisyphus, who for a lifetime's deeds struggles endlessly to push an enormous boulder up a hill. When he reaches the top, it rolls back down again. Orpheus passed and he played, and for a moment Sisyphus was able to sit upon his rock to rest.

And a little farther along, there was Tantalus, whose unspeakable offense against the gods dooms him to torture by burning thirst and stabbing hunger, while he stands neck-deep in a pool of water that recedes from his lips every time he stoops to drink, and just within reach of luscious grapes that wither away when he stretches to pick them. Orpheus passed and he played, and Tantalus too was given a moment of rest.

So were the Danaides, who stabbed their husbands on their wedding night, and for that deed must try eternally to scoop up water in a sieve. Next he saw the fiery winged wheel, on which Ixion spins in torment forever because he committed mankind's first murder, the murder of his brother. At Orpheus's song, for a moment the wheel ceased its spinning.

Even the Furies—the terrible goddesses who inflict these punishments and who keep the dead from escaping Hades to return to the upper world—even they were moved. Orpheus passed and he played, and for the first time ever, the faces of these dread powers grew wet with tears.

At last, Orpheus stood before the thrones of Hades, the dark-browed king of the Underworld, and his queen, Persephone, her fair face veiled by the shadows of that terrible place. What could he say to the god and goddess of death that would persuade them to give Eurydice back to him? He plucked the strings of his lyre, and put his whole heart into the song that would plead his cause:

> *You who rule this dark and silent world*
> *are masters of all who walk on the Earth.*
> *Every one of us will come to you,*
> *even the most beautiful and best loved belong to you at last.*
> *You are the creditor who must always be paid.*
> *We only belong to the upper world for a short time,*
> *and then we are yours forever and ever.*
> *But there is one who came to you too soon,*
> *a bud that died before it ever grew into a flower.*
> *I tried to bear the loss, but it was too great.*
> *O king, I could not bear it. Love was too strong.*
> *Hear me and weave again the web of life,*
> *put together the threads cut from the loom too soon for my Eurydice.*
> *I ask you only for a loan, and not a gift to me,*
> *for she'll be given back to you when her years are full.*

Orpheus's music was so compelling that even the ice-hard heart of Hades melted. Persephone whispered a plea in his ear, and tears flowed from his eyes. Just this once, he had to yield before the force of love.

Hades called for Eurydice, and she came forth from among the newest shades, still limping from her wound. Orpheus's wish was granted. But there was one condition: she must follow in his shadow and he must not pause, or speak, or turn to look on her until they reached the upper world.

Of course, Orpheus agreed, and at once the couple turned away from the throne of death to begin their difficult journey back. Through dark and tortuous passageways, through the chill of death, they made their way in terrible silence. Orpheus listened with all his being to hear the footsteps of Eurydice in the shadows behind him. At each step, he desperately wanted to turn, to make sure she was still there, and even more, he longed to look upon her face. But he controlled his yearning and kept going, up and up, until utter darkness began to change to only black, then gray, and then lighter gray, and at last he could see the light of day ahead.

Some people say that what happened next was just a moment of forgetfulness. Others maintain that Orpheus had reached the sunlight and turned to help Eurydice, believing she was out, too. There are those who think he didn't trust Hades, and had to see that she was really there, or that he couldn't hear her steps and was overcome by a terror that she was no longer following him. But you might believe—and I believe it too—that his great love for her overwhelmed him. He could not keep himself from turning around, just to see her beloved face at last.

At the very instant he turned, Eurydice was snatched away for the second time, this time forever. He heard a faint cry— "Farewell!"—and knew that it held no tone of reproach. How could she blame him when his only fault was loving her too much?

Desperately, Orpheus stretched out his arms and called her name: "Eurydice!" But it was too late. His arms clasped only the cold air, and a long deep sigh echoed from the darkness. He would never see her again while he lived.

In vain, Orpheus tried to follow his bride. But this time the Underworld was firmly closed to him. No other mortal had broached it once, and certainly he was not going to get a second chance. The power of his music failed him at last. Charon turned a deaf ear to his pleas, and all the gods agreed that a living mortal could not enter the world of the dead again.

For seven days and seven nights, Orpheus remained at the entryway, unable to sing or even speak, taking no food or drink, wishing for death. But even death refused him. Finally, he had no choice but to get up and go back into the world. Once there, he avoided every scene of joy, and turned his back on women, although there were many maidens who would have liked to make him forget Eurydice.

Orpheus traveled into the mountain forests, seeking solitude or the companionship of beasts rather than men. Although he still played his lyre, he played only to melt the hearts of tigers, to move the mountains and the oak trees. His songs were so sad that no human could bear to listen to them.

One day, as Orpheus slept in a clearing, a band of Maenads, women driven to madness by their worship of Dionysus, came upon him and demanded that he join their revels. Horrified, he refused them. In their fury, they closed in on him like hunters on a deer. First they stoned him, then smashed his precious lyre. Finally, in a frenzy they tore his body to pieces and threw him into a stream. From there he floated out to sea, and people say that as he floated he still sang the name of Eurydice. His body was washed ashore on the island of Lesbos. There it was buried by the Muses, who lamented for their beloved Orpheus.

And to this day, the nightingales sing more sweetly on that island than anywhere else in the world.

The Prize Princess:
Hippodamia

HIPPODAMIA WAS THE DAUGHTER OF OENOMAUS, KING OF PISA. SHE WAS A BEAUTIFUL AND winsome girl, and many princes came to ask the king for her hand in marriage. But he did not want her to marry, for he had been warned by an oracle that his daughter's husband would be the cause of his death.

Still, how could he continue to refuse all her suitors, when there was no apparent reason to turn any of them down? Oenomaus puzzled over this problem. At last he thought he knew how he could keep his daughter from marriage without seeming to withhold his permission unreasonably. He would put each of Hippodamia's suitors to a harsh test, one he was sure they would all fail.

"Any man who wishes to marry my daughter must compete with me in a chariot race," he declared. "I want to make sure that her husband is worthy to take my place in caring for her. She deserves a man of great courage, daring, and skill in horsemanship. Then I know he will guard her against any dangers that may come to her."

The king himself laid out the course, and he made it long and difficult. He felt sure that he would always triumph because he owned a pair of very swift horses, a gift from Ares, the god of war. Then he declared the terms of the competition. If a suitor should win the race, his prize would be to marry Hippodamia; but if Oenomaus won, the suitor's head would be cut off and placed on a stake by the palace gate. Already there were twelve stakes at the gate, with twelve heads, enough to discourage any but the most determined suitor.

Pelops, the son of Tantalus, was just that kind of man. He knew that he wanted to marry Hippodamia, and what's more, she wanted to marry him, too. She was tired of waiting while all her suitors competed with her father and lost their heads. And Pelops looked to her exactly like the man she had been wishing for in her prayers.

Pelops was not only determined and courageous; he was also very wise for one so young. He suspected that Oenomaus had offended the deities by the slaughter of all those men whose only offense was wishing to marry Hippodamia. It would be wise to enlist one of the gods on his side, he decided.

Pelops turned to Poseidon, praying for help, and the sea god's response was all he could have wanted. He gave Pelops a splendid chariot to drive in the race, with a team of immortal horses to draw it. Now the young man felt sure that he would win.

At this point the story becomes a bit unclear. What happened during the race is certain; so is what happened the night before. But who was the person, hidden in a long cloak, who secretly visited Myrtilus, the king's charioteer? Some say it was Pelops, while others swear it was Hippodamia herself who slipped into the stables and offered the charioteer a bribe.

Whichever of the young people had paid Myrtilus to do what he did, the outcome of the competition was never in doubt. For on the morning of the race, Myrtilus took out the metal pins that fastened the wheels onto Oenomaus's chariot, and substituted pins made of wax.

The race began, and for a time it looked even. First Pelops would pull ahead, then Oenomaus. Faster and faster they drove, and the wheels of their chariots began to grow warm, then hot. Then, just as the king was turning a corner, the wax pins melted from the heat and the wheels flew off his chariot, throwing Oenomaus to his death.

Pelops succeeded where twelve before him had failed; he won the hand of Hippodamia. They married, and Pelops became the new king of Pisa. Afterwards, he threw Myrtilus into the sea, where the charioteer died cursing him.

Whether it was Pelops who had bribed Myrtilus, or Hippodamia, the new king was visited by remorse, both for the way he had won the race and for sending the charioteer to his death. Pelops set up a monument to his victims at Olympia, and later, to commemorate his own contest, he started the Olympic Games. Today, among the ruins at Olympia, you can still see the course where the earliest races were run, starting and ending at the tomb of Pelops and Hippodamia.

The Nymph of the Orchard: Pomona and Vertumnus

IN THE CENTER OF A LOVINGLY TENDED GARDEN, THERE ONCE LIVED a woodland nymph named Pomona. Nobody was as skillful at growing things as she. Flowers sprang up at her touch, and fruit trees bore wonderfully when she tended them. The orchard was her specialty; indeed, that's how she got her name, for Pomona means "apple."

Unlike most wood nymphs, Pomona cared nothing for other trees, the shady green woods, or the rivers. Hunting was not her sport; she never carried a spear or a javelin, only a pruning knife. With it she shaped the fruit trees and trimmed the hedges around the orchard, or cut back the rosebushes and cherries to keep them from spreading too far. Her trees never went thirsty, for she had made an irrigation system that watered every root. To save an ancient tree, she would slit the bark and graft on a new twig. It always worked; you could say she had a green thumb. Pomona's orchard bore the most fruit, and the largest and sweetest, too.

Romance meant nothing to her; the fruit trees were her love, her passion. Yet Pomona was nervous about men, and to keep lovers away she built a high wall around the orchard, its gates tightly locked.

Many were the men and gods and demigods who tried to woo the nymph. They did everything they could think of to catch her attention. They danced around her wall with their hair wreathed, singing words of love. Among them all, none fell as hard for her as the young god Vertumnus, but he had no better luck in winning her affections than any of the others.

Still, he remained undiscouraged by the nymph's indifference. Vertumnus had an advantage over mortals: he could take any shape he wanted. Sometimes he came to her orchard gate dressed as a harvester, and offered Pomona baskets of grain. He looked as if he had just come in from the fields, with a band of hay tied around his brow. Other times he would come up with an ox goad in his hand as if he had just turned his cattle out to pasture. Or he would be the very image of a hedge trimmer, carrying a pruning hook. Next he would appear with a ladder on his shoulder, as if his only interest in life were picking apples. With a sword and battle dress, he would seem to be a soldier; with a rod and tackle, he was a fisherman.

Such disguises gave Vertumnus many opportunities to see Pomona, and for a while he was happy just to be near enough to gaze at her beauty. One afternoon, he grew bolder still. He put on wisps of false gray hair and bound a bright scarf around his head. Then, leaning on a stick, he hobbled up to the nymph's gate, walking around the garden walls bent over as if he were a very old woman. Pomona let him into the orchard, where he admired the fruit, saying how wonderful the apples were, and the peaches.

"But you, my dear, are even better-looking," he suddenly said, "more beautiful and more charming." And he kissed her, not just once but over and over. No old woman ever kissed like that! Then the poor old creature, bent almost double, sank down on the grass, and gazed up at the branches overhead, with their heavy load of autumn fruit.

Just across from where they sat was an elm tree, whose trunk and branches were interwoven with a grapevine bearing thick clusters of rich, gleaming grapes. Vertumnus stared at them as if he were hypnotized by the sight of the two plants growing so close together, the elm and the vine. At last he sighed and said, "Just imagine! If the tree had not married the vine, but stood there alone, we would look at it because its leaves were pretty, but that's all. And if the vine had remained unmarried to the helpful tree, it would be lying along the ground and it would fade away, choked by weeds and grasses, not bearing such luscious fruit."

He looked at Pomona and said, softly, "You have not understood the fable of the vine and the tree. You haven't married, and you say you don't want to. If you would change your mind, you'd have more suitors than Helen ever did, or Odysseus's wife, Penelope. You already have a thousand, although you shun and scorn them—men and gods and demigods, every man in these hills and all those who have divinity in them.

"Now, if you are wise, and would make a good match, choose your man today. Listen to the words of this old woman, who loves you more than all the others—yes, more than you can imagine! Forget these nobodies, the ordinary men who come around, and take the best. I mean Vertumnus! I speak for him—I know him just as well as he knows himself. I tell you, he is no vagabond roaming around the world. He lives nearby, and knows the hills and land around here like his right hand. He's not fickle like most young men, loving one girl after another, falling in love with every new one he sees. You'll be his first love and his last; he'll give his life to you.

"And then consider this: he's young and charming, and can fit himself into every mood. He can change into any shape that suits you, be anything you want him to be, no matter what you ask. Your tastes are the same; the things you love, he loves. He's always the first one to cherish the sweet apples from your orchard. But what he really longs for is not the fruits from your trees, nor the tender plants you grow in your garden. No, it's just you—you alone.

"Take pity on him, be kind to him. Be more than kind! He loves you so. Can't you hear him pleading through my lips? Give him his heart's desire. What's more, you ought to fear the vengeance of the gods, especially Venus, who hates a stony heart in a human body. Let me tell you a story that shows what can happen to those whose hearts are cold and hard when somebody loves them." And the lover, still disguised, told Pomona the story of the stony-hearted Anaxarete. (You may read this story, which follows.)

When Vertumnus had finished telling his tale, he saw that it was all in vain. Pomona was not to be moved by the advice of an old woman. His disguise was worthless. He threw off the dress, the hair, the scarf, and appeared before her in his proper shape, in the form of a young god. The light of his radiance shone like the sun when it breaks through the clouds and rain. Dazzled by the beauty of his godlike figure, Pomona fell joyfully into his arms. Love had triumphed again.

*This is the tale Vertumnus, the lover in the previous story,
told to persuade his beloved, Pomona, that she should not reject his love.*

The Girl with a Heart of Stone:
Anaxarete

THERE WAS A YOUNG MAN OF HUMBLE BIRTH NAMED IPHIS, WHO HAD SEEN A PRINCESS AND HAD fallen in love with her on the spot. She was Anaxarete, born of an ancient noble line. Knowing how unequal their stations in life were, Iphis fought with all his might against the fires of his passion. But his reason could not overcome his feelings. Every day he came to her door like a beggar, pleading for her love.

Anaxarete remained deaf to his entreaties, taking no more notice of him than the waves that surge on the sea in a winter storm. She was harder than iron forged in the fire, stonier than rock deep-rooted in earth.

One day, Iphis confessed his feelings to Anaxarete's nurse and implored her to help him win her charge's love. "If you love her," he said, "and hope for her happiness, look on my suit kindly, and talk about me with her. Tell her I am worthy of her love." Then, in an anxious voice, he coaxed Anaxarete's many maids to do him favors. He gave them love notes to carry to her, full of sweet words, carved into tablets of soft wax. He hung garlands of flowers on her doorposts, damp not with dew but with his own tears. He lay down on her threshold all night, reproaching the bolts and bars for not letting him in.

None of these things helped Iphis win Anaxarete's love. She despised him and laughed at him, taunting him with proud, haughty words and cruel actions, until at last he lost hope entirely. He could stand it no longer, this awful, drawn-out agony. In torment he stood at her door and cried out his last words.

"Anaxarete, you win! I won't bother you anymore. Prepare a triumphal parade, sing hosannas, and crown your head with laurel. You are victorious, and I am glad to die! Be happy in my death, you stony-hearted woman!

"Still, there must be something about me you can find to praise, something to admire, something that will make you admit I was good enough for your love. Perhaps at the least you will value my faithfulness! Remember that I loved you, and my love ended only with my death. And you won't hear it from some rumor that's being spread around! No, I myself will be here right in front of you, Iphis in person, so that you may feast your cruel eyes on the sight of my lifeless body.

"O gods, if you do see all the acts of mortal beings, remember me! My tongue can speak no more; this is its final prayer. Let my story be told in far distant times; let the years that I have lost from my life be added after I am dead to keep my fame alive!"

Then Iphis lifted up his tear-filled eyes and his pale, weakened arms to the doorpost he had so often adorned with wreaths of fresh flowers. Standing on a bench, he hung a rope over the beam, and at its end he tied a noose. "Here's a wreath for you, cruel and wicked girl—one that will finally make you happy!" And, thrusting his head into the noose, Iphis turned to face the door for one last time. Then he stepped off the bench.

The door, struck by the convulsions of his feet, seemed to shudder and then groan with sounds of grief, and flew wide open, revealing the awful sight. Servants screamed and lifted the body down, but it was too late to save the tormented lover. They carried him to the house of his widowed mother. When she saw her son, she caught him up in her arms, embracing his cold limbs; she spoke the words of grief so natural to a parent, and mourned as a mother must mourn at such a time. Then through the streets she went, leading a tearful funeral procession, with the death-pale body carried high on his bier, to be laid on a pyre in the town center.

Now it happened that Anaxarete's house looked out onto the street through which the sad procession wound its way. The sound of wailing reached the ears of the proud girl. At the dismal noise, she was moved in spite of herself. She thought, "I'd better go and see what is causing all these tears, this lamentation." Some god of vengeance was driving her on.

Anaxarete climbed the stairs to an upper room, threw open the wide windows, and looked out. Just at that moment, the mournful procession passed by, with the pale body of Iphis on his bier. The instant she caught sight of the young man, her eyes grew stiff, the warm blood cooled in her body, and her face became entirely white. She tried to step back from the window, but she could not move from her place. She tried to turn her face away from the sad sight, but she could not do that either. Slowly, little by little, the stone that had always filled her heart spread over her whole body and petrified her limbs.

Vertumnus ends his tale with these words:

This story is true, and you can see the proof with your own eyes: a marble statue in Salamis, with a temple in her honor that bears the inscription "For the Venus who looks out the window."

Remember this, fair nymph, and be warned by Anaxarete's fate. Put off your pride and disdain, and give your love to the one who loves you. Then the frosts of spring will never come to nip your tender buds, nor rough winds shake the blossoms off your boughs.

A Love
Made of Ivory:
Pygmalion and Galatea

ALL THE GIRLS ON THE ISLAND OF CYPRUS WERE CRAZY about the handsome young sculptor, Pygmalion. Not only was he wonderful to look at, but his talent was astonishing. Nobody could carve ivory or marble as he could, giving the figures a warmth that made them seem as if they were alive, and not just some cold artist's material. Even more intriguing was the fact that Pygmalion would have nothing to do with the girls. None of them embodied his ideal of pure womanhood, and he swore never to marry. His disdain only made the girls of Cyprus more determined to win his attention. But they were doomed to disappointment.

What they didn't know was that his art was all-absorbing to the young sculptor. How could he be interested in mere earthly beauty when there was a world of beauty that so far surpassed the promise of the Earth—a world that he could almost touch when he took his tools in his hand and began to sculpt?

It was this ideal that Pygmalion had in mind when he started to carve an ivory likeness of a woman. It would be the figure of one he had never seen, but only imagined: what the perfection of beauty must be. Day after day he labored over the statue, lovingly cutting and scraping the ivory as he tried to release from its rich tones the essence of female beauty he knew must exist, somewhere.

At last the statue was finished, and Pygmalion regarded it with awe. He felt all the triumph of one who had created a superb work of art. How perfect it was! How surpassingly beautiful it—no, she—appeared! Before the eyes of its maker, the sculpture seemed to glow, even to pulse with life. Nothing could be added or taken away.

The longer Pygmalion stood in admiration of his statue, the more wonderful it seemed to him. She was so lifelike, this woman, this perfection of beauty! If only she had breath, she might speak to him—and oh, if she only could, what would he not say to her? He could tell her anything, and she looked at him as if she could understand everything he meant.

At last Pygmalion was in love, helplessly, passionately in love. But what use is it to love a figure of ivory, cold and smooth as death itself?

And yet she felt more like life to him than death. He had worked the ivory so tenderly, capturing the play of light and shadow across the carved surfaces, that the statue almost had a human warmth. It was too much, this torment of looking at an almost-living figure of perfection. At any moment, he thought, she might step down from her pedestal and speak to him. She was so real to him, he had to give her a name. Galatea. Yes, that was perfect!

The sculptor began to behave in a manner that would have given satisfaction to all those scorned girls of Cyprus, if only they could have seen him. He was paying for his coldness now. Indeed, they might have thought that love had made him mad.

First, he constantly had to touch the ivory to make certain he was not mistaken about what Galatea actually was. Surely this was living flesh! Did he not feel some warmth beneath his hands as he ran them along the ivory arms? Didn't the skin yield to his touch? Now he held her in his arms. Perhaps, he thought, he was too rough, and there would be a bruise!

He kissed her lips, and now and then he fancied that his kisses were returned. He spoke to her and paid her compliments, then waited for her to answer him. But of course, in his saner moments, Pygmalion knew that she could never respond to any of his advances.

Now he began to play with the statue in the way that children play with a doll, pretending she was alive. He brought her little gifts of the kind girls enjoy: shells and polished stones, pet birds and lilies, flowers in every color of the rainbow, painted balls and chunks of amber. He dressed her in beautiful clothing, trying out first one effect and then another, pretending to see which one pleased her more. Jewels of every kind he heaped on her, rings for her fingers, necklaces, earrings.

At night Pygmalion put his Galatea to bed tenderly on a couch of crimson silk with the softest of feather pillows, and tucked her in under a coverlet of purple down. He would pretend that she was his wife and gently say, "Goodnight, my darling!"

But the sculptor was not really insane, and he knew that this behavior was far from normal. At last he acknowledged to himself that he was being ridiculous, and gave up in despair. He loved someone—no, something—that could never return his love, however he might pretend. He was the most wretched of men!

Then came a day of celebration: the feast day of Venus, the goddess of love. This was a time of special rejoicing for Cyprus, because it was on this island that the goddess had landed after being born from the foam of the sea. Everyone was in a festive mood, and they brought to the altars snow-white heifers, garlanded with bright flowers, their horns all tipped with gold. The sweet aroma of incense spread through the air.

Unhappy lovers thronged the temples to beg the goddess for help. Pygmalion too knelt and made his offering. But he was timid. How could he ask for what he really wanted? It was too silly! He phrased his request in the mildest of terms.

"If you can, O goddess," he whispered, "give me a wife ... um, a wife that ... um ..." How could he come right out and say, "Give me my statue for a wife?"

He tried again. "Please," he choked, "O goddess, help me find a wife like my ivory maiden, a girl as lovely as my work of art."

Venus was there beside him, and she understood what Pygmalion was really asking. Her heart was ready to help a young man so devoted to love. Suddenly, the flame on the altar before which he knelt flared up three times, leaping high into the air.

Pygmalion hardly dared to take this sign as a favorable omen, and yet hope sprang in his breast. He had to see if Venus had granted his prayer. The sculptor ran home as fast as he could, back to his statue, his beautiful Galatea. There she stood on her pedestal, in still, ivory perfection.

He touched her arms, and they seemed to have more warmth than they had before, although he could not be sure. Trying her lips with a kiss, he felt certain that there was a tenderness in them beyond what he just imagined. He held her in his arms, and the ivory softened beneath his touch, as wax softens in the warm rays of the sun. This could not be true! But as he gently caressed her, a pulse began to beat beneath her skin.

Imagine the praises he gave to Venus, his prayers of thanksgiving! The lips he was kissing were real lips; Galatea could feel his kisses, and responded to them just as he would wish. She was shy at first, blushing and a little afraid, but as she raised her eyes to his—eyes that were seeing the world for the first time—he knew that she loved him just as he loved her.

Of course, they invited Venus to their wedding, and the goddess was glad to come. She blessed the newly married couple and wished them happiness forever.

Pygmalion, the artist who had held himself aloof from the girls of Cyprus, had found love. And the woman he had created out of ivory had also created him, from flesh—a complete human being at last.

The Princess and the Bull: Europa

ONE MORNING, JUST BEFORE SHE AWOKE, Europa had a strange dream. In the dream, two continents were fighting over her. The first was Asia, who said, "You belong to me because you were born here." The other continent had no name, but it whispered, "Zeus shall give you to me!"

When she awoke, the princess—for Europa was the daughter of the king of Tyre, in Phoenicia—could not shake off the dream. Rising from her bed, she threw open the window and looked out on a bright, sunny day, the most beautiful day so far that spring. She was filled with a joy she could not explain, even to herself. It made her restless.

Europa had to share her feeling of wonder. She called together the noble maidens of the kingdom, her friends and attendants. "Let's go out to the meadows and gather flowers!" she cried, strangely elated. "Somehow, I know that today is going to be special!"

Who could say no to such an invitation? Infected by Europa's excitement, the girls all picked up their baskets and went out merrily into the spring sunshine.

The place they loved most was a green and flowery stretch of meadow that ran along the shore of the bright blue sea. There the girls often went to dance and sing, to bathe in the cool water at the mouth of the river, or pick blossoms. This morning the meadow seemed unbearably beautiful to them, and they exclaimed with joy. Spring had covered the land with a glory they had never seen before. They began to fill their baskets with sweet-smelling flowers: purple and yellow crocus, white narcissus, hyacinths, violets, and the bright crimson wild rose. Soon the colors and scents of the flowers filled the air with their rich beauty.

The blossoms Europa had gathered seemed the most beautiful of all. Her basket was made of gold, wonderfully worked into scenes that depicted the story of her father's ancestor, Io, who had been changed by Zeus into a white cow.

Suddenly Europa's gaze was drawn away from the beauty of her flower-filled basket. Ambling through the meadow toward the girls came not a white cow, but a handsome white bull. His coat gleamed in the spring sunlight, and his horns shone like the crescent moon. Around his brow, the bull wore a circlet of silver.

How could Europa know that this was not a bull at all, but the great god Zeus in disguise? He had been looking down from Olympus, examining the rich lands of Phoenicia, when he spotted the maidens picking flowers in the bright spring sunshine. All of them were as lovely as the blossoms they were gathering, but even so, Europa's beauty shone like the goddess of love herself.

Once again, Zeus had fallen in love. He decided to visit the Earth, where he could meet this wonderful mortal. In order to approach her more naturally—and perhaps to keep his wife Hera from becoming suspicious—Zeus turned himself into the splendid white bull, who seemed to graze innocently on the meadow with the rest of the herd.

Now the bull came trotting up to Europa and the other maidens, looking at them with big soft eyes, and moving so gently that they were not at all afraid. He began to play with them, frisking and making little mock charges, until they were laughing in delight, charmed by this playful animal. They wove wreaths from the flowers they had gathered and hung them about his neck and horns. Giggling, they gave him more of their blossoms to eat.

Europa felt herself oddly drawn to the white bull. When she stroked his gleaming neck, he lowed in tones so musical that all the girls were rapt at the sound. He lay down on the grass and whispered to the princess, "Climb on my back. Don't be afraid. I will take you on a journey you could never imagine." Of course, she was entranced! Although she did not know it, this was the voice of Zeus himself. How could she resist?

Lightly, Europa seated herself on the bull's broad back. At once he leapt to his feet and galloped toward the sea, where he flung himself into the waves. The frightened girl clung to his neck with all her might. Where was he taking her? Terrified, she looked back longingly at the land that was receding so fast, but she didn't dare to jump off the bull's back.

To her amazement, when the bull began to swim, the sea smoothed out in front of him. It seemed that nothing could hinder him. Resigning herself to the inevitable, Europa settled down for a long ride, grasping a long curved horn with one hand, while the other held up her purple dress above the waves to keep it from getting wet.

In the moonlight, dolphins and Nereids rose out of the sea, frolicking around the bull and his rider as they passed over the water. Tritons blew on their horns as they went; even the sea god himself appeared beside them. All night the bull swam, swift and strong, as Europa clung to his horns, and in the morning they landed on a beautiful island. Gently, the bull set Europa down on the sand.

Now at last, the god appeared before her in his own form. "I am Zeus," he told the wondering girl. "I have brought you to Crete, my own island, where my mother hid me after I was born, and where I grew up. I give this land, my favorite place on Earth, to you because I love you. Here you will marry me, and here you will bear glorious sons who will rule over all men of the Earth."

When Zeus had finished speaking, the Seasons came to dress Europa in her bridal clothing. Then Aphrodite appeared, to assure the princess that the god's love for her was not only an honor, but that it would last forever. A whole new part of the world, Aphrodite said, would be named after her.

Zeus gave Europa three wondrous gifts as bridal presents. The first was a spear that could never miss its mark; the second was the unconquerable hound Laelaps, who would always protect her. The last gift was Talos, a man made of bronze, who daily walked around Crete and drove off intruders.

In time, Europa gave birth to three sons, all of whom became great kings on Earth, noted for their justice. Two of them were awarded the eternal position of sitting in Hades as judges of the dead.

The dream of a young princess on that spring morning so long ago had proved to be prophetic. A new continent had indeed won her, and it would forever be called by her name: Europe.

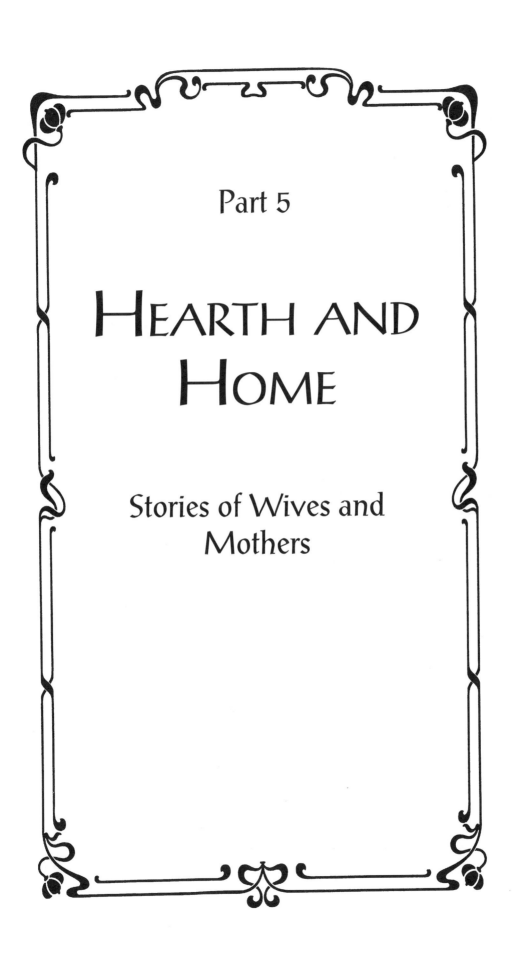

Part 5

Hearth and Home

Stories of Wives and
Mothers

FAITHFUL WIVES

The Goddess of Hearth and Home: Hestia

HESTIA, THE OLDEST OF THE CHILDREN OF CRONOS AND RHEA, STAYED CLOSE TO HOME, ENJOYING the comforts and tranquillity of domestic life. She was the most peace-loving of all the gods and goddesses, the only one who never took any part in war, or even in quarrels. Hestia was revered as the mildest, most merciful, and most upright of all the Olympian deities.

Like Athena and Artemis, Hestia received many offers of marriage; like them, she chose to remain a virgin. At one time, Poseidon and Apollo were rivals for her love, but she turned both of them down, taking an oath by the sacred head of her brother Zeus that she would never marry.

Although she was single, the goddess of the hearth was the symbol of a steady and happy family life. Hestia herself had invented the art of building houses, and in every home she provided protection for those who lived there. Offerings were made to her at the beginning and end of each meal, and newborn babies had to be carried around the house in her honor before they were considered part of the family.

Since public places, too, had hearths, Hestia was also the goddess of public buildings such as the city hall, where citizens could seek her protection. In the public hearth, her fire was sacred, never allowed to go out. If a new colony was formed, the inhabitants carefully carried coals from her fire with them when they moved, so that the sacred hearth of the new city could be lighted by the same fire that had protected the old one.

In Rome, the goddess was called Vesta. The fire of her temple in the Forum was tended by six virgin priestesses, called the Vestals. Vesta's protection was considered so important to the city that if, by any chance, the Vestals let her fire go out, they were punished very severely, while the fire was rekindled by the rays of the sun.

The Constant Wife: Penelope

OF ALL WIVES, THE FAITHFUL PENELOPE MAY HAVE HAD THE HARDEST TRIAL. FOR YEARS SHE HAD TO WONDER: was her husband alive or dead? There was no way she could know. Her husband was the king of Ithaca, the famous warrior Odysseus, who had gone off to fight in the Trojan War, while Penelope stayed behind, as wives did, and waited for him to return.

Her wait called for unusual patience. Odysseus had been gone for twenty years and that was a long time to live with no news at all. Nobody knew what had happened to the great hero. At last, only Penelope and their son Telemachus still believed that he would return to them someday.

And now people were beginning to put pressure on Penelope. After twenty years, they said, it was safe to assume that Odysseus was dead. She must marry again. No woman should live alone, especially one as rich as she had become. For Penelope controlled a great property, much land, and almost endless herds of cattle.

But when she thought about her life, both past and future, Penelope's mind was filled only with love for her husband. She remembered how Odysseus had come to woo her when she was just a girl, a princess of Sparta. Many young men had wanted to marry her, but she had made her choice. It could only be Odysseus for her.

The day of their marriage arrived, and everyone was pleased. At the very last moment, when the time had come for her to leave home, her father, Icarius, begged her not to go. He could not, he said, bear to part with his beloved daughter. Odysseus gave her the choice: she could stay with her father or go with her husband. That was easy; Penelope had already decided what her future was to be. She said nothing, but she dropped her veil over her face, and her father knew what she had chosen. She would stay with her husband forever.

They had been married for just a year when the Trojan War began, and Odysseus had to leave his home and his young wife. The night before he went away, he took Penelope in his arms.

"I know you will be lonely," he said, "but hold these words to your heart. I love you most tenderly, and will think of you every day. All I ask of you is to remain faithful to me and wait for me to return to you.

"However long it takes me," he added, "I will come home to you. That's a promise."

Soon after Odysseus had gone, Penelope gave birth to their son, Telemachus. Now she wanted only one thing: for her husband to come home and see his son, for them to be together once more.

So, no matter how long it had been, Penelope could not even think of marrying again. It didn't matter to her how many people tried to persuade her, to whisper in her ear about this suitor or that, and how happy she would be if she would choose him, or him. She held fast to her belief that Odysseus was alive and would return to her someday. All she wanted to do was wait for him.

But now her house was in a state of siege; suitors had come from all the islands and the country around to win Penelope's consent to marry them. She detested every one of them, and would have nothing to do with them, but they refused to leave. She was fighting a war of her own, one that was hard for a woman to win.

Penelope's suitors spent week after week living in the palace, courting her—or so they said. In fact, they acted as if it were one long party for them, and a very unmannerly party at that. They seemed to have no standards of behavior at all. How could they imagine she would be interested in any of them when they behaved so rudely, destroying her property, getting drunk every night, going against all the rules of courtesy? They acted as if they owned the place! They gave orders to the servants, they broke up the furniture, and day after day they slaughtered her husband's cattle for their huge feasts, cutting down his woodlands to make the fires that cooked his beasts. They even threatened the life of young Telemachus. The suitors swore they would never leave until Penelope agreed to marry one of them.

Penelope and Telemachus felt powerless against such a violent crew of men. What could a woman and a boy do to hold them off? Desperately she stalled for time, until at last she thought of a ruse.

"I cannot even dream of marrying again," she said, "until I have performed my last and most sacred duty to my husband's family. I must weave a perfect piece of cloth, a shroud magnificent enough for my husband's father to be buried in, when his time comes to die."

Every day, Penelope sat at her loom, weaving the beautiful fabric, and the suitors could see her hard at work. And every night, when they were asleep, she unwove the cloth she had made that day. A good trick, but it couldn't work forever. The suitors became suspicious when they noticed that the shroud seemed to grow no larger. Finally, a serving woman told them the whole truth, how her mistress labored through the night to undo the threads she had so painstakingly woven during the day.

At this, the suitors lost all patience. They demanded that Penelope make up her mind to marry one of them, and if she didn't do it soon, they would choose one for her and force her to marry him. And they became ruder and more destructive than ever.

Although nobody yet knew it, Odysseus was indeed alive. He had been trying to reach home ever since the war had ended. At last the gods had taken pity on him, and after his years of wandering through the world, they brought him to the shores of Ithaca, his homeland. Athena appeared to him in a dream, in which she warned him about what was happening. He needed to be cautious, she said, and advised him to disguise himself as a beggar before he approached the palace. Then he could avoid suspicion, and find out for himself what he must do.

In the morning, the goddess brought Odysseus's son, Telemachus, to his side so that father and son could know each other at last. Delighted by their meeting, they agreed to work together to cleanse their house of the unwanted suitors.

When the two men reached the palace—Odysseus dressed in rags, with his hair and beard all wild and uncombed—they found the suitors still in place, wildly eating and drinking, as usual. At the sight of the tattered old beggar, all the men laughed uproariously, sneering at his age and the way he was dressed.

But when she heard what was going on downstairs, Penelope was angry. However poor and ragged, no one should be insulted in her house as that old man had been. She sent for him, and asked him who he was and how he had arrived in Ithaca. She did not recognize her husband—after all, it had been twenty years since she had seen him.

"In Troy," the beggar said, "I met the king Odysseus. He asked me to visit Ithaca, where his wife would offer me hospitality."

Weeping, Penelope recounted the story of her husband's disappearance, and how bitterly she missed him, how she had never given up hope that he would return. Somehow, she felt compelled to confide in this man, but still she did not realize who he was.

Now the moment of crisis had arrived. Ever since the suitors had learned the truth about Penelope's weaving, they had become completely uncontrollable. At last the queen had reached a point of utter despair. How could she hold them off any longer? If she didn't agree to marry one of them, they would destroy everything—her son, her husband's palace, lands, livestock, everything!

Desperate, she called them all together. "I have something to tell you," she said quietly, "something that I think must be an omen. Last night I had a dream, a very odd dream. I saw an eagle kill twenty geese. Who knows what such a dream might mean?

"It made me think, though, and I have come to a decision. I will marry whichever of you can win an archery contest. My husband, Odysseus, owned a great bow and a set of keen arrows that nobody else has ever been able to use. No one has ever had the strength to pull back the bow, and no one has ever been able to hit the target he used to practice with. But if one of you can, I will become his wife."

Penelope hung up a row of twelve axes to dangle from the ceiling, each with an open ring in its handle. She swore she would give her hand to the man who sent one of the arrows through all twelve rings using her husband's bow.

The suitors were eager to try their skill, for the reward was great. In turn, each of them tried to string the bow; in turn each failed. Not one had the strength to pull back its great weight. They agreed to postpone the contest until the next morning. Then, they thought, they would feel stronger, and one of them surely would be able to do this simple task!

Imagine their laughter when the old beggar spoke up from his place in the corner. "Every man in the room has had his chance at this contest; I should be given my turn, too!" Then imagine their dismay when he pulled the bow with ease and sent his arrow flying through all twelve rings without even touching their sides!

Suddenly, the old man, who for some strange reason looked younger now, turned his arrows toward the suitors. With his son Telemachus handing him the arrows, Odysseus killed each of the men in turn, finally cleansing his house of their rudeness and impieties.

Now Odysseus could go to his wife and tell her who he was. At first, Penelope did not understand. She had waited so long for this moment—and he was so much older than the husband she remembered! How could she believe what she so much wanted to believe? But when he told her what only her husband could know—how he had carved their marriage bed himself, out of a great branching olive tree—she knew that this was indeed Odysseus, come home at last. She rejoiced.

The couple kissed and embraced each other. "Nobody," he said, "has had a wife more loyal, more true, more loving than you, Penelope. I count myself luckiest among men." And they talked the night through, telling each other everything that had happened during the years they had been apart.

Then Odysseus told Penelope what the old seer Tiresias had predicted for him. There would be many more travels ahead of him, but death would come to him gently, after an easy old age. And husband and wife would be together for the rest of their days.

The Devoted Couple:
Alcyone and Ceyx

N O COUPLE HAD EVER BEEN MORE DEVOTED TO EACH OTHER THAN ALCYONE AND HER BELOVED husband, Ceyx. She was the daughter of Aeolus, who controls the winds, keeping them imprisoned in a cave and releasing them whenever he wishes or the gods command him to. Ceyx was the son of the morning star, and king of Thessaly, a peaceful and just ruler.

Since the day this couple married, they had never willingly parted from one another. But a time came when Ceyx knew he had to undertake a journey. His mind was deeply troubled; strange things had happened that made him uneasy about what lay in store for his kingdom. For one, his warlike brother, Daedalion, grieving for his daughter's death, had been transformed into a hawk. There had been other portents too, and Ceyx feared for the future. He knew he had to travel to Claros, to consult the oracle of Apollo and learn if the gods were hostile to him, and, if they were, find out what he must do to appease them.

When he told Alcyone his plans, she was stricken with terror. Her bones felt as cold as ice, her face turned pale as the boxwood leaf, her cheeks were wet with tears. Three times she tried to speak, but three times she could get no words out, for crying.

At last she managed to say: "Oh, my dear, what have I done to turn your heart away from me? You used to care for me above anything! What's happened to that love? How can you leave me so calmly? You're going away from me; the journey will be long, yet you seem happy.

"I'm so frightened of this trip! If you were going by land, I would be sad, but the very idea of a sea voyage fills me with terror. Just yesterday, when I was walking on the beach, I saw piles of wreckage from broken ships, and above the shoreline there were rows of empty tombs, with the names of sailors written on them.

"Don't feel confident just because my father rules the winds. Once he lets them loose, even he can't control them. Then both land and sea are at their mercy, and in the sky they quarrel and collide, sending red lightning flying all across the heavens. I often saw them in my father's house when I was a little girl, and I know them too well.

"If you are determined to go, take me with you, I beg you. Side by side, we can face the storms, and I'll be able to bear what happens because we're together. If you go without me, I'll suffer so much worse from imagining the agonies you might be going through!"

Her husband was deeply moved by Alcyone's words, but he could not give up his journey, and he could not bear to expose her to such danger. Unable to soothe her fears, he said at last, "Every hour we're apart seems like a lifetime, I know. But by the fires of my father, the morning star, I swear I will return to you before the moon has made its way around the sky twice."

Alcyone was comforted by this promise, but when she saw the ship fitted out and ready to sail, she was again filled with premonitions, again she shuddered and wept. She held Ceyx in her arms and managed to whisper only one word: "Farewell!"

Ceyx could delay no longer; he had to board the ship. The crew was young and eager to be underway, and they pulled hard at the oars. Alcyone could see her husband standing in the stern, waving to her, and as she watched, his figure grew smaller and smaller until it faded out of sight. Still she stood, staring out to sea until the ship dropped below the horizon. Then, with a leaden heart, she made her way back home, where she lay down on her bed and wept. She was already lonely: part of her life, part of her very self, it seemed, was gone.

The ship had cleared the harbor and was heading out to sea in a freshening wind. The captain gave orders to pull in the oars and spread the sails wide. By nightfall they were halfway across, when the waves began to roughen and rise, and the sea to whiten. "Lower the yards and reef the sail!" the captain shouted, but the wind had grown so strong and the ocean so loud that his words were carried away. Some of the crew had sense enough to fasten down the oars and close the portholes; one or two tried to lower the sails; some frantically began to bail out the water that was pouring into the ship.

Everything was confusion as the wind kept rising and the waves grew high as hills. In the darkness, the captain lost his bearings entirely. Even he was terrified. He admitted that he had no idea what shape the ship was in, and he could give no orders. The storm itself was in control. Nothing could be heard over the terrible din: the shouts of the men, the clatter of the rigging, winds roaring, waves crashing, and thunder like cannon fire. The sea seemed to break against the skies, the very clouds wet from its spray. The water turned yellow with sand swept up from the seabed, then black as the River Styx. Over it all spread white sheets of foam.

The only master of the ship now was chance. At one moment they seemed to be on a mountaintop, looking down into the yawning gorges of the Underworld; at the next, they thought they were in the pit of Hell itself, looking up at the heights of Heaven. Waves struck the sides of the ship like a battering ram against a fortress. Now the decks began to crack, the ship's seams to break open. Rain fell from the sky in sheets, as if Heaven and sea were one. Not a star shone, and the storm's blackness only made the darkness of night more absolute, except when flashes of lightning reddened the sky and lit up the waves.

Nine times the sea had battered at the sides of the ship, but the tenth wave proved to be its final thrust. Water filled the hold, and everyone saw that this was death. One man began to cry, another sat dazed and silent; one thought enviously of landsmen who could receive a proper burial, one called on the gods in prayer; many shouted the names of their children, parents, brothers, and sisters.

But Ceyx had only one thought: Alcyone. Even though he felt agony at their separation, he gave thanks that she was not sharing his fate. He wanted to turn his face toward her, but in the darkness and chaos of the storm, he couldn't tell which way home lay.

Now the whirling wind shattered mast and rudder, and one last wave, tall as a mountain, crashed down on the ship and sent it to the bottom of the sea, not to rise again. Most of the crew went down with it, or were sucked under by the whirlpool, except for a few who clutched at fragments from the wreck. Ceyx himself grasped a plank in his hand, the hand that once had held a scepter. In vain he cried for help from his father and from his wife's father; but mostly his lips called out the name of Alcyone. His last fervent prayer was that the waves might carry his body to her so that her beloved hands could prepare him for burial. As long as he had breath, he murmured her name, until at last a huge black wave towered over him, salt water filled his mouth, and he was drowned.

Of course, Alcyone knew nothing of this. She was counting the days until Ceyx would come home, keeping herself busy by weaving cloth to make a robe for him to wear, and another for herself to put on in celebration when he returned. Every day she burned incense to all the gods that live in the heavens, but most of all she offered petitions to Juno. She knelt before the goddess's altar to pray that her husband would come back safely and that he would never love another woman, but remain faithful to her. Of these wishes, only the second would be granted.

Juno could no longer stand all these sad prayers for a man already dead. Those hands should be mourning, not praying at her altar. Calling for the rainbow goddess Iris, Juno said, "Trusty friend and honored messenger, please do me a favor. Fly down to the drowsy hall where Sleep lies heavy-eyed in bed. When you find him, tell him to send Alcyone a dream of Ceyx, showing her the very image of her drowned husband, to let her know what has happened to him." Iris, clad in her mantle of a thousand colors, arched down through the sky to seek the palace beneath the clouds where the sleep king reigned.

Far, far down under the mountains of Cimmeria lies a cavern that is the home and hiding place of lazy Sleep. The sun's beams never penetrate the shadows of this cave— morning, noon, or evening—only a dim twilight, shrouded in mists. No cock crows in the morning to wake the sleepers, no dog barks, no goose cackles, no cow lows. The boughs of trees do not stir and rustle; people do not speak in human voices. Silence alone dwells there. From the base of the rock trickles a small stream, carrying the waters of Lethe over a shallow bed of pebbles to murmur "Sleep!" and again, "Sleep!" At the mouth of the cave, above damp ferns and grasses, grow poppies and other herbs whose juices are scattered nightly to sprinkle sleep across the darkening Earth.

The cavern has no door with hinges that could creak, no guardian at the entrance. In the center of dark, velvet-draped walls stands a high couch of ebony, all downy and soft, with a sable comforter. And here lies Sleep himself, stretched out in languor on the counterpane. Around him drift insubstantial forms, empty dreams, as numerous as the ears of wheat at harvesttime, as leaves on the trees, or grains of sand along the seashore.

Iris entered the cave and brushed the dreams aside. Her gleaming robes cast a radiance into the darkness, waking the god, who lifted his heavy eyelids with some difficulty. His head nodding in drowsiness, he asked her why she had come.

"O quiet god," Iris addressed him, "gentlest god, who brings peace to all the Earth and comfort to the hurting soul, rest for the weary body, and renewal of our strength so that we can meet tomorrow, Juno sends an urgent request. Make an image of King Ceyx and let him appear to his widowed queen in a dream, to tell her of the shipwreck that drowned him."

After she delivered her message, Iris left the cavern as quickly as she could get away, for she felt drowsiness stealing over her. She soared back up the rainbow arch by which she had come down. Then, from among his thousand sons, Sleep chose Morpheus, who can take any shape he wishes, to carry out these commands. The god himself instantly sank back down in slumber.

Wasting no time, Morpheus flew to Alcyone's chamber, where she lay sleeping. He laid aside his wings and stood at the foot of her bed, taking on the form of Ceyx, naked and deathly pale, water streaming down his beard and hair, and his eyes flowing with tears.

"My poor wife," this image whispered, "do you recognize your husband? Look at me—I am your husband's ghost, not the living man. Your prayers were not answered; you must give up your hopes. I am dead, drowned in a storm in the Aegean Sea. I died calling your name, Alcyone. Rise! Put on mourning clothes and weep for me so that I will not join the spirits of the Underworld unlamented."

In her sleep, Alcyone wept. Then her own voice woke her. She was calling out, "Wait for me! Let me come with you!"

Her servants, roused by her cries, saw her beating her breast and tearing her clothes, and tried to comfort her. But she sobbed, "Alcyone is gone, she is nothing, she died with her beloved Ceyx! Don't try to comfort me—I saw him with my own eyes, changed and pale, my husband's ghost! Oh, Ceyx, why didn't you take me with you on that terrible journey? It would have been better for us both if I had sailed with you, so that death could not come between us! But I will not live on to suffer such grief! Even though our bones can't lie together, I will join you now!"

Sadly Alcyone rose, and seeing that morning had come, she made her way down to the seashore. When she found the place where she had stood to watch her husband sail away, she relived that last day, thinking, "It was just here that they cast off, and here that he kissed me good-bye."

As she stood gazing out to sea, Alcyone caught sight of something floating far out on the waves. It looked like a body, and suddenly she felt certain that it was a man who had drowned in a shipwreck. The omen moved her to tears of pity. "Alas, poor soul, I grieve for you, and for your unhappy wife, if you are married," she murmured. The body floated in toward the shore, and as it drifted closer, she knew him. It was Ceyx! "Oh, my dearest love, must you come home to me this way?" she called to him. "Wait! I'm coming for you!"

Running out on a jetty built to break the force of the waves, Alcyone leaped into the sea. But she never fell. Before she could touch the water, she found herself skimming the surface on newly sprouted wings. Her sad cries of mourning came, birdlike, from a slender bill. When she reached the lifeless body of her husband, she embraced it in her wings and tried to kiss the cold lips with her hard beak.

Nobody knows exactly what happened then. Was it the waves that made him lift up his face, or had Ceyx felt Alcyone's kiss? Whichever it was, he too rose, flying. The gods had taken pity on this loving couple, and had changed them both. They had become beautiful birds, the kingfishers.

Now they are together again as one, although so strangely transformed. Their love lives on, and their strong bonds. They breed and rear their young, and each year, in the winter season, they are given seven days of peaceful weather. This is the time when Alcyone broods over her nest, floating on the surface of the water, which lies calm and quiet.

Aeolus watches over his grandchildren: for these halcyon days of calm, he keeps his winds in chains and forbids storms to trouble the seas.

Hosts to the Gods: Baucis and Philemon

UP ON THE PHRYGIAN HILLS, AN OAK TREE AND A linden grow, so close their branches interlace and their trunks seem as one. Around them stands a low wall of stone. Nearby, the land is marshy, with stagnant pools and fens. Once this area was habitable, but now it is all water, the playground of ducks, of coots and diving birds.

At this place, a long time ago, Jupiter came to Earth dressed as a mortal. With him came his son Mercury, who had also laid aside divine garments, his wand, and his wings. In this disguise the gods went from house to house, pretending to be weary travelers looking for rest and food. They stopped at a thousand homes, and a thousand homes were bolted tight against them. No welcome could they find anywhere, no words of kindness or offers of refuge for wanderers.

But at last one house opened its doors to them. It was a tiny cottage, thatched with reeds and straw. Here they were greeted warmly by a kind old couple, the good Baucis and her husband Philemon. These two had joined their lives in marriage when they were very young, and had grown old together in this same cottage. Although they were poor, the couple had a cheerful spirit; they made light of their hardships and bore poverty with content. To them it seemed no shame to be poor. They were rich in love and honesty. They had no servants, but did all the work themselves.

The two gods had to stoop to enter the low doorway of the little home. Pulling out a rustic bench, which Baucis first covered with a simple homespun cloth, Philemon begged them to rest their weary limbs. The good wife stirred up the ashes of yesterday's fire in the hearth, and fanned the embers to revive their heat. On the embers she laid leaves and bark, blowing the sparks to flame with a feeble breath. Then she took kindling, fine-split wood and little twigs, which she broke up over her knee, and built a good roaring fire.

Over the fire there hung a little copper pot. Into it Baucis put a cabbage her husband had harvested from their well-tended garden, first stripping off the outer leaves. With a forked stick, Philemon lifted down from the smoke-darkened beams overhead a side of bacon, one they had been saving up for a long time. From it he cut a portion of meat to add to the boiling pot.

While the food was cooking, the old couple helped the time pass pleasantly in conversation with their unknown visitors. A beechwood bowl hung from the wall on a peg, and they filled it with warm water for their guests to wash and refresh themselves after their travels. Then Philemon and Baucis brought out an old couch, whose frame and feet were of willow. On it they put a soft cushion stuffed with sedge grass from the nearby marsh, and spread over that an antique cloth, which they used only on great occasions. It hadn't cost much when it was new, and it had worn thin over the years, but it was their very best, and they didn't hesitate to offer it for the comfort of their guests.

As the gods reclined on the couch, Baucis went about setting the table, with her skirts tucked up so that she would not trip over them. Her hands trembled as she worked. The table wobbled a little because one leg was short, but she placed a broken piece of pottery under it to make it steady. Then she scoured the table clean and fresh-smelling with a handful of green mint.

On the table, Baucis placed olives, both black and green, cherries preserved in wine, endive and radishes, creamy cheese, and eggs that had been lightly roasted in the ashes of the fire. The dishes were all of earthenware, and the bowl for the wine was made of the same inexpensive material. The goblets were carved of beechwood, coated inside with wax.

Soon the hot food was ready, and the couple brought out more wine—not a very good vintage, but the best they had. The gods set to this meal with hearty appetites. Before long Baucis had to clear the table for the second course, which consisted of nuts, dried figs and wrinkled dates, plums and apples piled in wide baskets, purple grapes just gathered off the vine, and in the middle, almost hidden, a pale and gleaming honeycomb dripping with sweetness. All this good food was made even tastier by the willing generosity and kindness of the hosts. There was nothing skimpy or poor in that! Smiling faces beamed all around the table.

But now the hosts noticed that something very strange was happening. As soon as the cups were brimming and the wine bowl was empty, it filled up again, all by itself. The frightened old couple guessed at once that their visitors were not what they seemed to be. They must be gods!

Trembling, Baucis and Philemon raised their hands and prayed, "Oh, please, forgive us for our humble home and the simple food we've given you!" Eager to make their offering more acceptable, they determined to sacrifice their prized possession: their one goose, which they kept as guardian of their little estate. But the goose ran too fast for the two old people to catch, and as they grew exhausted from chasing it, it flew to the deities for protection.

"Don't kill the goose!" Jupiter cried. He continued, "You must know by now, we are indeed gods. Everyone in this wicked neighborhood is going to pay a stiff price for their meanness, their terrible lack of generosity. Don't be alarmed; you will not be hurt. But you must leave your house and come along with us, up to the mountaintop."

The two old people obeyed and laboriously followed the gods. With the help of their walking sticks, they went slowly, slowly up the side of the mountain, reaching as close to the peak as one shot from an archer's bow would take the arrow. When they turned around to look below, they were astonished. The land was flooded, everything covered with water except their own little house. They wept for their friends and neighbors.

But as they stood marveling, the old cottage began to change right before their eyes. It had been small even for the two of them, but now it became larger and larger. At last it turned into a shining temple. The wooden props that had supported it were now marble columns, and the yellow thatch of the roof grew yellower still, until it was pure gold. The low doors were richly carved gates, and the ground that had been bare was paved with marble.

Jupiter spoke to Baucis and Philemon in gentle tones. "Tell us, good old man and good old woman, you who are so faithful and so worthy of each other, what might be your dearest wish? Ask us any favor, and we will grant it to you with pleasure."

The old couple conferred quietly for a few minutes. What did they most wish? Then Philemon answered for them both.

"What we would like is to be named priests, to become the guardians and caretakers of your temple. And since we have lived together so long and happily, we have one more dear desire. Please let us die together, so that neither of us ever has to bury the other, or see the other's grave."

Their wish was granted. Baucis and Philemon watched over the temple for many years, as long as life was given to them.

One day, when they had grown very old indeed, they were standing just before the temple steps, talking about times past. Suddenly each of them saw the other begin to sprout leaves. As the crowns of trees grew over their heads, they reached toward each other, and while they still had words to speak, they said, "Farewell, dearest love!" Then bark closed around them, sealing their lips.

Today the peasants of that district still love to point out to strangers two trees, a linden and an oak, growing, it seems, from a single trunk.

Faithful to Death:
Egeria, Evadne, and Alcestis

Egeria

In a fountain in Italy lived a water nymph named Egeria, who was as smart as she was beautiful. Numa, the second king of Rome, fell in love with her, and she became his source of wisdom as well as his wife. The nymph and her husband would meet by night for secret conferences, at which she instructed him in statesmanship and religion. Through these lessons, Egeria taught her husband how to turn the savage, war-loving people of the new nation into those who love peacefulness and law.

When Numa died of old age, all the people of Rome mourned for him. Egeria was inconsolable. She left the city and hid herself deep in a forest, where her pitiful moans shook the shrine to Diana. In vain the other nymphs tried to console her; in vain people told her tales of others' sorrows to make her feel less alone. Egeria only cried harder, and threw herself at the foot of the mountain, dissolving in tears.

At last Diana took pity on her. The goddess changed Egeria's flowing eyes into a clear, cooling fountain, and her slender body, stained and drenched with weeping, became a river that flows forever, like her tears.

Evadne

Famous far and wide for wifely devotion, Evadne was married to Capaneus, one of the Athenians who attacked the city of Thebes. When Zeus heard Capaneus boast that he would make his way into the city in spite of the god's will, he struck with his mighty thunderbolt, destroying Capaneus right there on the ladder he was mounting.

After the battle, all the dead warriors were placed on a funeral pyre, which was lit and fanned into bright flames. Suddenly, on the heights above, appeared the figure of a woman. It was Evadne. Crying "Death is sweet when I die with the one I love," she leaped from the cliff into the blazing pyre. Now Evadne could go with her husband into the Underworld, where they would be together forever.

Alcestis

A happier ending was reserved for Alcestis, a wife whose name resounds with heroic self-sacrifice.

When the time was ripe for Alcestis to marry, her father imposed a strange condition. He would, he said, give her hand only to a man who came for her driving a chariot harnessed to a lion and a boar.

With the help of the god Apollo, the Thessalian king, Admetus, accomplished this astounding feat. An angry Zeus had sentenced Apollo to live on Earth for a time as a mortal and a slave, and for the past year the god had served Admetus as his herdsman. He had come to cherish his kind master, and helped him in any way he could.

Admetus claimed Alcestis for his own, and the couple drove off happily in the chariot, still drawn by the lion and the boar. Their marriage was blessed with healthy children and great love between the two partners.

But there came a sad time. Admetus fell deathly ill, and no remedies could heal him. The Fates were about to snip the thread of his life when Apollo once more intervened on his behalf. He begged the Fates to change the course of destiny, and they consented, but only on one condition. "Let him find someone who will agree to die in his place," they said, "and we will let Admetus off, for now."

Hearing this, the king rejoiced. At once he began to search for a person who would accept such an exchange. How strange that he found none! His friends begged him not to ask them, saying, "Even though we love you, dear friend, we find we love life better." His servants looked the other way when he came near, and became very busy.

At last, Admetus approached his mother and father, who were both very old, already at death's door themselves. Surely they loved him enough to be taken in his place! But both parents refused to give up what was left of their own lives for their son.

Deeply disappointed, Admetus returned home, where his beloved Alcestis was waiting for him. As soon as she saw him, she said, "I will gladly die for you, my husband." In horror he cried out, "No! Not you, my love! Never would I let you make such a sacrifice!"

But it was too late. The condition of the Fates had been met. Someone had agreed to exchange her life for his.

Alcestis began to sicken. She grew pale and weak, while Admetus sat by her side weeping. The queen begged, "I only ask one thing, my dearest husband. When I have died, don't marry again; don't give our children a stepmother, for she might not treat them well."

He promised that in all his life he would have only one wife, his cherished Alcestis. When she received that word of comfort, she died. Beating his breast in grief, Admetus dressed himself in mourning clothes and began to prepare for her funeral.

As luck would have it, at just that moment the hero Heracles knocked at the door. The rules of hospitality decreed that the king must admit him and offer food and entertainment, never letting his guest know the sad situation in the house. Although the hero questioned his host about his reddened eyes and his mourning garments, Admetus would say only that a woman, a stranger, had died within the house.

After the grieving king left for the funeral, Heracles sat on, blithely eating and drinking— a little too much, if truth be known. He began to behave in a generally rowdy way. Finally, one of the servants could stand it no more, and scolded him.

"How can you be so obnoxious? Anyone can plainly see that we are all in mourning for our dear queen, who has just died!"

Heracles was horrified to learn the truth of the situation. His behavior, he realized, was indeed inexcusable. He must make amends for what he had done. He thought hard. Suddenly he grabbed the servant.

"Which way has Death gone?" he shouted, and, hearing that Death had left the house only a short while ago, he ran off in pursuit.

The next morning, Admetus sat alone outside his house, weeping for his lost wife. Looking up, he saw Heracles coming down the road, leading a veiled woman by the hand. They drew up before the king.

"Admetus," the hero said softly, "will you forgive me for my rudeness by taking this woman in marriage?"

The king was thunderstruck. Such a request, at such a time! He thought of his love for Alcestis and his promise to her. Besides, this veiled figure was very disturbing, for she had much the same shape and the same way of carrying herself as his wife. He began to refuse, angrily. At that moment, her veil flew off and he recognized the loved figure of Alcestis herself, brought back from the dead.

For three days she could not speak. She could barely move, but gradually life flowed back into the body of Alcestis, the queen who had given her very life for her husband. Now she was restored to him, and they lived together for many long happy years.

LOVING MOTHERS

Goddess of the Earth and Fruitfulness: Demeter and Persephone

O F ALL THE GODDESSES ON MOUNT OLYMPUS, DEMETER WAS THE GENTLEST, THE KINDEST, THE most helpful to mortals. It was she who brought forth the growing things of Earth, the plants and trees, the grasses and flowers. Most of all, Demeter gave the gift of grain, golden wheat that women could grow and harvest to make into bread, the great giver of life.

Demeter had one daughter, the lovely Persephone, whom she loved more dearly than anything in the world. The girl was like the spring itself, warm and rosy, and so happy that she gladdened the hearts of everyone who saw her. Because her daughter was both beautiful and innocent, Demeter knew that she would be attractive to gods and men alike. The mother watched over her closely.

But one fine morning, she gave Persephone permission to join a group of friends who wanted to celebrate the beautiful day. Carrying their baskets, the girls joyfully went out to gather flowers in their favorite meadow, which lay in a green valley beside a wooded lake. There it is always spring; the hot rays of the noonday sun never penetrate, and the cool ground is covered with blossoms, wildflowers of every kind. Persephone had wandered a little away from her companions, filling her basket and her apron with lilies and violets, when she spotted the most beautiful flower of all. It was a narcissus, dark blue, with a hundred blooms springing from its root, and a scent like Heaven itself.

Just as Persephone reached out her hand to pick the flower, the earth suddenly opened wide, and out of the gaping hole burst Hades, the god of the Underworld, driving a golden chariot drawn by blue-black steeds. He took Persephone by the wrist and pulled her up beside him. Then he turned his horses back toward the land of the dead. The girl screamed for help, "Mother! Mother!" But although the hills and the seas echoed her cries, nobody heard her. Only the Sun saw what was happening.

Hades spurred on his horses, calling each by name. Faster and faster he sped, until he reached a curving bay. There a water nymph named Cyane bravely tried to stop him. Raising herself waist-high out of the water, she cried, "Sir, you shall not pass this way! You cannot become a son-in-law of Demeter against her will. Persephone deserves a better wedding, with a gentle courtship, not to be taken off by force!" She put out her arms to stop him, but Hades only looked at her with rage. Then he took out his royal scepter and flung it to the depths of the pool. The Earth sprang open, and the chariot plunged down into the deep abyss, all the way to Hell.

Persephone found herself in the dark realm of Death. Bitterly she mourned the loss of her flowers, of the fresh air and sunshine, of all the good things of Earth. Most of all, the unhappy girl longed for her mother. She wept and sighed, and would touch no food.

When Demeter learned of her daughter's disappearance, she was terrified. She began to search for Persephone, looking through every land, into every sea, the world over. Nothing could stop her, not the morning dews that soaked her hair nor the setting sun of evening. She lit two torches at Mount Etna, and guided only by their light, went on through the frosty dark. For nine days and nine nights she searched, refusing to eat or drink all that time.

At last Demeter came to Cyane's clear pool. The nymph would have told her where her daughter had been taken, but alas, she could not say what she had witnessed. Grieving at Persephone's fate and her own inability to help the girl, Cyane had wept and wept inconsolably, until she had melted and mingled with the waters of her pool. Now she could no longer speak at all. All she could do was to show Demeter Persephone's sash, which had come off in her passage through the pool.

That was enough to make the goddess suspect the truth. Searching ever more frantically, Demeter met Hecate, who knew of the abduction and led her to the Sun, Helios, the only witness to Hades's deed. He told her the whole story.

"Zeus consented to the marriage," he said. "He didn't consult you because he knew you would never agree to a wedding between your daughter and Hades, never agree to let her live underground forever. Zeus himself planted a flower so unusual that it would be sure to entice Persephone away from her companions.

"And I agree with him," Helios went on. "The marriage is very suitable. After all, Hades is the brother of the great god. What better match could you ask for?"

But Demeter was stricken with grief. How could her beautiful, springlike girl—the daughter of the Earth goddess herself—live in the dark shades of the dead, away from the light, from growing things? It was horrible, unthinkable!

In her anger, the goddess turned on the Earth that had allowed such a thing to happen. She cursed the land, breaking the ploughs that turn the soil, and killing both farmers and their cattle. She ordered the tilled fields to betray their duty, to spoil the seeds, to lie completely barren. Crops died as soon as they were planted, either from too much sun or too much rain; stars and winds both turned hostile; birds gobbled up the planted seeds; weeds overran the fields and choked out the crops.

Now Arethusa, the nymph who had been turned into a spring, rose from the water, shaking her streaming hair from her eyes, to beg mercy for the Earth.

"Don't be angry at the land, divine Mother," she pleaded. "It is innocent. Hades alone is responsible for Persephone's fate. I saw him cut a passageway to the Underworld and drive her there. Her face was wet with tears and had a look of terror, but she held herself like a queen. You would have been proud of her."

But the nymph pleaded in vain; Demeter was inconsolable. In her grief she left Olympus, to dwell in disguise among the mortals, wandering from place to place. For a year, she refused to allow the Earth to be fruitful. Nothing grew anywhere; no green sprouts broke the soil, no ripening grain made the countryside rich with golden promise. It seemed as if all of mankind were doomed to die of famine.

Zeus was worried. He sent each of the gods in turn to beg Demeter to return to Olympus, offering her gifts if she would only relent. She would listen to none of them. "Never," she swore, "never will I set foot on Olympus, never will I let any crops spring out of the ground, never will I make the grass and trees and flowers grow again! Not unless I have my daughter back!"

At last Zeus realized that he himself must intervene. If the race of mankind died out, who would there be to make sacrifices to the gods? An unthinkable situation! Since Demeter was adamant, he would have to get Persephone back for her.

There was, however, one thing over which even Zeus had no control. Long ago, the Fates had decreed that anyone who ate or drank in the Underworld could never return to the land of the living. If Persephone had eaten anything while she was there, Zeus himself was powerless to help.

Hermes, the messenger of the gods, was sent to the Underworld with orders to persuade Hades that he must let Persephone go. The god of the dead really had no choice when it was Zeus who commanded. He begged his wife to reconsider. "It's no shame to be married to me," he urged. "After all, I am one of the great gods! Why shouldn't you think kindly of me?" When she refused even to look at him, Hades was forced to agree to release the girl.

Imagine her happiness! At last she would see the sun again, and the beautiful Earth. Best of all, she would be with her mother. Hermes helped the joyful girl into the golden carriage. Just as they were about to leave, Hades said, "You must be hungry! Here, take this pomegranate." Absently, Persephone accepted the fruit. Then Hermes drove the black horses up, up through the Earth, right to the temple where Demeter was eagerly awaiting her daughter's arrival.

The goddess rushed out to meet her. With a cry of joy she took her daughter in her arms. At once, all of the seeds that were lying sterile in the ground began to sprout; the trees bore leaves and flowers; sunshine warmed the cold soil. Then Demeter begged Persephone to tell her everything that had happened during her long adventure.

After the girl had finished her story, her mother asked anxiously, "Did you eat anything while you were down there?"

At first Persephone denied it. "No, no, I was too sad to eat!" she answered. Then she remembered the pomegranate Hades had given her, and how she had nibbled at it while Hermes drove. "Well," she added, "I had nothing but four little pomegranate seeds."

Just four seeds—but that was enough to doom her. Zeus could not override the will of the Fates. Still, knowing what Demeter would do if Persephone were returned to Hades, he worked out a compromise that everyone had to agree to. Persephone would have to live in the Underworld for four months of every year, one month for each of the seeds she had eaten. The other eight months she could spend with her mother above the ground.

Now, each year when Persephone leaves for her sojourn in the Underworld, the flowers die, grain ceases to grow, trees sadly drop their leaves, and Earth turns cold and barren. Four months later, when she returns, she brings the spring with her. Once more the Earth becomes fruitful and green, and mortals can grow the crops that sustain life, storing enough to last through the sad four months when Persephone dwells in the world of the dead.

The Unknown Guest: Metanira

D URING THAT TERRIBLE TIME WHEN Demeter was wandering the Earth searching for her lost daughter, Persephone, she happened upon two families with children. How eagerly she must have greeted them, hoping to be reminded of the happiness of mothers and children! But if that was the case, she was sadly disappointed by the first family she met.

Demeter had disguised herself as an old woman, and after nine days and nights without rest, she was tired and thirsty. Neither food nor drink had crossed her lips during all that time, until at last she knew she must stop for a moment to refresh herself. Her eyes fell on a small cottage, roofed with straw. When the goddess knocked on its low door, an aged woman came out and looked at her keenly. Hearing that her visitor was thirsty, the woman went inside the cottage and brought out a cup of sweetened barley-water.

While Demeter drank, a little boy stared at her boldly, smirking and making faces. He began to make fun of the goddess, calling her greedy and laughing that she drank too fast and too much.

Angered by such bratty behavior, Demeter threw the rest of her drink, with the grains of barley still in the bottom of the cup, into the boy's face. At once his cheeks were covered with little spots. Where his arms had been, legs now grew, and a long tail dropped down behind him. He shrank until he was tiny, even smaller than a lizard.

He might still be naughty, but at least now his mischief would be harmless. The old woman watched all this, amazed, but when she stooped to pick the little creature up, he skittered away between the stones and disappeared. Now that boy has a name to match his skin: the starry-spotted newt.

Demeter went on her way, still calling Persephone's name. She had reached the city of Eleusis when utter exhaustion overtook her, and she sank down on a rock to rest for a while. Veiled and dressed in simple clothes, with dark robes that covered her to her slender feet, her face disguised to look aged, the goddess seemed like the kind of person who might be a servant in somebody's house. Most people passed by without even noticing her, she looked so unimportant.

But four lovely young girls, who were coming to draw water from the well, did notice the old woman. They looked at her with kindness and pity. When they asked if she was in need, Demeter invented a sad story. Her name was Doso, she said; she had been captured by pirates, who meant to sell her into slavery, but she had managed to escape. Now she was stranded, helpless, here in this town where she knew nobody.

Without hesitation, the sisters urged Doso to come to their own house. There, they assured her, she would find rest and nourishment, and as much help as she needed to make her way home again. As it happened, the girls were the daughters of Celeus, the king of Eleusis, and his wife, Metanira. In their home, Demeter found a warm welcome indeed.

The goddess entered the palace, where Metanira sat in the hall with her young son in her lap. When the queen looked up and saw her visitor, she had a fleeting impression of radiance, but it vanished as the old woman drew her veil closer around her face. Invited to sit down, Doso did so solemnly; offered a cup of sweet wine, she refused. All she wanted, she answered, was a little barley-water flavored with mint. This she drank as if it were a sacrament—for indeed it was the drink given to worshipers of the goddess.

Metanira and her daughters were so kind and thoughtful that Demeter felt almost calm at last. How different the children in this house were from the last one she had seen! Demeter asked if she might hold the baby, and when Metanira saw how tenderly she nursed him in her arms, and how happy he seemed to be there, the queen asked her to stay and be the boy's nurse. The goddess was pleased to do so, as a way to repay this family for their sympathy and generosity to one so apparently poor, so genuinely distressed.

The child thrived under his new nurse's care. He grew like a god, for every day Demeter anointed his limbs with ambrosia; then every night she held him in the heart of the fire. By doing this, the goddess could make the boy immortal and eternally young.

One night Metanira kept herself awake. How was this new nurse treating her son? She wondered, determined to find out for herself. When she saw Demeter lay the baby in the roaring fire, she screamed in horror. The goddess snatched the boy out of the fire and put him on the ground.

"Foolish woman!" she snapped. "You should have trusted me! Because you didn't, your son will never be able to escape death and the Fates, as I had intended. In the fire, I would have burned away his mortality, but now that can never be.

"Still," she said, looking fondly at the boy, "he has rested in my lap, and because of that, he will always be honored throughout his life. In later times, the people of Eleusis will hold contests in his name."

Now Demeter threw off her disguise and revealed herself in all her radiance. Light blazed from her body and lit the whole house; the air was filled with a lovely fragrance. Beauty shone all around.

"I am Demeter," she announced to the women, "the bringer of blessings and joy to gods and men alike. If you want to win back my heart and my favor, you must build a temple on the hill behind the city with an altar dedicated to me. I myself will teach you the rites you must perform. I loved you well, and would be glad to be reconciled with you."

The goddess left the house, while everyone who had seen her trembled with awe. The four girls lifted up the crying child and held him tenderly, but he could not be consoled. He was used to the arms of a more skillful nurse than they could ever be, no matter how much they loved their brother.

After Metanira told her husband everything that had happened, the king gathered the people together and revealed the words of the goddess. Willingly, they set to work to build her temple, and when it was finished, Demeter returned.

There in the beautiful temple she sat, sorrowing over the loss of her daughter, while outside, the Earth remained barren and cold. It would be a long year before Persephone was given back to her mother, and before the fruits and flowers returned to make the land happy once again.

Today's environmentalists have much in common with the ancient Greeks, for whom damaging or destroying trees was a serious offense, even if the act was unintentional. The story of Dryope is told by her sister Iole, who saw these events take place.

My Sister Dryope

MY SISTER DRYOPE WAS THE MOST BEAUTIFUL OF ALL the girls in our country. She was her mother's only child (for we were half sisters; I had a different mother). Dryope and her husband Andraemon were a very happily married couple, and not long before the sad events I am about to tell, they had become the parents of a baby boy.

Near where we live, there's a lake with a sloping shore. At the top stands a lush grove of myrtle. One sunny day, Dryope and I came to this spot, laughing and joking, in a festive mood. At her bosom she carried her young son, not yet a year old, feeding him as we went along. How could we guess the terrible fortune that awaited my lovely sister? She had brought garlands to honor the nymphs of the lake, and that makes what happened to her then even more unjust.

Not far from the dreamy lakeshore grew a water lotus, blooming that day in beautiful crimson flowers, a sign of rich ripe berries soon to come. Dryope picked a little bouquet of the flowers for the baby to play with. I was about to do the same thing when I saw drops of red juice, red as blood, dripping from the stems of the blooms she had plucked. The boughs were shuddering as if they felt horror. You see, this shrub—as the peasants who lived nearby could have told us, although they had not bothered to—was really the naiad Lotis. Some time earlier, she had been transformed into a flower to escape the god Priapus, but although her body had been changed, she had kept her name.

My sister didn't know this story, and so she never thought twice about gathering the lovely blossoms for her son. She had said her prayers and made her offerings to the nymphs, and now she was ready to leave. But when she turned to go, she found she could not move. Her feet were rooted to the ground! Terrified, Dryope struggled to free herself, but she could move only the upper part of her body. From the ground up, a rough covering like bark was creeping around her legs, and rising steadily. Her hands moved to tear her hair in horror, but they only pulled the lotus leaves that were now growing from her head. Her little boy felt his mother's body harden as he lay in her arms.

I saw all this while it was happening, but there was nothing I could do. I had to stand there watching, helpless to save my sister from this awful fate, although I tried. I clung to her and held her in my arms, praying that the same bark would grow over me, too. But it would not.

Just then, Andraemon and our father came along, looking for Dryope, and asked me where she was. I could not speak for tears. I only pointed to the lotus. At once they understood what I could not find the words to tell, and embraced and kissed the wood. It still felt warm. Sobbing, they threw themselves on the ground, where they hugged the roots of this new plant. Nothing was left of my sweet sister except her face; all the rest was tree. I could see her tears falling onto the leaves that were growing over her head, and while she still could move her lips, she lamented, saying these words:

"If my misery can convince you that what I say is true, listen to me. By all the gods I swear I have not deserved this dire fate! I never intended to commit a crime, but even so, I am punished. My whole life has been innocent! I've never wanted to hurt anyone. If I'm lying, let my leaves dry up and fall off, let axes cut me down, let me be burned in the brightest flames!

"Oh, sister, I have one final wish—please do this for me! Take my baby from my branches, and find a nurse to care for him. Let him drink his milk under this tree and play in my shade. When he learns to talk, teach him to say, 'My mother is hidden in this trunk.' Teach him to be afraid of ponds and pools, too, and never to pick blossoms from trees, but to imagine that every bush might be a goddess in disguise.

"And now farewell, dear husband, dear Father, dear sister! If you love me, I beg of you, protect me from further harm. See to it that no pruning knife will ever come near me, that my leaves will never be eaten by some grazing flock. Oh, I cannot bend down to touch you! Please reach up and let me kiss you while I still can. And lift my little son so I can see him before this lotus covers me entirely. Now I can say no more. I feel the bark creeping up over my neck, and moving down across my forehead. Don't close my eyes with your hands. The bark is spreading over them and it will darken them before I die."

Those were the last words her lips could speak, she was so quickly changed. But for a long time, the branches held a glow of warmth from her body.

The Tragic
Mother of Troy:
Hecabe

ONE BY ONE, THE CHILDREN OF THE QUEEN OF Troy suffered tragic fates. Her son Paris had brought on the Trojan War, the cause of all their deaths. Deiphobus and Polites were both killed in the war. Troilus, and then Hector, who was the greatest of the Trojan warriors, were slain in battle by Achilles. Paris finally killed Achilles, but soon he himself was shot. Cassandra, the unhappy prophetess, was taken captive by the victor, Agamemnon, and killed by his wife.

Now Troy was defeated, and the surviving Trojan women were dragged, mourning, from the tombs of their loved ones and thrown into Agamemnon's ship. The last woman to board was the queen, Hecabe, cradling the ashes of her son Hector, on whose tomb she had dropped tears and a tress of her white hair. All she had left were her daughter Polyxena and one son, Polydorus, who as a child had been sent away to Thrace for safety.

What Hecabe could not know was that Polydorus too was dead. His guardian, King Polymestor, was not the friend that Hecabe and her husband Priam had hoped. Instead, he was a man whose greed outweighed all his loyalty. Priam had sent a great treasure to Thrace with his son, and when Troy fell, Polymestor saw his chance to win it for his own. He took his sword and slit Polydorus's throat, then threw the boy's body from a cliff into the waves below.

By coincidence, it was just off the shore of Thrace that Agamemnon now moored his fleet, waiting out a storm that made sailing impossible. Suddenly the ghost of Achilles rose from the Earth, furious and threatening. He roared, "Greeks! Are you going to forget me and how my feats won Troy for you? My tomb must be honored! I demand a sacrifice: you must slay Polyxena, the last of Priam and Hecabe's children. Her shade will be my companion in the Underworld."

The Greeks could not deny their greatest hero. At once, Polyxena was torn from her mother's arms and led to the altar. The girl was as brave as any of the Trojan heroes, and when she realized what was in store for her, she looked straight at Achilles's son, who had readied his knife.

"Here—be quick about it!" she said. "My blood is noble; choose where you will take it from: throat or breast!" and she bared her bosom to the knife. Polyxena was not sorry to die. She would never be a slave, she was determined about that.

The girl continued, "You won't please the gods by this deed, though. I only wish that my mother didn't have to know my fate. Her tragedy is her life, not my death. That's what she ought to mourn!

"Now, let me go to the Underworld of my own will. Whoever it is you seek to appease by my sacrifice will prefer blood that's freely given. Let no man touch my body—remember it's a king's daughter who is speaking, not a slave—but give it to my mother, who will pay you in tears instead of gold."

When Polyxena finished speaking, everyone was weeping, even the priest who unwillingly drove the knife home. To the very last, the princess kept her look of fearlessness, and as she fell, she swept her robe around her to keep her body covered.

Hecabe embraced her, crying as she so often had: scalding tears for her country, her sons, her husband, and now her daughter. Beating her breast, the mother kissed Polyxena's face.

"I thought, because you were a woman, you might be safe from steel, which killed your brothers! But he who destroyed your brothers has also destroyed you—Achilles, the doom of Troy and my bereaver. For him I bore all my children! When Paris killed him, I thought, 'Now we are safe from Achilles!' But he rises from his grave and demands more death.

"Only yesterday I was a queen, with sons, daughters, husband, a family, and a country. Now I am poor, an exile, a slave. Why doesn't my heart break? Cruel gods, why do you keep me alive? The dead are happy: Priam is happy, not seeing his daughter's body. I have only one thing left: my youngest son, my only reason for living."

Hecabe called on the Trojan women to give her an urn so that she might carry seawater to wash her daughter's body. But when she walked down to the beach, the unhappy mother saw the corpse of Polydorus, cast up by the waves, with a great gash in his throat. Struck speechless with anguish, Hecabe stood like a rock of granite, staring at the ground, then at Heaven, then at her son's face and his wounds.

The mother's fury rose, and as her anger towered high, Hecabe became a queen again. Her whole being turned to thoughts of vengeance. Like a lioness whose cub is stolen, and who, wild with rage, tracks down her enemy, so Hecabe forgot her years and made her way to Polymestor, the murderer. When she spoke with him, she told him that she still had a store of gold hidden for her son. She wished to show him where it was, she said.

Polymestor did not know that Hecabe had discovered Polydorus's body, and passionate with greed, as usual, he agreed. They set a time and place for the meeting. When he arrived, the king cried, "Quick, give me the gold, and I'll give it to your son. I swear it to Heaven!"

Hecabe looked at him with rage in her eyes. At this perjury, her wrath boiled over. Anger gave her supernatural strength. Shouting to the other captive women, she grabbed Polymestor and dug her fingers into his lying, treacherous eyes. She gouged out his eyeballs, and continued to tear at him.

The Thracians were horrified to see their king attacked so. They came after Hecabe with stones and sticks, but she just snapped at the stones and chased them, snarling. When she tried to say words, only a barking sound emerged.

The spot where Hecabe stood remains today, and because of what happened there, people call it The Place of the Dog. It is said that, because of those ancient wrongs, her voice still howls in sorrow through the land of Thrace.

The fate of that unhappy mother moved all hearts to pity, friend and foe alike. Even the gods in Heaven were struck with horror, and declared it unfair. Hecabe had not earned such misfortune.

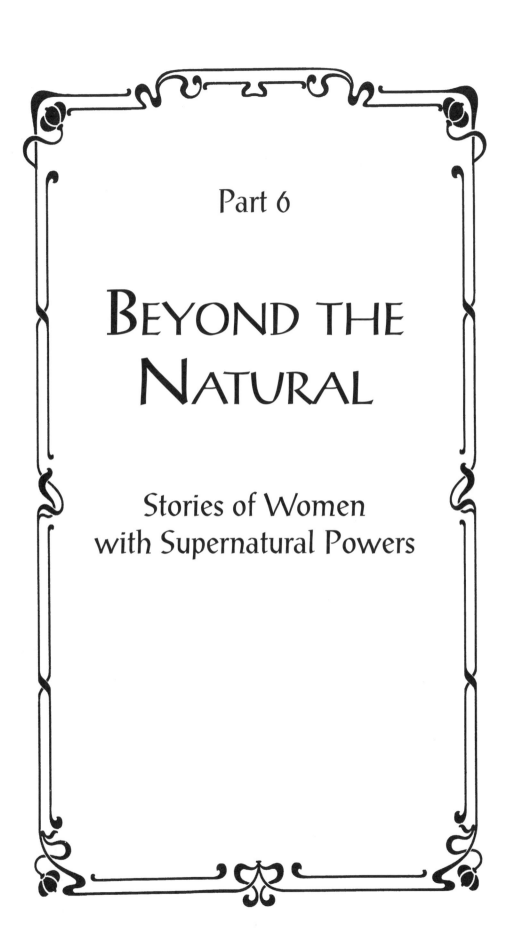

Part 6

BEYOND THE NATURAL

Stories of Women
with Supernatural Powers

WITCHES AND MONSTERS

The Goddess of Enchantment: Hecate

A MYSTERIOUS GODDESS WAS HECATE, THE GODDESS OF MAGIC, OF WITCHCRAFT, OF THE DEAD, of the dark side of the moon. Was she frightening or helpful? Even in ancient times, attitudes toward this goddess were mixed.

Hesiod, one of the earliest writers of the myths, calls her the greatest of the goddesses, honored by Zeus above all the others. The mighty god gave the Earth, sea, and heavens into her keeping. When the gods won their battle with the Titans, Zeus allowed Hecate, a Titan, to keep all her privileges, including great power over mortals. When she was well disposed toward someone, Hecate would grant anything the person wished for: victory and glory in battle or in athletic contests, success in fishing or farming—in fact, prosperity in any endeavor. She concerned herself equally in the affairs of the great and the small: she was a wise advisor to kings, and the nurse of the young.

As triple goddess of Earth, Heaven, and the Underworld, Hecate had three bodies and three heads, one a lion, one a dog, and one a mare.

Later, she became identified with two other goddesses. Living in the Underworld, she was a close friend of Persephone, the queen of that realm, the land of the dead. Both Persephone and Hecate represented not death, but regeneration and fertility, the Earth coming alive again after the winter.

But Hecate also stood for the things we fear. She came to be seen as an aspect of Artemis, the goddess of the moon. Hecate represented the dark of the moon, the terrors of those nights when the moon does not shine and the world is bathed in darkness. She was said to walk the Earth by night, accompanied by her dogs, invisible except to earthly dogs, whose barking warned of her presence. In this form, Hecate was the goddess of witchcraft and of dark acts, her name and help invoked by those who would perform black magic. Since crossroads were important places for magical rites, she was sometimes known as the Artemis of the Crossroads.

Enchanting Circe

CIRCE LIVED ON AN ISLAND CALLED AEAEA. HER LARGE house, made of purest marble, stood alone in a circular clearing in the woods. Around the house wandered animals of all kinds: lions and wolves, bears, asses and pigs. These animals were not fearsome: when anyone approached, they would fawn on the newcomer, bending their heads to lick his feet. In fact, these were not really beasts at all. They were men who had been transformed by powerful magic.

For Circe was a sorceress. She knew the secrets of all the herbs that grew in the woods. She understood what juice to mix with what leaf by the dark of the moon, how to compound love potions or healing draughts. She had a potent magic wand and a vast store of spells and incantations, magic words she chanted to help the herbs work her will.

More than anything else, Circe loved turning men into beasts. Usually she transformed them into the animals they most resembled. It would be bad enough just to become a pig or an ass, but the most terrible part of this metamorphosis was that the men kept their minds and their memories. Although beastly in form, they understood what had happened to them.

One day, the wandering hero Odysseus and his men landed on Circe's island, drawn there by some unknown force. Climbing up a rocky point near shore, Odysseus looked out over the island. He saw smoke rising from a clearing, but caution suggested that not everyone should go to investigate; some should stay behind for backup. Odysseus divided the men into two platoons, himself commanding one, his friend Eurylochus the other. They drew lots to see which group would go, and the lot fell on Eurylochus.

The general and his twenty-two companions set off. When they reached the clearing, they found the tame wolves and lions, wagging their tails in greeting. From inside the white stone house they heard the sweet voice of Circe, singing as she nimbly worked her loom, weaving a delicate fabric, while her attendants sorted herbs and flowers into different baskets. When she invited them to enter, they all crowded in eagerly—all, that is, except Eurylochus. He alone was suspicious and hung back.

Inside the house, Circe seated the men on thrones. "You must be hungry and thirsty!" she exclaimed, and gave them a wonderful meal of creamy cheese, toasted barley, and amber honey mixed with wine. To this drink she secretly added a few drops of her magic potion. As the men drank deep, Circe touched each of them lightly with her wand. At once, they felt bristles begin to sprout on their bodies, their noses broaden into snouts, their voices change to swinish grunts. Then she herded them into a pen, where she tossed them acorns and berries, proper food for pigs.

Eurylochus had watched all this through a window, and now he ran back to the ship to tell Odysseus of his crew's awful metamorphosis. Without hesitation, Odysseus started off for Circe's clearing. Eurylochus begged him not to go there. "She will do the same to you, I know!" he pleaded. But Odysseus could not rest until he had freed his men.

As he made his way through the silent woods, his path was suddenly barred by a beautiful youth holding a golden wand. It was Hermes, the messenger of the gods, who spoke: "I can tell you how to avoid Circe's spell and free your men." The god held out a potent herb, a white flower with a black root.

"It is called *moly*," Hermes said, "a plant that only gods can dig. When Circe gives you the enchanted cup, put this flower in it, and your senses will remain clear. Then, when she comes near with her wand, pull out your sword; show her its sharp cutting edge. She will be afraid, and will do what you wish."

Odysseus did as the god had told him. As soon as he drew his shining sword and held it to her throat, Circe fell back in terror. "Spare me," she cried, "and I will free your men. I'll even marry you!" Before he agreed, Odysseus made her promise to work no more enchantment. Fervently, she swore to obey him. Then she sprinkled the swine with magic herbs and touched their heads with the other end of the wand, singing charms and spells. Gradually, the pigs began to rise from four legs to two, their cloven hooves became feet again, and the bristles fell off their bodies.

A year passed, and the men remained men, even though they feasted nightly at Circe's table. She had kept her oath. When it was time for Odysseus to continue his journey, she told him where he must go next, then gave him a beautiful shirt and cloak. At dawn, the men made their way back to the ship, to find that Circe had been there before them. A black ewe and a black ram were tied on deck, ready for the journey. But they saw nobody: unless a goddess wishes to be seen, she will remain invisible to mortal eyes. Circe did not want to say good-bye.

The Beautiful Witch:
Medea

FROM HER VERY EARLIEST CHILDHOOD, MEDEA WAS adept in the arts of sorcery. For as well as being the daughter of Aeetes, king of Colchis, Medea was the niece of the great enchantress Circe. Like her aunt, the princess was a devotee of the goddess Hecate. By the time she reached young womanhood, she was unsurpassed in the powers of witchcraft.

Now there came a hero in need of help: Jason, the leader of the Argonauts, who was nearing Colchis in his quest for Aeetes's famous Golden Fleece. And luckily, help was on its way. Jason was a favorite of Hera's, but the goddess knew that, left to his own resources, he could never win the prize he sought. The princess Medea alone could aid him. Hera consulted with Aphrodite, and the two goddesses hatched a plot. They promised little Cupid that they would give him an enameled golden ball if he could make Medea fall in love with Jason. Delighted, he agreed.

When Jason reached Colchis, the king welcomed the Argonauts with hot baths and food. Medea, curious about the strangers, entered the chamber quietly. At the very moment her eyes fell on Jason, Cupid shot his arrow, which struck her full in the heart. The sweet pain of love washed over her.

Medea fled to her room, filled with confusion. How could she have fallen so deeply in love with a total stranger? It went against all reason, and yet his handsome face filled her every thought—his youth, his strength.

After the guests were comfortable, King Aeetes asked them, "Who are you and what do you want here?" Jason answered, "We are men of noble birth, and we are seeking the Golden Fleece. We'll do anything you ask in return for it, fight for you, anything you want."

The king was furious. Was this their repayment for his hospitality, to take his treasure? He replied, "I will give the Fleece only to a man who can prove he's as brave as I am, by doing what I once did. Here's the test: he must harness my two bulls, who have feet of bronze and breathe fire. Then he must plow a field and sow it with the teeth of a terrible dragon. From the teeth will spring up a host of armed men, whom he must kill. If he can accomplish these deeds, he is indeed worthy of the Fleece."

Jason was taken aback. These were fearful tasks! How could any man do them? And yet he must try, or admit defeat.

Medea had spent this time arguing with herself. She knew what her father would demand, and she knew that she had the power to help Jason win. But wouldn't that be betraying her father for a stranger? Still, she loved Jason too much to let him die. She sent word to him to meet her secretly in the forest, at the shrine of Hecate.

As soon as Jason saw the beautiful princess, he returned her love. Before the altar of Hecate, he swore that if she helped him, he would marry her. Medea took out a magic ointment she had prepared from powerful herbs. "Rub this on your body and your weapons," she said, "and for a day neither fire nor iron can harm you." Then she told him what he must do to fulfill her father's tasks.

The next morning, Jason went into the field, which was surrounded by spectators. At a signal from the king, splendid in his purple robes, the bulls were loosed. They flew at Jason, their bronze hoofs gleaming in the sun, their lowered heads snorting fire that singed the grass. But he stood, unmoving, and when the bulls came up to him, he did not feel the flames; such was the power of the charm Medea had given him. Instead, he stroked their necks and yoked them together, forcing them to draw the plough through the field, which had never before been touched. Everyone was astounded.

Next, Jason took out the dragons' teeth and scattered them over the freshly cut furrows. As soon as the teeth touched soil, armed men sprang out of the earth, their spears pointed at Jason. But he remembered what Medea had told him to do, and when they advanced on him, he threw a heavy rock in their midst. At once they turned against each other, and in the terrible fight that ensued, all were killed.

Jason had triumphed. But Medea knew that her father would not keep his bargain, and that he would have the Argonauts killed. "We must flee!" she whispered. "But you earned the Golden Fleece. I'll help you get it away from the dragon who guards it."

That night while everyone slept, Medea led the men into the sacred wood where the Fleece was kept. Chanting a spell, she dipped a sprig of juniper into a magic potion and sprinkled it over the raging dragon. It stood for a moment, motionless, then shut its great eyes and fell down, fast asleep. Jason snatched the Fleece from the oak tree on which it hung. Then he turned and fled to his ship, taking Medea with him. They sailed at once and, with Hera's help, made their escape. Aeete's fleet pursued them as far as Phaeacia, where they married. The king offered them his protection, and at last they were able to return to Jason's home.

The only thing that troubled Jason now was that his father, Aeson, was too old and infirm to join in their celebration. He turned to his wife and tearfully asked her, "Can your magic powers do one thing more for me? Can you take some of my youthful years and give them to my father?"

Sadly, Medea thought of her father, so far away. Perhaps helping Jason's father would make up, a little, for betraying her own. She answered: "I can't take years away from your life! That's forbidden by Hecate, and it's not right of you to ask it of me. But if she will stand by me, I'll do something even better: I'll win back your father's own youth."

Three nights she waited, until the moon was full. Then, when all creatures of the Earth were fast asleep, Medea went out of the house. She was splendid in her flowing robes, barefoot, her hair streaming over her shoulders. Everything was still; only the stars glittered in the sky.

She stretched out her arms to the heavens, turning around three times, three times uttering a wailing cry, and three times sprinkling her head with water. Then she knelt on the stony ground and prayed:

"O night, the mother of mysteries, o golden stars and moon that follow the fires of day! O Hecate, divine, three-formed goddess, you know all my desires and teach enchantment; you, Earth, of the magic herbs; you, winds and breezes, mountains, lakes and streams; O forest gods and gods of night, come to me now! Through your power, I have sent rivers flowing backward, stilled the angry ocean, and made calm waters wild; I have made clouds gather or disperse; I have called the winds and silenced them. You have seen me shatter the fangs of serpents, overturn rocks and mighty oaks, move the forests and shake the mountains, call forth ghosts from the graveyards. I can make the moon turn dark, the sun pale. You helped me tame my father's bulls and turn the dragon-born warriors against each other, lull to sleep the guardian of the Fleece.

"Now I need herbs whose power can turn old age to youth, and bring back the early years. I see that you will help me, for the stars flash bright, and my chariot, drawn by winged dragons, has come for me."

Medea stepped into the chariot and caressed the dragons' necks. Then she shook the reins and soared up into the sky, turning toward places she knew from long ago. Nine days and nights she roamed the world, gathering powerful herbs. When she returned, the dragons were sleek, shining in bright new skins, although they had only smelled the magic plants, not tasted them.

Now Medea built two altars, the right dedicated to Hecate, the left to Hebe, goddess of youth, and covered them with foliage. She sacrificed a black sheep and poured wine and frothing milk, called up the deities of Earth, and commanded Death to leave Aeson alone.

Forbidding Jason or anyone else to enter the room, Medea charmed the old king to sleep. Her cauldron was bubbling with a rich mixture: root-herbs from Thessaly, seeds and flowers, gemstones from the Orient and ocean sands, hoarfrost gathered at the full of the moon, wings and flesh of owls, a werewolf's entrails. Now she added the fillet of a water snake, the liver of a stag, and eggs and heads of ancient crows. All of these were in the cauldron, along with a thousand other things, things without names, not of this world. She stirred the mixture with a dry, dead olive branch, and the branch grew green and burst into leaf, then was covered with fat olives. Where some drops had spilled over, spring bloomed, and everywhere there were sweet meadow flowers.

Seeing this, Medea drew her knife and slit the old king's throat. When the blood had all run out, she filled his veins with her elixir. At once, Aeson's hair and beard, for years so white, turned black; his wrinkled skin grew smooth; his limbs became strong and sleek. When he awoke, Aeson marveled to see himself as he had been forty years ago.

Such wonders Medea could perform! But she did not always use her powers for good. It was rumored that she and Jason had escaped from her father's fleet by killing her brother. When they went to Circe, asking to be cleansed, Circe was horrified at their crime, but consented to sacrifice to Zeus, who forgave them.

Now Medea offered to rejuvenate Pelias, Jason's uncle, who had stolen Aeson's throne. Although she pretended to want only good for him, her real motive was revenge for her husband and his father. She demonstrated her skill to Pelias's daughters by throwing an old ram into her cauldron, where it became a tiny bleating lamb. Then she told the daughters that they must slit their father's throat, and she would replace his blood with the elixir. But when they had reluctantly done so and turned to Medea to perform the next step, she had disappeared.

Revolted by this crime, Hera now abandoned Jason and Medea, and things turned sour for them. In Corinth, where they went to live, Jason proved false.

Everything Medea had done, good and evil alike, she had done for him. Now, to ingratiate himself with Creon, the king of Corinth, Jason divorced her and became engaged to the king's daughter, Glauce. To make matters worse, Creon told Medea that she and her children must leave Corinth to wander, friendless, in exile. That meant her children would become slaves. And Jason agreed to this outrage.

What a reward for her love, to be betrayed like this! Medea sat brooding in sorrow and anger, remembering her father long ago, her brother's blood that had stained her conscience, the passion and loyalty she had given Jason. When she taxed him with his faithlessness, he only laughed, claiming that all his help had come from the goddesses, not from her at all.

Burning with anger, Medea set about her revenge. She sent a wedding present to Glauce, a beautiful robe she had anointed with a magic charm. When the bride put on the dress, she was instantly devoured by flames.

Slavery was worse than death, Medea thought. To save her children from one terrible fate, she inflicted the other: she herself killed them. Jason was stunned with horror. Defiantly, Medea told him she would take the children's bodies to Hera's temple and bury them with her own hands, safe from all her enemies, including him.

Then out of the sky came a chariot, drawn by the winged dragons. Medea put her children into it and stepped in. The chariot moved away, high into the sky, and disappeared.

The story of Medusa is one of the most frightening of the transformation stories, for not only was the punishment of this woman unjust, but her metamorphosis made her a terrible monster who brought suffering to others.

The Terrible Medusa

ONCE MEDUSA WAS A LOVELY YOUNG GIRL, whose fame for beauty was widespread. Chief among her assets was her gorgeous hair, so glossy and thick it was the envy of everyone. Many a man courted her and longed to marry her. She seemed to be headed for a happy life.

Then she fell victim to the jealousy of the goddess Athena. Did she boast of her beauty, saying she was more beautiful than Athena? Some tell the story that way. Others say that Poseidon made love to Medusa on the grounds of Athena's temple, against the girl's wishes. Whichever is true, Athena visited a terrible wrath on her. She transformed her into a hideous monster, the kind of being who destroys others simply by existing. Medusa's face became so terrible that a single look at her would turn any living thing— creature and plant alike—to stone. Her most terrifying feature was her hair, which Athena changed into a writhing, hissing mass of poisonous snakes.

One day Perseus, the son of Zeus and Danae, made a rash and foolish boast. He would kill Medusa and bring back her head as a gift for his mother's wedding! But how could any mere human accomplish such a daunting task? Why, Perseus didn't even know where she and her sisters, the Gorgons, lived! It looked as if, once again, arrogance would prove the undoing of a mortal.

Fortunately for Perseus, Athena wanted to see Medusa dead, and she decided to help him. As he began to wander in search of the monster, he came across a marvelous figure, a radiant young man wearing winged sandals, a winged cap, and carrying a winged staff. This could be none other than Hermes, the messenger of the gods. Perseus could accomplish his mission, Hermes assured him, but he would need a great deal of help. He must have special equipment, and that equipment was in the possession of certain nymphs who lived in a far, remote land. To learn the way to their dwelling place, he would have to visit the Gorgons' sisters, the Graiae, who lived in a cave on the side of Atlas's mountain, and ask them.

He himself would accompany Perseus on this venture, Hermes assured him. First they must travel to the land of the Graiae, the Gray Ones, a land that was itself completely gray. Neither sun nor moon ever shone there; only dim twilight illuminated both the day and the night. In the heart of this gray scene lived the three old women, wrinkled and gray as their landscape. They had human heads but bodies shaped like swans, with arms and hands hidden beneath their wings. The strangest and most dreadful thing about the three was that they shared a single eye among them, passing it back and forth as it was needed.

Then Hermes told Perseus how to get what he wanted from the Graiae. He must stay hidden until the moment came when one of them was handing the eye to another. Then he should seize it and refuse to give it back until they had told him how to find the nymphs.

Suddenly Athena appeared, standing at Hermes's side, and offered Perseus her shield for protection. The only way to keep from being turned to stone, of course, was never to look at Medusa's face directly. But how could he kill her without looking at her? If he used the highly polished bronze shield as a mirror, Athena told him, he could see the Gorgon well enough by looking only at her reflection. Then Hermes gave Perseus his own curved sword of adamant—a substance so hard the Gorgon's scales could not break it—the only weapon that could ever kill her.

The plan worked perfectly. They arrived at the land of the Gray Ones, and silently entered their cave. When one of the women plucked the eye from her forehead, Perseus snatched it out of her hand. For a moment the sisters sat in utter darkness, not realizing the eye was gone; each thought one of the others had it. When they understood the situation, they were desperate to get back their only eye. Eagerly, they gave Perseus the information he needed.

The god and the mortal continued their journey together. Following the Graiae's directions, they found the land of the nymphs, which lay in the far north at the back of the North Wind. The nymphs were happy to entertain the travelers with feasting and music, and at once brought out three wonderful gifts for Perseus. First they presented him with a pair of winged sandals like the ones Hermes wore. Then came a magic bag that would always be just the right size for whatever he wanted to carry in it. Last, the most precious gift of all, was the cap of invisibility, which would allow the wearer to go anywhere without being seen. Now that Perseus was completely equipped for his task, it seemed less daunting.

Putting on the shoes and cap, Perseus flew over Ocean's stream to the land of the Gorgons, a land of strange, stony forms, men and animals that had chanced to look on Medusa and had been petrified just as they were. There he found the Gorgons asleep in their cave. In the mirror of the shield he could see their scaly bodies and terrible hair. At this crucial moment, both Hermes and Athena stood by his side, and they told him which of the three was Medusa. Still looking only at the shield, he swooped down and to cut off her head with a single stroke, his hand guided by the warrior goddess. Quickly he stuffed the head into the bag, where he would not have to see it.

Medusa's sisters awoke in a tremendous rage. Who had dared to do this deed? The sisters, who were immortal, would have been impossible to defeat if they had found their enemy. But because he wore the cap of invisibility, Perseus was able to escape from their wrath.

During his return, of course, Perseus was delayed by another adventure, the rescue of Andromeda from a fearsome sea-serpent. But at last he returned to Athena and presented her with the head of Medusa. The goddess set the head in the middle of her shining bronze shield, and carried it there forever.

Scylla and Charybdis

IN THE NARROW CHANNEL THAT SEPARATES ITALY AND SICILY, KNOWN TODAY AS THE STRAIT OF MESSINA, there lived two terrible female monsters. They lay in wait, hoping to destroy any sailors who were brave—or foolish—enough to dare to pass by. These monsters were known as Scylla and Charybdis.

Charybdis was a powerful whirlpool. Three times a day, she sucked in the water of the sea, creating a vortex so strong that any passing ship would be drawn down into its depths. Then she cast the water out again in a powerful stream that wrecked ships against the nearby rocks.

On the opposite shore lived Scylla, a frightful beast whose waist was circled by a ring of dogs' heads. Scylla had twelve feet and six heads; in each head gaped a mouth lined with triple rows of sharp teeth. With these she lashed out at the unlucky sailors whose ships she had lured to approach her rocks, devouring as many of the crew as she could snatch up.

The strait was so narrow that it was almost impossible to avoid these monsters altogether. Any ship's commander had to face a difficult question: which of the two would be worse? Odysseus chose to risk Scylla, since she would most likely take only part of his crew, while Charybdis would destroy the whole ship and everyone on it. He lost six men, but the rest survived.

Poor Scylla! This frightful monster had once been a beautiful maiden, loved by the fisherman Glaucus. Then, in a fit of jealousy, the witch Circe changed her forever.

From Maiden to Monster: Scylla and Glaucus

GLAUCUS WAS PERFECTLY HAPPY IN HIS LIFE AS A FISHERMAN. EACH DAY HE WENT DOWN TO THE sea or to the river and cast his nets, bringing in an ample catch, for he was skilled at his trade. One fine summer morning, he found himself a new place to fish, and it looked promising: a lovely island in the river, covered with lush green plants. The grass was untrampled, which meant that no cattle had been pastured there, and, even better, nobody had been there before him to disturb the fish.

When Glaucus brought up his nets, they were filled with a wondrous catch. Fish of every kind and color spilled out onto the grass. He sat down to dry the nets, when suddenly he noticed something unusual. The fish were beginning to stir and move as if they were alive, making swimming motions on the grass. Then, before his startled eyes, they began to move toward the river, and in a moment they were all back in the water, swimming gaily away.

Glaucus scratched his head in bewilderment. Nothing like this had ever happened to him before! What could have caused such a strange thing? Had some god chosen to revive the fish, or could there be something peculiar about the grass he had spread them on? Did it have some supernatural power?

"Hmm," he said to himself, "I'll have to see about this! That kind of plant could be very valuable." He pulled up a handful and touched his tongue to it. "Not bad," he thought, and putting the rest of the grass into his mouth, began to chew.

The moment Glaucus tasted the luscious juices that came from the herb, he was seized by an overpowering desire to plunge beneath the waters of the river. He didn't hesitate for a moment, but threw himself in at once. The gods of the seas and rivers greeted him graciously, welcoming him into their company.

It was so beautiful in that world under the water that Glaucus had no desire to return to the Earth. When the gods asked if he would like to stay with them, he accepted with pleasure. Ocean and Tethys, the rulers of the sea, agreed to wash away all that was mortal in the fisherman. They sang a magic song, repeated nine times, then a hundred rivers poured their waters over him. He lost consciousness.

When he came to, he was a different Glaucus, no longer a man but an immortal. His shape, too, had changed. His hair was long and green; when he swam it trailed behind him through the water. His shoulders broadened, and in the place where his legs and thighs had been there grew a beautiful, flexible fish tail. Glaucus looked at his image reflected in the water and smiled. "What a handsome fellow I have become!" he exclaimed.

One day, as he was swimming through the bay, Glaucus came upon something beautiful. It was the Nereid Scylla. She had spent the morning on land with the other water nymphs, but when they left to swim in the peaceful bay, Scylla stayed behind. She was afraid of the deeps of the sea. The nymph amused herself by strolling on the beach; now and then, when she felt too warm, she found a little landlocked cove where she could splash in the cool water.

Scylla was playing in an azure pool when she heard a sea-call, a shell being sounded. Suddenly breaking the surface of the sea came Glaucus, enjoying his newfound freedom in the water.

When he saw the nymph, his heart was transfixed. Never had he beheld anyone so lovely! He began to talk to her without thinking, blurting out the first words that came to him. But she was frightened and turned to run. Her fear gave her strength to climb the nearby cliff, a great peak whose height cast a long shadow over the trembling waters of the bay. From her place of safety, she turned to look at this being who had spoken to her out of the depths.

The sight of Glaucus struck her with wonder. Scylla gazed at his color and form: the blue-green skin, long flowing hair, and the scaly fish tail where his legs should be. What was this creature, a monster or a god?

Glaucus understood her thoughts. He leaned against a nearby rock and laughed. "Fair maid," he said, "I'm neither fish nor fowl, no monster or savage beast. Something much better, indeed! I am a sea god, more powerful than Proteus or Triton. Once I was a mortal, but even then I was dedicated to the sea." And he told her the story of the strange island with its magic grasses, and how he had been transformed into a god.

"But what's the good of being so handsome," he went on, "or of being a god at all, if you won't look at me with love?" He would have spoken more, but again Scylla fled in fear. Her abrupt rejection struck him as very rude. Glaucus needed help, and he knew just where to get it: he would visit the golden court of Circe, daughter of the glorious sun.

Circe welcomed him. "Dear goddess," he entreated, "I've come to ask a favor of you. Have pity on a god, I beg. No one but you can help me. I'm in the worst kind of love affair, love that's not returned, and your island is full of magic herbs and flowers. I understand the power of plants, believe me, for they changed me from a man into a god.

"You may have heard my story, how I saw Scylla and loved her, but approached her too rashly. I blush to remember what I said to her—the promises, the begging, the flattering words. If you have magic spells that can charm her, give me one quickly, or if your herbs are stronger than spells, use them on her. Make her less cold, make her love me! I don't want to be cured of love myself; I just want her to feel the same kind of fire that consumes me."

But Circe had fallen in love with Glaucus herself. She replied, "Go find another girl, one who is warmer-hearted, eager for love. You should be pursued, not have to pursue someone who doesn't return your feelings! Trust yourself and your handsome good looks, your power to charm; be bolder! Here's a goddess who would be glad to have you—I mean myself, the daughter of the sun, mistress of magic. Forget the one who doesn't want you and open your arms to the one who does!"

Glaucus was astonished at this outpouring, which he had not invited. He blurted out the first thing that came to his mind: "Leaves will grow in the sea and seaweed on the mountains, before my love for Scylla fades. While she lives, I can love only her!"

Circe's heart was filled with rage. However offended and hurt she was, she could not strike out at Glaucus, for she loved him too dearly, but Scylla was another matter. "I'll get my revenge on that little nymph!" she promised herself. "If it weren't for her, Glaucus could be mine. She'll see what it is to thwart the great Circe!"

Now Circe took herbs, all the ones that she knew had the most fearful power. As she ground the ghastly plants and mixed them together, she sang the spells she had learned from Hecate. At last the brew was ready.

Circe put on a robe of the deepest blue and left her palace, moving through the throng of animals—pigs, wolves, and lions—who leapt at her to kiss her feet. She crossed the dancing ocean waves lightly, as if she were walking on solid ground.

Just beyond the beach there was a little rock-ringed pool, not very deep, and curving like a bow. This was a lovely, peaceful spot, one of Scylla's favorite retreats. She loved to come here in the middle of the day when the sun was hottest and the trees offered no shade. Into this pool Circe poured her drugs, the bitter poisons she had brewed from venomous roots and herbs. As she poured, the sorceress uttered the darkest spells anyone had ever known, saying them nine times, then three times more.

Now Scylla came to wade in her pool. When she was waist-deep, she realized, to her horror, that the water was full of monstrous beasts, all barking and snarling at once. The nymph tried to push the horrible heads away; she tried to flee. But what she ran away from, she took with her. The monsters were part of her! Looking for her thighs, her legs, her feet, she saw only the heads of vicious dogs, jaws gaping wide like those of Cerberus himself, the guardian of the Underworld. From her waist down, there was nothing but a pack of raging beasts.

When Glaucus saw what had become of Scylla, he wept, but there was nothing he could do. He swam away to escape from Circe, whose magic was too powerful for him. But Scylla remained where she was, as if she had been rooted to the spot. She raged at Circe, her hatred matching Circe's hatred of her.

In her misery, Scylla's nature turned as ugly as her body. She would stay where she was forever, part of the sheer rock along a narrow strait. There she would wait for ships to pass, and when they came close enough, her beastly heads would snatch sailors right out of the ship and devour them.

Mistress of the Riddle: The Sphinx

ECHIDNA WAS A NASTY CREATURE, HALF BEAUTIFUL woman, half voracious serpent. She was the mother of many hideous beings, including the fire-breathing Chimera, part goat, part lion, and part snake; Cerberus, the three-headed dog who guarded the gates of Hell; and the frightful, many-headed Hydra.

Another of Echidna's offspring was the Sphinx, a winged monster with the body of a lion but the head and breasts of a woman. When this creature took up residence along the road leading to Thebes, she threatened the very existence of the city. Apparently she had been sent by one of the gods, who wanted to punish Thebes for some offense.

And the punishment was terrible. The Sphinx lay in ambush at a lonely place near the road, where she waylaid travelers; sometimes, unexpectedly, she would fly up to the city walls to trap an unwary youth. Wherever she found her victims, she would perch on a rock or on the wall and challenge them to answer her riddle. If they could not, she carried them off, killed, and devoured them. No one had been able to solve the riddle, and the young men of Thebes were becoming scarcer by the day. Even one of King Creon's sons had tried to answer the Sphinx, and failed. He too had been killed.

Now the city was in a state of crisis. Nobody could enter, nobody could leave, and starvation was not far away. The citizens had eaten everything they could find within the walls, starting with their livestock, and ending up with rats and mice.

At last King Creon grew desperate. He offered to give his kingdom to anyone who could answer the Sphinx's riddle and rid Thebes of this terrible scourge.

Several heroes risked their lives to come to the city and challenge the monster, but each of them failed. Then, one day, the young prince Oedipus arrived just as heralds were announcing the challenge.

"Why not?" he thought to himself. "My life isn't worth much. The oracle has foretold a terrible doom for me, and I could ask nothing better than to escape Fate by dying. It might as well be this way as another!"

So the city elders led Oedipus out to the stony, bone-strewn ground where the Sphinx lurked. At once, he challenged the monster. "Give me your riddle!" he demanded.

The Sphinx looked at him and asked: "What is the creature who is two-footed, three-footed, and four-footed, the only creature of earth, air, or sea who changes its nature? It has four feet in the morning, two at noon, and three in the evening, and is weakest and slowest when it has the most feet." She sat back and smiled at Oedipus with her cruel mouth and cold stone eyes, anticipating her next feast.

Oedipus only laughed. "That's easy!" he exclaimed. "It's human beings you mean. When we walk the Earth, as babies we go on hands and knees; as adults we stride firmly on two feet; and in old age, we walk leaning on a stick as a third foot."

Of course, the Sphinx was furious that someone had answered her riddle correctly. Still glaring at Oedipus, she gave a raucous cry, something between a screech and a scream, hurled herself against her rock, and died.

SEERS OF THE FUTURE

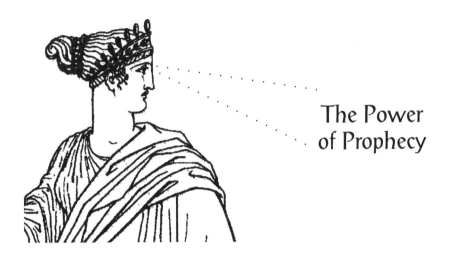

The Power
of Prophecy

W HAT WOULD IT BE LIKE TO SEE INTO THE FUTURE? WE HUMANS HAVE ALWAYS WONDERED what is going to happen, and wished that we could find out. Knowing what's in store should help a person decide how to act so that something good will occur or something bad can be avoided. But is the future already determined, or can it be changed? Perhaps it's better not to know!

Classical mythology is rich with stories of oracles and prophets, strange beings who can see what is inevitably going to happen.

An oracle was a priestess through whose lips a deity could speak to someone who badly wanted advice; it is also the shrine dedicated to that foretelling. Oracles knew everything and always spoke the truth. The catch is that what they said was often incomplete or disguised, or told in the form of a riddle, which the hearers had to interpret for themselves. So people usually weren't much wiser for the advice, but were left once again to make their own decisions on how to behave.

The most famous shrine was at Delphi, a beautiful spot high on the side of a mountain. This oracle first belonged to Gaia, Mother Earth, who was the source of prophetic powers, along with so much else. Then she gave it to the Titaness Themis.

The Goddess of Justice: Themis

THEMIS WAS GAIA'S DAUGHTER, SOMETIMES IDENTIFIED WITH the Earth goddess herself. She knew things that even the great Zeus did not know: the secrets of the future. He was wise enough to understand this, and sought her wisdom and knowledge to help him make decisions. After all, her name means "The Right" or "Divine Justice" or "Law." Themis sat at Zeus's side to advise him, especially when he was making judgments. She is often pictured holding up a scale, with which she weighed the arguments of opposing sides.

Some of Themis's most famous prophecies had great impact on the lives of gods and mortals. She knew, for instance, that Zeus must not wed the beautiful Thetis, for the Fates had decreed that Thetis's son would be greater than his father. If Zeus had married her, his son would have overthrown him, just as Zeus did his father, Cronos.

Later, when Zeus destroyed the world with his great flood, the only two surviving mortals, Pyrrha and Deucalion, sought the temple of Themis and asked her what they should do. The goddess appeared in person to tell them, "Shroud your heads and throw over your shoulders the bones of your mother." When they had rightly interpreted "mother" as Mother Earth and her bones as stones, they were able to repopulate the world.

Themis raised the infant Apollo, because his mother was still being persecuted by Hera. When he was four days old, she fed him nectar and ambrosia, the foods of the gods. At once he burst out of his swaddling clothes to stand before her full-grown, demanding a bow and a lyre. Later, having taught Apollo the art of prophecy, Themis gave the oracle at Delphi into his keeping.

Among her own children were Prometheus and Astraea, goddess of innocence and purity. But her power is shown most clearly by the names and actions of her other children. For Themis was the mother of the Hours (the Seasons), of Justice, of Peace, and of the three Fates who determine the lives of every mortal.

The Sibyl of Cumae

SIBYL WAS A NAME GIVEN TO MANY ANCIENT seers, after Sibylla, a famous prophetess who received the oracular gift from Apollo. Sibyls could be found in many places, but the most famous was the Sibyl of Cumae.

When Aeneas returned from Carthage, he wanted nothing so much as to talk to his father. But his father had died. How would it be possible to reach him? Aeneas sought the help of the Sibyl, who received him in her rocky cave near the sacred grove of Artemis and Apollo. She told him how to find the powerful Golden Bough that would allow him to enter the Underworld. When he returned with it, she agreed to accompany him on his journey through the dark realm below.

Together they descended, and were allowed to cross the River Styx. Passing by many chambers of the Underworld, they saw the shades of babies who had died in infancy, of those who were falsely condemned and those who killed themselves, of those who died from cruel love, of war heroes. At last they entered the Elysian Fields, where Aeneas met his father's spirit, who revealed to him the workings of the universe. Then the Sibyl brought Aeneas back up into the light of day.

This same Sibyl, it was said, was attractive to the god Apollo. Hoping she would love him in return, he offered to give her anything she wanted. She asked to live as many years as the grains of sand in a pile of dust, which numbered a thousand. Apollo granted the wish, but alas, her powers of prophecy had failed her. She forgot to ask for eternal youth, and as the years went by, she grew older and older, more and more shriveled and weak. At last she hung from the ceiling of her cave in a leather bag, from which she continued to utter her prophetic words.

Oenone, the Healer

A LOVELY NYMPH CALLED OENONE RECEIVED two wonderful gifts from the gods: the gift of prophecy from Rhea, and the gift of healing from Apollo. Oenone lived on Mount Ida, where Paris, a prince of Troy, was abandoned at birth. A kind shepherd found the baby and raised him as his own. As he grew up, nobody, including himself, knew who the boy was, and he was happy living the life of a shepherd.

The two young people saw each other every day, days they spent hunting together or tending their flocks. Inevitably, they fell in love. As they wandered through the woods, Paris would carve Oenone's name into the bark of beech and poplar trees. At last they married, ready to settle down to a joyful life together.

But then came the fateful day when Hera, Athena, and Aphrodite asked Paris to judge which of the three goddesses was the fairest. Enticed by Aphrodite's promise to give him the most beautiful woman in the world, Paris chose her. True to her word, the goddess offered to take him to meet Helen. Oenone tried to warn him of the dangers she could foresee, but he ignored her words and abandoned her without a thought. She stayed on the mountain, heartbroken.

Many years later, Paris was mortally wounded in the Trojan War. His companions carried him to Mount Ida, where he begged Oenone to heal him. Still deeply hurt by his actions, she refused, and he was carried back to Troy to die. Almost immediately she relented, for she loved Paris in spite of everything. She ran to the city, carrying her basket of healing herbs. But it was too late: Paris was dead. Stricken with grief and remorse, Oenone threw herself off the city walls.

The Centaur's Daughter: Ocyrhoe

MANY OF THE CENTAURS WERE RUDE AND BAD-MANNERED, TO SAY THE LEAST. THESE CREATURES, half man and half horse, once broke up a wedding feast to which they had been invited, behaving so coarsely that they actually started a war.

One Centaur, though, was different. This was the wise old Chiron, revered for his many skills. In his youth, Chiron had been taught by Apollo and Artemis, and he became a famous hunter. From Apollo he also learned the arts of music and medicine. As Chiron grew older, he became a distinguished teacher, numbering most of the great Greek heroes among his students.

Admiring his vast knowledge, Apollo trusted his son Aesculapius to the wise Centaur's care. One day, as he was instructing the boy in the art of medicine, Chiron saw his daughter approaching, her red-gold hair gleaming in the sunlight. The girl had been born to the nymph Chariclo in the long grasses along the banks of a flowing river, and was given the name Ocyrhoe, which means "swift-flowing."

Ocyrhoe knew all her father's art, but beyond that, she had learned prophetic singing: she could foretell the dark secrets of the Fates. Just now, as she drew near Chiron and Aesculapius, the fires of prophecy flared up in her heart. She looked at the child and cried: "Blessed boy! Grow quickly, grow strong. You will become a healer and strength-giver to the whole world. Again and again, mortals will owe their lives to you. You will even have the power to win back to this world souls that have just departed for the Underworld.

"But when you have performed this daring act just once, the gods will learn what you have done. Zeus will strike you with his thunderbolt and you will fall dead, then rise again to godhood, born a second time!

"And you, my dearest father, although you are now immortal, you will long to die on the day when you are wounded and your wounds poisoned by a serpent's blood. In your agony, you will beg for death. The gods will grant your wish and make you mortal; then the Fates will cut short the thread of your life."

There was more Ocyrhoe had to say, but she could only utter a long sigh from the depths of her heart. She began to weep bitterly.

"The Fates are keeping me from speaking; they forbid me to tell you any more. What was my power of prophecy worth if it only brings the wrath of Heaven down on me? I wish I had never received the gift of future-knowing!

"Oh, Father, help me! I feel myself changing, growing less human! All at once I want to do nothing but canter across the meadow and graze on the long green grass. I'm turning into a mare—I know it's a shape that is familiar in our family, but at least you have always been half human, Father! Why am I becoming entirely horse?"

But Ocyrhoe's last words were lost in the new sounds coming out of her mouth, more like a whinny or a neigh than a human voice. Her arms lengthened, touched the earth, and began to move among the grasses, the nails of her fingers and toes fused into hard, rounded hoofs. Her mouth grew larger and her neck longer. The dress that had flowed behind her so gracefully became a tail; her lovely golden-red hair fell over her shoulder in a thick, rich mane. Ocyrhoe had been transformed into a horse, changed entirely—her voice, her figure, even her name was different. Now she was called Hippe, which means "mare."

The Prophetess Nobody Believed: Cassandra

CASSANDRA WAS ONE OF THE YOUNGER CHILDREN OF Hecabe and Priam, the Trojan monarchs. By all accounts, she was the most beautiful of their daughters. But there was something else that set her apart. Cassandra and her twin brother, Helenus, both had the gift of prophecy.

How was this princess given her power to see into the future? As little children, says one story, the twins were taken into a temple of Apollo to celebrate their birthday. Tired from excitement and play, the children fell asleep in a dark corner. When their parents gathered the family to return home, nobody noticed that the twins were not with them. Hecabe soon realized they had been left behind, and hurried back to find them. She entered the temple, where, to her horror, she saw the sacred serpents licking her children's ears and mouths. The mother screamed out in fear. Instantly the serpents slithered into a pile of green laurel boughs and disappeared. But from that moment, Cassandra and Helenus were both able to foretell the future.

A second story is very different. In this version, the princess did not receive her gift until she became a young woman, whose beauty outshone all the other Trojan girls. One day, she fell asleep in the temple, where the god Apollo saw her and fell in love. To woo her, he taught her the most precious of his arts, how to read the future, hoping that she would love him too. But she rejected all his advances. In anger, Apollo wished to take back his gift of prophetic power, but even a god cannot do that. So he did something even worse: he made it her fate that her prophecies would always be true, but that nobody would ever believe them. This was to have terrible consequences for Troy.

Cassandra foresaw everything that was to happen, falling into an ecstatic trance from which her voice rang out its terrible utterings. Even her family believed her to be mad. They were glad enough when she recognized that the young man who came to the city was their son Paris, who had been left exposed on Mount Ida as a baby. They accepted the prince with joy. But no one paid attention when Cassandra tried to keep him from visiting Sparta, where she knew he would meet the beautiful Helen and abduct her, leading to the war that was to destroy Troy. Nobody believed her stories about what the war would be like, or its dire end after ten long years. In fact, to avoid scandal, her father locked her up in a pyramid, ordering the woman who attended her to report everything she said. He heard his daughter's prophecies, but believed nothing.

Even after so many of her predictions came true, nobody paid any attention to Cassandra. When, late in the war, the Greeks fooled the Trojans into believing that they had fled, leaving behind a great wooden horse as a gift to Athena, Cassandra tried to warn them. She knew that the horse was in fact filled with Greek soldiers, but ignoring her pleas, the Trojans wheeled it into the city walls, which until then had kept the intruders out. That night, of course, the soldiers left the horse to capture and burn the city. That was the end of Troy.

What a terrible gift: always to know the tragedies that lay ahead, and never be able to avert them! But Cassandra was to suffer a still worse fate. When Troy burned, she sought the protection of Athena in her great temple. As she was clinging to the statue of the goddess, a man called Little Ajax entered and saw her. Although the other Greeks did not dare to lay hands on her in the temple, Little Ajax had no such qualms. He grabbed Cassandra and dragged her out of the sanctuary, still clinging to the statue, which had turned its eyes away in horror. None of his companions protested at this violation.

Athena's wrath was great. She asked Poseidon, the god of the sea, to help her avenge this sacrilege. He agreed to raise a terrible storm as the Greeks set sail for home, with violent whirlwinds to drown many ships, and reefs on which the rest would be wrecked. In the tempest, Agamemnon's fleet was nearly destroyed. Little Ajax at first survived the sinking of his ship, but as he swam away to a nearby reef, he made the mistake of shouting that no sea could drown him. Of course, Poseidon would not take that insult! He broke off the piece of rock to which the culprit was clinging, then carried him away to his death.

Meanwhile, Cassandra had been awarded to Agamemnon as a prize of war. He returned home with her, little dreaming that his wife, Clytemnestra, was plotting his murder. "This is Priam's daughter," he told his wife, "the most noble of all the captive women. Treat her well." Then he entered the palace, followed by Clytemnestra.

Left in the street, Cassandra was seized by her prophetic power. "Earth!" she screamed. "Mother!" And the bystanders looked at each other uneasily. The seeress continued. "Apollo! My destroyer! You have destroyed me twice! Where have you brought me? What house is this?"

Cassandra knew what was about to happen, not just to Agamemnon. She knew that she too would die in that house. "This is a house of blood!" she cried, and began to describe the murders that would be committed. "Look out! Look out! Oh, I am breaking! Fate is so hard!" She went back over everything that she had foreseen for Troy, and its awful outcome.

Then she pulled herself together and turned toward the palace. "There's no escape!" she sighed. "Enough of life! I must go in now." And she opened the door to enter the place of her doom.

GLOSSARY

A

Abydos (uh BYE dus): A city on the Asian side of the Hellespont, home of Leander.

Achaea (uh KEE uh): A country in the northern Peloponnese; also another name for Greece.

Achilles (uh KIL eez): A Greek hero of the Trojan War.

Acis (AY sis): The lover of Galatea, turned into a river god.

Actaeon (ak TEE un): A hunter turned into a stag and killed by his own dogs.

Admete (ad MEE tee): A girl who wanted the Amazon queen Hippolyta's girdle.

Admetus (ad MEE tus): King of Thessaly, husband of Alcestis.

Adonis (uh DAHN is): A handsome man loved by Aphrodite and Persephone.

Aeaea (EE uh): The island on which the enchantress Circe lived.

Aeetes (ee EE teez): King of Colchis, Medea's father.

Aegean Sea (uh GEE un): An arm of the Mediterranean, between Asia Minor and Greece.

Aegeus (EE jee us): King of Athens, the father of Theseus.

Aegina (a JIE nuh):(1) A woman deceived by Zeus; (2) the kingdom of King Peleus.

Aegis (EE jis): The great breastplate of Zeus and Athena with the Gorgon's head in the center.

Aegisthus (i JIS thus): Clytemnestra's lover, slain by her son Orestes.

Aello (EE lo): A Harpy.

Aeneas (i NEE us): A hero of Troy who escaped; he was loved by Dido and later founded Rome.

Aeolus (EE uh lus): The king of the winds.

Aesculapius (es cue LAY pee us): The god of medicine.

Aeson (EE sun): Father of Jason.

Agamemnon (ag uh MEM non): King of Mycenae, victor of the Trojan War.

Aglaia (uh GLAY uh): Youngest of the three Graces.

Alcestis (al SES tus): The wife of Admetus.

Alcinous (al SIN oh us): The father of Nausicaa.

Alcithoe (al SITH oh ee): Daughter of King Minyas, turned into a bat.

Alcmena (alk MEE nuh): The mother of Hercules.

Alcyone (al SIGH uh nee): The devoted wife of Ceyx, turned into a kingfisher.

Alecto (uh LEK toh): One of the three Furies.

Alphenor (al FEE nor): One of the sons of Niobe.

Alpheus (al FEE us): A river who pursued the nymph Arethusa.

Althea (al THEE uh): The mother of Meleager.

Amazons (AM uh zonz): A nation of warrior women.

ambrosia (am BRO zhuh): (1) The food of the gods; (2) an ointment or perfume used by the gods.

Amor (AY mor): A Roman name for Eros.

Amphion (am FIE un): The husband of Niobe; a musician and king of Thebes.

Anaxarete (an ax ARE ee tee): The princess who spurned Iphis, turned into a statue.

Andraemon (an DREE mun): The husband of Dryope.

Androgeus (an DRAHJ ee us): Son of King Minos.

Andromeda (an DRAHM i da): Daughter of Cassiopeia.

Antigone (an TIG uh nee): (1) Daughter of Oedipus; (2) a girl who was turned into a stork.

Antiope (an TIE uh pee): An Amazon queen.

Aphrodite (af ro DITE ee): The Greek goddess of love and beauty.

Apollo (a POL loh): The Greek god of the sun, music, and healing.

Arachne (a RACK nee): A girl who was turned into a spider.

Arcadia (ar KAY dee uh): A beautiful region of the southern Peloponnese, associated with the Golden Age.

Arcas (AR cus): The son of Callisto, turned into the Little Bear.

Ares (AIR eez): The Greek god of war.

Arete (uh REE tee): The mother of Nausicaa.

Arethusa (air uh THU zuh): A wood nymph turned into a spring.

Argonauts (AR guh nawtz): Fifty sailors of the ship *Argo* commanded by Jason on the quest for the Golden Fleece.

Argos (AR gos): An ancient city in the northern Peloponnese.

Argus (AR gus): A monster with a hundred eyes; Hera set him to guard Io.

Ariadne (ar ee AD nee): The daughter of King Minos of Crete.

Artemis (AHR ti mis): The Greek goddess of the hunt and the moon.

Asterie (as TEAR ee ee): A woman deceived by Zeus.

Astraea (a STREE uh): The Greek goddess of innocence and purity.

Atalanta (at uh LAN ta): The swift runner, turned into a lion.

Athena (a THEEN a): The Greek goddess of wisdom and war.

Athens (A thuns): The great city–state of ancient Greece; capital of modern Greece.

Atlas (AT lus): A Titan who supports the heavens on his shoulders.

Atropos (A truh pahs): One of the three Fates.

Aulis (AW lus): A harbor in eastern Greece.

B

Bacchanals (bah kuh NAHLS): Followers of the god Bacchus.

Bacchus (BOCK us): The Latin name for Dionysus.

Baucis (BAW sis): The devoted wife of Philemon, turned into a tree.

Bellerophon (buh LEHR uh fahn): A hero of Corinth.

Beroe (BEHR oh ee): Semele's old nurse.

bier (BEER): A coffin and its platform or stand.

Briareus (bry EHR yoos): A hundred-handed monster, son of Gaia and Uranus.

C

Cadmus (KAD mus): The founder of Thebes.

Calchas (KAL kus): A Greek soothsayer in the Trojan War.

Calliope (kuh LIE uh pee): The Muse of epic poetry, mother of Orpheus.

Callisto (kuh LIS toe): A follower of Artemis, turned into a bear and then to the constellation Great Bear.

Calydon (KAL uh don): The kingdom of Oeneus.

Canens (KAH nens): A nymph with a beautiful voice, who turned to mist.

Capaneus (KAP an yoos): The husband of Evadne.

Carthage (KAR thuj): One of the greatest of ancient cities on the Mediterranean coast of northern Africa.

Cassandra (kuh SAN druh): Daughter of Hecabe and Priam; a prophetess whose words nobody believed.

Cassiopeia (kas ee uh PEE uh): The queen of Ethiopia and mother of Andromeda, turned into a constellation.

Celaeno (suh LEE no): A Harpy.

Celeus (SEE lee us): The king of Eleusis, husband of Metanira.

Centaur (SEN tawr): A creature half man and half horse.

Cepheus (SEE fee us): King of Ethiopia, husband of Cassiopeia, and father of Andromeda.

Cerberus (SUR bur us): The three-headed dog who guards the entrance to the Underworld.

Ceres (SEAR eez): The Roman name for Demeter.

Ceto (SEE toh): A sea creature, perhaps a whale, mother of the Gorgons and Graiae.

Ceyx (SEE ix): Devoted husband of Alcyone, turned into a kingfisher.

Chaos (KAY os): The shapeless nothingness before anything existed.

Chariclo (KAR i clo): A nymph, mother of Ocyrhoe.

Charon (KEHR un): The ferryman who carries the souls of the dead across the River Styx into the Underworld.

Charybdis (kuh RIB dis): A whirlpool off the coast of Sicily.

Chimera (ki MEER uh): A fire-breathing monster, part goat, part lion, part snake.

Chiron (KIE ron): A wise Centaur, teacher of Aesculapius and many Greek heroes.

Chrysothemis (kris AH thuh mis): A sister of Iphigenia, Electra, and Orestes.

Cinyras (sin EYE rus): A father whose daughters were turned into marble steps.

Circe (SUR see): An enchantress who turned men into animals and performed other deeds of magic.

Claros (KLAHR os): The site of an oracle of Apollo.

Clio (KLIE oh): The Muse of history.

Clotho (KLOH thoh): One of the three Fates.

Clytemnestra (kly tem NES truh): Wife of Agamemnon and mother of Iphigenia, Electra, and Orestes.

Clytie (KLIE tee ee): A nymph who loved Apollo, turned into a heliotrope.

Coeus (KOH ee us): A Titan, the father of Leto.

Colchis (KOL kis): Ancient region at the eastern end of the Black Sea.

Colonus (koh LO nus): The place near Athens that offered refuge to Oedipus and Antigone.

Corinth (KOR inth): A leading city of ancient Greece on the Peloponnese.

Corona Borealis (kor OH nuh bor ee AL us): Ariadne's crown, turned into a constellation.

Creon (KREE ahn): (1) The uncle of Antigone; king of Thebes; (2) the king of Corinth, father of Glauce.

Crete (KREET): An island in the Mediterranean Sea ruled by King Minos.

Cronos (CROW nus): A Titan, son of Gaia and Uranus.

Cupid (KYOO pid): A Roman name for Eros.

Cyane (SIGH uh nee): A fountain nymph, turned into water.

Cyclopes (SIGH klo pees): One-eyed giants, children of Gaia and Uranus. The singular is Cyclops.

Cyprus (SIGH prus): An island in the Mediterranean Sea.

D

Daedalion (deh DAY lee un): The brother of Ceyx.

Daedalus (DED uh lus): An Athenian inventor; the architect of the labyrinth.

Damasichthon (da MAS ik thon): One of the sons of Niobe.

Danae (DAN uh ee): The mother of Perseus.

Danaides (duh NAY idz): Women eternally punished in the Underworld.

Daphne (DAF nee): A nymph, Apollo's first love, turned into a laurel tree.

Deino (DAY no): One of the Graiae.

Deiphobus (dee IF uh bus): A son of Hecabe and Priam.

Delos (DEE lohs): The tiny floating island on which Leto gave birth to Artemis and Apollo.

Delphi (DELL fee): The site of the most famous oracle of Apollo.

Demeter (di MEE tur): The Greek goddess of grain, agriculture, and fertility.

Deucalion (doo KAY lee un): Son of Prometheus and husband of Pyrrha.

Diana (die AN uh): The Roman name for Artemis.

Dido: (DIE doh): The founder and queen of Carthage who loved Aeneas.

Dionysus (die uh NIE sus): The Greek god of wine.

Doso (DO so): A name Demeter adopted for disguise.

Dryad (DRY ad): A nymph of the trees and woodlands.

Dryope (DRY uh pee): A young mother turned into a lotus.

E

Echidna (e KID nuh): A monster, half woman, half serpent; mother of the Sphinx, Cerberus, Chimera, and Hydra.

Echo (ECK oh): A wood nymph who faded away for love of Narcissus.

Egeria (e JEER ee uh): An Italian nymph, wife of Numa.

Electra (e LEK truh): Daughter of Agamemnon and Clytemnestra.

Eleusis (e LOO sus): The city where Demeter found shelter with the king and queen.

Enyo (EN yo): One of the Graiae.

Epaphus (EP uh fus): Son of Io and Zeus.

Epimetheus (ep uh MEE thee us): Brother of Prometheus and husband of Pandora.

epithet (EP uh thet): A word or phrase used along with or in place of someone's name.

Erato (AIR uh toh): The Muse of love poetry.

Erebos (AIR uh bus): The darkness, born of Chaos.

Erinyes (i RIN ee eez): The Furies, goddesses of vengeance and justice.

Eris (AIR is): The Greek goddess of discord.

Eros (AIR ahs): The Greek god of love.

Eteocles (i TEE uh cleez): The brother of Antigone who was honorably buried.

Ethiopia (ee thee OH pee uh): A country in Africa on the Red Sea.

Euippe (yoo IP pee): The mother of the Pierides.

Eumenides (yoo MEN i deez): Another name for the Erinyes or Furies.

Euphrosyne (yoo FRAHS uh nee): One of the three Graces.

Europa (yoo ROH puh): The princess abducted by Zeus in the form of a white bull.

Euryale (yoo REE uh lee): One of the three Gorgons.

Eurydice (yoo RID uh see): A wood nymph who married Orpheus.

Eurylochus (yoo RILL oh kus): A companion of Odysseus.

Eurynome (yoo RIN oh mee): (1) In one creation story, the Goddess of All Things, the first born out of Chaos; (2) mother of Leucothoe.

Euterpe (yoo TUR pee): The Muse of lyric poetry and music.

Evadne (e VAD nee): The wife of Capaneus.

F

Fates (FATYZ): Three goddesses who determine the course of human life.

Faunus (FAWN us): The god of the countryside.

Furies (FYUHR eez): The Erinyes, goddesses of vengeance and justice.

G

Gaia (GEE uh) or Ge (GEE): Mother Earth, the primal Earth goddess, created after Chaos.

Galanthis (guh LAN thus): A serving maid of Alcmena, turned into a weasel or ferret.

Galatea (gal uh TEE uh): (1) The statue loved by Pygmalion; (2) Nereid loved by both Acis and the Cyclops Polyphemus.

Glauce (GLAW see): A princess of Corinth.

Glaucus (GLAW kus): A fisherman changed to a sea god.

Golden Fleece (GOLD un FLEECE): The fleece of a ram sent by Hermes to rescue a youth from being sacrificed.

Gorgons (GOR gonz): Three monstrous sisters; one glance at them turned living creatures to stone.

Graces (GRAY suz): Three goddesses of beauty, grace, and friendship.

Graiae (GRAY ee): The Gray Women, sisters of the Gorgons.

H

Hades (HAY deez): (1) The Greek god of the Underworld; (2) a name for the Underworld.

Haemon (HAY mahn): The son of Creon, engaged to Antigone.

Hamadryad (ham uh DRY ud): A wood nymph who presided over a specific tree.

Harmonia (har MOAN ee uh): The wife of Cadmus; mother of Semele.

Harmony (har MOH nee uh): The mother of the Amazons.

Harpy (HARP ee): A winged monster, half bird and half woman.

Hebe (HEE bee): The Greek goddess of youth.

Hecabe (HECK uh bee): Queen of Troy, wife of Priam. The Latin name is Hecuba.

Hecate (HECK uh tee): The goddess of witchcraft and enchantment.

Hector (HECK tor): The greatest of the Trojan warriors.

Helen (HEL un): The most beautiful woman in the world.

Helenus (HEL uh nus): Twin brother of the seeress Cassandra.

Helicon (HELL uh kon): One of the mountains sacred to the Muses.

Helios (HEE lee ahs): The Greek god of the sun.

Hellespont (HEL us pohnt): A narrow strait between Asia Minor and Europe, today called the Dardanelles.

Hephaestus (heh FES tus): The Greek god of fire.

Hera (HEER uh): The wife of Zeus.

Heracles (HAIR uh klees): A great Greek hero.

Hercules (HER kyu leez): The Roman name for Heracles.

Hermes (HERM eez): Zeus's son, the messenger of the gods.

Hero (HEER oh): A priestess of Aphrodite, lover of Leander.

Hesiod (HEE si od): One of the earliest writers of Greek myths, about the eighth century B.C.

Hestia (HES tee uh): The Greek goddess of the hearth.

Hippodamia (hip uh duh MY uh): Princess won by Pelops in a chariot race against her father.

Hippolyta (hip PAHL i tuh): A queen of the Amazons.

Hippolytus (hip PAHL i tus): The son of the Amazon queen Antiope and Theseus.

Hippomenes (hip POM uh neez): A suitor of Atalanta's, turned into a lion.

Homer (HOH mur): The great Greek writer of epic poetry, around 1000 B.C.

Horae (HOH ree): The Hours, goddesses of the changing seasons.

Hours (OURZ): The Horae.

hubris (HYOO brus): The sin of pride.

Hydra (HIGH druh): A many-headed monster, killed by Heracles.

Hymen (HIGH men): The Greek god of marriage.

I

Icarius (i KAR ee us): The father of Penelope.

Iliad, The: Homer's great epic poem about the Trojan War.

Ilioneus (il ee OH nee us): One of the sons of Niobe.

Ilithyia (ill uh THIE yuh): The Greek goddess of childbirth.

Inachus (IN uh kus): A river god, the father of Io.

Ino (EYE noh): Semele's sister, who raised the god Dionysus.

Io (EYE oh): The daughter of Inachus, turned into a white heifer.

Iole (EYE uh lee): Narrator of the story of her sister Dryope.

Iphigenia (if i juh NYE uh): Daughter of Agamemnon and Clytemnestra.

Iphis (EYE fus): Unhappy lover of Anaxarete.

Iris (EYE ris): The goddess of the rainbow.

Ismene (is MEE nee): The sister of Antigone.

Ismenus (is MEE nus): One of the sons of Niobe.

Ithaca (ITH uh kuh): The island home of Odysseus.

Ixion (IX ee un): A man eternally punished in Hell for wickedness.

J

Jason (JAY sun): Commander of the *Argo*; the husband of Medea.

Jove (JOHV): The Roman name for Zeus.

Juno (JOO noh): The Roman name for Hera.

Jupiter (JOO pi tur): The Roman name for Zeus.

L

Labyrinth (LAB uh rinth): The maze in Minos's palace on Crete.

Lachesis (LACH i sis): One of the three Fates.

Ladon (LAY don): The river where Syrinx turned into reeds.

Laelaps (LEE laps): The unconquerable hound, a wedding present from Zeus to Europa.

Latona (la TONE uh): The Roman name for Leto.

Leander (lee AN der): The young man in love with Hero.

Leda (LEE duh): A woman deceived by Zeus; mother of Helen.

Lesbos (LEZ bos): The island where Orpheus's body rests.

Lethe (LEE thee): The Underworld River of Forgetfulness.

Leto (LEE toe): Daughter of the Titans Coeus and Phoebe; mother of Artemis and Apollo.

Leucothoe (loo KOTH oh ee): A girl loved by the Sun.

libation (lie BAY shun): A sacrificial offering to the dead, usually wine, milk, or hair.

Little Ajax (AY jaks): The Greek who snatched Cassandra from refuge in Athena's temple.

Lotis (LOH tis): A naiad, turned into a flower.

Lucina (loo SEE nuh): The Roman name for Ilithyia.

Lydia (LID ee uh): A country in Asia Minor.

lyre (LIER): A stringed instrument resembling a harp.

M

Macedonia (ma suh DOHN ee uh): An ancient country in the northeast corner of the Greek peninsula.

Maenads (MEE nadz): Worshipers of Dionysus.

Manto (MAN toh): A seeress of Thebes.

Mars (MAHRZ): The Roman name for Ares.

Medea (meh DEE uh): A powerful witch, wife of Jason.

Medusa (meh DOO suh): One of the Gorgons, killed by Perseus.

Megaera (meh GEE ra): One of the three Furies.

Megara (meh GAH ra): The city ruled by Nisus.

Meleager (mel ee AY jur): A prince who hunted the Calydonian Boar with Atalanta.

Melpomene (mel PAHM uh nee): The Muse of tragedy.

Menelaus (men uh LAY us): King of Sparta and husband of Helen.

Mercury (MUR kyu ree): The Roman name for Hermes.

Metamorphosis (met uh MOR foh sis): A change from one form to another.

Metanira (met uh NYE ruh): The queen of Eleusis.

Minerva (mi NER vuh): The Roman name for Athena.

Minos (MY nus): The king of Crete, father of Ariadne.

Minotaur (MIN uh tawr): A monster, half bull and half human.

Minyas (MIN yas): King of Thessaly; father of Alcithoe and her sisters, who were turned into bats.

Mnemosyne (nee MAHS uh nee): A Titaness, the personification of memory; the mother of the Muses.

Morpheus (MOR fee us): The god of sleep.

Mount Etna (mount ET nuh): A volcano in Sicily.

Mount Ida (mount EYE duh): The mountain where Paris was abandoned as a baby; home of Oenone.

Mount Pierus (mount pie EAR us): The birthplace of the Muses.

Muse (MEWS): One of the nine daughters of Zeus and Mnemosyne, who inspire artists.

Mycenae (my SEE nee): The kingdom of Agamemnon, noted for its riches.

Myrtilus (MUR ti lus): The charioteer who was bribed to help Pelops win his race.

N

Naiad (NIE ad): A nymph who dwelt in rivers, springs, brooks, and fountains.

Narcissus (nahr SIS sus): A handsome youth who fell in love with his own face and turned into a flower.

Nausicaa (naw SIK ay uh): The princess of Phoeacia who rescued Odysseus after a shipwreck.

Naxos (NAK sohs): An island in the Aegean Sea.

Nemesis (NEM uh sis): The Greek goddess of revenge.

Neptune (NEP toon): The Roman name for Poseidon.

Nereid (NEER ee id): A nymph who dwelt in the sea.

Ninus (NYE nus): Pyramus and Thisbe planned to meet at his tomb.

Niobe (NYE oh bee): Wife of Amphion, king of Thebes, turned into a weeping statue.

Nisus (NYE sus): The king of Megara, father of Scylla.

Numa (NOO ma): The second king of Rome, husband of Egeria.

O

Oceanid (oh SEE uh nid): A nymph of the oceans and rivers.

Oceanus (oh SEE uh nus): A Titan, married to Tethys; Hera's foster father.

Ocyrhoe (oh SIR oh ee): A seeress, daughter of the Centaur Chiron, turned into a mare.

Odysseus (oh DIS ee us): King of Ithaca, a hero of the Trojan War.

Odyssey, The: Homer's epic poem that recounts the adventures of Odysseus on his way home from the war.

Oedipus (ED uh pus): King of Thebes, Antigone's father.

Oeneus (EE nee us): King of Calydon, Meleager's father.

Oenomaus (ee NOH may us): King of Pisa, Hippodamia's father.

Oenone (ee NOH nee): (1) A nymph with the gift of prophecy; (2) a Pygmy queen, turned into a crane.

Okypete (oh kuh PAY tee): A Harpy.

Olympus (oh LIM pus): A mountain in Thessaly; the home of the gods.

Ophion (oh FIE on): A serpent created by Eurynome.

oracle (OHR uh kul): (1) A priestess through whom a god foretold the future; (2) the shrine in which the priestess dwelt.

Oread (OHR ee ad): A nymph of the mountains.

Oreithyia (ohr EE thee uh): An Amazon, sister of Antiope.

Orestes (oh RES teez): The son of Clytemnestra and Agamemnon.

Orpheus (ORH fee us): Son of Apollo and Calliope; husband of Eurydice.

Ortygia (or TIJ ee uh): The place in Sicily where Arethusa became a spring.

Otus and Ephialtes (OH tus and ef ee ALL teez): Giants; brothers who loved Artemis and Hera.

P

Pallas (PAL us): Another name for Athena.

Pan (PAN): The Greek god of nature and the countryside.

Pandora (pan DOHR uh): The first woman.

Paris (PAIR is): A prince of Troy, who eloped with Helen.

Parnassus (par NAS sus): A mountain near Delphi, sacred to Apollo and the Muses.

Pelasgus (puh LAZ gus): The founder of an early Greek people.

Peleus (PEE lee us): King of Aegina, husband of Thetis.

Pelias (PEE lee us): Jason's uncle.

Peloponnese (pel up uhn EEZ): A major peninsula of Greece.

Pelops (PEE lahps): A son of Tantalus; husband of Hippolyta.

Pemphredo (pem FRAY doh): One of the Graiae.

Penelope (puh NEL uh pee): The wife of Odysseus.

Peneus (puh NEE us): A river god, father of Daphne.

Penthesilea (pen thuh suh LEE uh): A queen of the Amazons.

Persephone (per SEF uh nee): Daughter of Demeter; wife of Hades.

Perseus (PER see us): The son of Zeus and Danae; husband of Andromeda.

Phaeacia (fee AY shuh): An island where Odysseus was shipwrecked.

Phaedimus (FEE di mus): One of the sons of Niobe.

Phaedra (FEE druh): The sister of Ariadne; wife of Theseus.

Philemon (fi LEE mun): The devoted husband of Baucis, turned into a tree.

Phocaea (fo KEY uh): An ancient Ionian city.

Phoebe (FEE bee): A name for Artemis as the moon.

Phoebus (FEE bus): A name for Apollo as the sun.

Phorcys (FAWR sis): A god of the sea, father of the Gorgons and Graiae.

Phrygia (FRIJ ee uh): A country between the Mediterranean and Black Seas.

Picus (PIE kus): The husband of Canens, turned into a woodpecker.

Pierides (pye EAR uh deez): Nine sisters who were turned into magpies.

Pierus (pye EAR us): Father of the Pierides.

Pleiades (PLEE uh deez): Daughters of Atlas.

Pluto (PLOO toh): The Roman name for Hades.

Polites (po LIE teez): A son of Hecabe and Priam.

Polydorus (pahl i DAWR us): The youngest son of Hecabe and Priam.

Polyhymnia (pahl i HIM nee uh): The Muse of sacred music and poetry.

Polymestor (pahl i MES tor): King of Thrace who murdered Polydorus.

Polynices (pahl i NYE seez): The brother of Antigone who was not given honorable burial.

Polyphemus (pahl i FEE mus): The Cyclops who loved the Nereid Galatea.

Polyxena (puh LIK suh nuh): The youngest daughter of Hecabe and Priam.

Pomona (puh MOAN uh): (1) A woodland nymph loved by Vertumnus; (2) a Roman deity of fruit.

Poseidon (poh SIGH dun): The Greek god of the sea.

Priam (PRY um): King of Troy at the time of the Trojan War.

Priapus (pry AY pus): The Greek god of gardens and fertility.

Prometheus (pro MEE thee us): The Titan who created mankind and stole fire for mortals.

Proserpina (pro SUR pi nuh): The Roman name for Persephone.

Proteus (PRO tee us): A sea god able to change his shape at will.

Psyche (SIGH kee): The princess who was married to Cupid and later became a goddess.

Pygmalion (pig MAY lee un): A Cretan sculptor who fell in love with his statue, Galatea.

Pylades (PIL uh deez): The companion of Orestes; husband of Electra.

Pyramus (PEER uh mus): The young man who loved Thisbe.

pyre (PIRE): A heap of combustible material, usually for burning a body in a funeral rite.

Pyrrha (PEER uh): Daughter of Epimetheus and Pandora; wife of Deucalion.

Python (PIE thon): A monstrous serpent who inhabited Delphi before Apollo killed it.

R

Rhea (REE uh): A daughter of Gaia and Uranus; wife of Cronos.

Rhodope and Haemon (ROH duh pee and HAY mun): A couple turned into mountains.

S

Salamis (SAHL uh mus): An ancient city on Cyprus.

Sarpedon (sahr PEE dun): A son of Zeus, a hero of the Trojan War.

Saturn (SAT urn): The Roman name for Cronos.

Satyrs (SAY turz): Deities of the woods and countryside.

Scylla (SIL uh): (1) A Nereid, turned into a six-headed monster; (2) the daughter of Nisus, turned into a seabird.

Semele (SEM uh lee): Theban princess loved by Zeus; the mother of Dionysus.

Semiramis (si MEER uh mis): The queen who built Babylon.

Sestos (SES tos): A city on the European side of the Hellespont, home of Hero.

Sibyl (SIB il): A prophetess; the most famous was the Sibyl of Cumae.

Sicily (SIS uh lee): An island in the Mediterranean, sacred to Artemis.

Silenus (sigh LEE nus): The oldest of the satyrs.

Sipylus (SIP uh lus): One of the sons of Niobe.

Sirens (SIE renz): Temptresses who lured sailors to their island by singing.

Sisyphus (SIS ih fus): A man eternally punished in Hell for wickedness.

Sparta (SPAR tuh): A powerful ancient Greek city–state.

Sphinx (SFINX): A winged monster with a woman's head and a lion's body.

Stheno (STHEE no): One of the three Gorgons.

Strait of Messina (STRAYT of meh SEE nuh): The channel between Italy and Sicily where Scylla and Charybdis lurked.

Styx (STICKS): The river separating the Underworld from the upper world.

Syrinx (SEAR inks): A nymph who was pursued by Pan, turned into a reed flute.

T

Talos (TAY lahs): A man made of bronze who guarded Crete.

Tantalus (TAN tuh lus): Niobe's father, eternally punished for his wickedness; also one of her sons.

Tartarus (TAR tuh rus): A name for the Underworld or Hell.

Tauris (TAW rus): A city in northwestern Iran, today called Tabriz.

Telemachus (tuh LEM uh kus): The son of Odysseus and Penelope.

Tempe (TEM pee): A valley in Thessaly.

Terpsichore (turp SIK uh ree): The Muse of dancing.

Tethys (TEE this): A Titaness, married to Oceanus; Hera was her foster daughter.

Thalia (thuh LEE uh): (1) The Muse of comedy; (2) one of the three Graces.

Thebes (THEEBZ): The capital city of Boeotia, in central Greece.

Themis (THEE mis): The Greek goddess of law and justice, mother of the Hours and the Fates.

Theseus (THEE see us): The son of Aegeus, king of Athens.

Thessaly (THEH suh lee): A fertile region in northeastern Greece.

Thetis (THEE tis): A Nereid; Eris threw the golden apple of discord into her wedding feast.

Thisbe (THIZ bee): The girl who loved Pyramus.

Thoas (THO us): King of Tauris.

Thrace (THRAYS): A region of Greece north of the Aegean Sea.

Tiber (TIE bur): A river in Italy.

Tiresias (tie REE see us): The blind seer of Thebes.

Tisiphone (ti SIF uh nee): One of the Furies.

Titan (TIE tun): Any one of the twelve children of Gaia and Uranus.

Triton (TRY tun): The son of Poseidon who blew on a conch shell to control the waves.

Troilus (TROY lus): A prince of Troy, son of Hecabe and Priam.

Trojan War (TROH jun war): A ten-year war between Greece and Troy; Troy was destroyed.

Troy (TROY): A great city in Asia Minor, destroyed in a war with Greece. Also called Ilium.

Tyndareus (tin DEHR ee us): The king of Sparta, father of Clytemnestra, and stepfather of Helen.

Typhoeus (tie FEE us): A snake-headed giant who revolted against the gods.

Tyre (TEIR): A great city in Phoenicia.

U

Underworld (UN der world): The realm of the dead, ruled by Hades; also sometimes called Hades.

Urania (yuh RAY nee uh): The Muse of astronomy.

Uranus (YUHR uh nus): Father Heaven, the personification of the sky; husband of Gaia.

V

Venus (VEE nus): The Roman name for Aphrodite.

Vertumnus (vur TUM nus): A god who loved the nymph Pomona.

Vesta (VEST uh): The Roman name for Hestia.

Virgil (VUR jil): A great Roman writer of epic poetry.

Vulcan (VUL kun): The Roman name for Hephaestus.

Z

Zethus (ZEE thus): Twin brother of Amphion.

Zeus (ZOOS): The Greek supreme god, ruler of Heaven, whose weapon was the terrible thunderbolt.

BIBLIOGRAPHY

Aeschylus. *Agamemnon.* Translated by Robert Fagles. New York: Penguin Books, 1966.

Bowra, C. M. *Classical Greece.* New York: Time, 1965.

Bulfinch, Thomas. *Mythology.* New York: Harper & Row, 1970.

Calasso, Roberto. *The Marriage of Cadmus and Harmony.* New York: Vintage Books, 1993.

Editors of Time–Life Books. *What Life Was Like at the Dawn of Democracy.* Alexandria, Va.: Time–Life Books, 1998.

Euripides. *Iphigenia in Tauris.* Translated by Philip Vellacott. London: Penguin Books, 1953.

———.*Medea.* Translated by Philip Vellacott. New York: Penguin Books, 1954.

Foss, Michael. *Gods and Heroes: The Story of Greek Mythology.* Lincolnwood, Ill.: NTC Publishing Group, 1994.

Grant, Michael. *Myths of the Greeks and Romans.* New York: Meridian Books, 1995.

Grant, Michael, and John Hazel. *Who's Who in Classical Mythology.* New York: Oxford University Press, 1993.

Graves, Robert. *The Greek Myths,* Vols. 1 and 2. London: Penguin Books, 1955.

———. *The Greek Myths.* Illustrated edition. London: Penguin Books, 1955.

Hall, James. *Dictionary of Subjects & Symbols in Art.* New York: Harper & Row, 1974.

Hamilton, Edith. *Mythology.* New York: New American Library, 1940.

Hesiod. *Theogony* and *Works and Days.* Translated by M. L. West. New York: Oxford University Press, 1988.

Homer. *The Odyssey.* Translated by Robert Fagles. New York: Penguin Books, 1996.

Larousse Encyclopedia of Mythology. New York: Prometheus Press, 1959.

Martin, Thomas R. *Ancient Greece from Prehistoric to Hellenistic Times.* New Haven, Conn.: Yale University Press, 1996.

Moncrieff, A. R. Hope. *Myths and Legends of Ancient Greece.* New York: Gramercy Books, 1955.

Ovid. *The Metamorphoses.* Translated by Horace, Gregory. New York: Mentor Books, 1960.

———.*The Metamorphoses.* Translated by Rolfe, Humphries. Bloomington: Indiana University Press, 1983.

———.*The Metamorphoses.* Translated by A. D. Melville. New York: Oxford University Press, 1986.

Shapiro, Max S., and Rhoda A. Hendricks. *A Dictionary of Mythologies.* London: Paladin Books, 1981.

Sophocles, *Antigone.* Translated by E. F. Watling. Middlesex, England: Penguin Books, 1947.

———.*Electra.* Translated by E. F. Watling. Middlesex, England: Penguin Books, 1953.

Storace, Patricia. *Dinner with Persephone: Travels in Greece.* New York: Vintage Books, 1996.

Switzer, Ellen, and Costas Switzer. *Greek Myths: Gods, Heroes and Monsters.* New York: Atheneum, 1988.

Index of Characters